FINANCING INDUSTRIAL INVESTMENT

FINANCING INDUSTRIAL INVESTMENT

John C. Carrington
and
George T. Edwards

First published 1979 by
THE MACMILLAN PRESS LTD
London and Basingstoke
Associated companies in Delhi
Dublin Hong Kong Johannesburg Lagos
Melbourne New York Singapore Tokyo

Printed in Great Britain by
Unwin Brothers Limited, Old Woking, Surrey

British Library Cataloguing in Publication Data

Carrington, John C
  Financing industrial investment
  1. Capital investments
  I. Title II. Edwards, George T
  332.6'09181'2   HG4028.C4

ISBN 0 333 24286 6

Contents

List of Tables and Figures

TABLES

Chapter 5

FIGURES

Preface

This book is primarily a comparative analysis of how industrial investment is financed in five countries (France, Japan, West Germany, the UK and the USA) and a consequent prescription for the improvement of UK investment-funding systems. At present, when North Sea oil is freeing Britain from the balance of payments constraint on economic growth, there seems to be common consent that there should be a higher level of industrial investment, but some doubt about how this objective could be achieved. It is therefore our view that the subject matter of this book could hardly be more pertinent to the current economic debate.

For example, the Committee to Review the Functioning of Financial Institutions is due to produce an interim report on its progress in November 1977. Sir Harold Wilson, the chairman of that committee, was reported, in advance of the report, as hinting strongly that the committee evidence seemed to suggest that the supply of external capital might not be a problem, although the associated costs and terms might be too high.[1] The comparative analysis conducted in this book seems to throw doubt upon such a conclusion, and casts some light on why investment levels are higher in other countries than in the UK.

The propositions advanced in Chapter 5 — that liquidity of a company takes precedence over considerations of profitability, and hence investment may occur up to the point at which the return on marginal investment projects is equal to the cash flow costs of investment capital — may explain part of the difference in national investment levels. But differences in government economic philosophies and attitudes to business, different levels of business savings, and different traditions in the degree of integration of the financial and industrial systems of countries, are also contributory.

While the bias in the final chapter is towards proposing possible methods of raising investment levels in the UK, there may also be lessons for other Anglo-Saxon countries — such as Australia, Canada, New Zealand, and the USA — in the suggested prescription for higher economic growth. The Anglo-Saxon traditions (of high internal funding of investment and the separation of the financial and industrial systems) are not restricted to Britain; they are largely shared by other English-speaking countries.

The subject matter of this book covers a vast area and it is difficult to ensure that a proper perspective has been arrived at for there is a great deal of potential source material. The authors have sifted and sorted, and earnestly hope that a proper balance has been struck between sources.

We wish to acknowledge permissions granted by the Controller of Her Majesty's Stationery Office to quote from 'National Income and Expenditure, 1973' and 'Economic Trends Annual Supplement 1976'; and by all of those other authors, publishers and authorities whose assistance has been so valuable and who are individually mentioned in the notes.

Thanks are due to all of those friends, colleagues, economists and correspondents who provided critical and helpful comment during our researches into this subject, from late 1971 to the present; errors in this book are, of course, our responsibility alone.

25 September 1977   J.C.C.   G.T.E.

1 Purpose and Plan of this Book

1.1 PURPOSE

This book attempts to place into context one of the factors which contribute to economic growth. Its primary aim is to show how industrial investment is financed in five developed economies — in France, Japan, West Germany, the UK and the USA — and to indicate from that analysis how the investment level may be stimulated in private industry in the UK. A secondary aim is to place the financing of capital investment into perspective as a contributory factor in assisting rapid economic development. This will involve a review of some of the current literature on the other possible reasons why the UK is growing slowly, relative to some of its major partners in the OECD.

To make such international economic comparisons is a hazardous venture. Nonetheless, it is a necessary exercise, for while economic comparisons may be uncertain (usually to several percent of their value) the reality of large differences in the investment rate between developed nations is virtually indisputable and calls for some explanation. Similarly, it may be difficult to determine the precise differences between the British and the Japanese growth rates during the 1960s, but the imprecision of the estimates leaves no room for doubts about which economy grew fastest. Our aim in this book is to arrive at estimates of investment financing which are of the correct relative magnitudes. These estimates can be no better than the data upon which they are based, and data sources are quoted in all cases. Yet, although estimates may not be accurate to two or three significant figures, we shall follow national accounting procedures in quoting the central estimate provided by sources or calculated by ourselves. The guide to the UK National Accounts, for example,[1] states that the reliability of estimates of the Gross Domestic Product in any one year may be less than $\pm 3\%$ but GDP is quoted to five significant figures. To say this is not to criticise the Central Statistical Office, for the GDP estimates are best estimates and

1

would not be improved by being replaced by (say) a range of values and probabilities, even if the biases could be so assessed. In practice, they cannot. Systematic errors and some degree of unreliability are inevitable in even the best-designed procedures for collecting statistics. The magnitude of these errors is sufficient to counsel caution in interpreting the data, but these errors are not generally so large as to render the results of analysis meaningless.

There is another difficulty in using economic data which results from the tendency of national authorities to alter some economic data with the wisdom of hindsight. The latest estimate is often therefore the best estimate, and it is quite possible to acquire several different estimates of (say) the GDP of a country in 1965, even from the same source of data. This usually does not matter, as revisions tend to be marginal for large economic aggregates such as investment or household saving. Nonetheless, it can occasionally change the total value of the estimate by several percent.

We shall throughout this book be comparing several economic variables in Britain with those of France, Japan, West Germany and the USA. To avoid frequent recourse to expressions such as 'the five countries under consideration' or 'the five countries being examined', we will usually say 'the five countries' or 'the five nations' when we intend to refer to these national economies. Britain will be used interchangeably with the United Kingdom to refer to the United Kingdom of Great Britain and Northern Ireland. (We are therefore not using the word 'Britain', as some geographers do, to refer to the United Kingdom minus Northern Ireland.) 'American' will also be used in its usual connotation, as an adjective pertaining to the USA alone. The national territories of the five countries did not change significantly during the period 1963 – 74, but a number of small points may be noted. French economic data excludes the Overseas Departments of French Guiana, Guadeloupe, Martinique and Reunion. The Ryukyu Islands (including Okinawa) were transferred to Japan from US jurisdiction on 15 May 1972. West German data includes West Berlin. Data for the UK does not include the Channel Islands or the Isle of Man, except when exports or imports are quoted.

This book necessarily contains a large number of tables. Practical economic analysis is dependent on statistics, and whenever it has been necessary to discuss the data, the relevant numbers have been quoted in a nearby table. Background information, or data referred to only in passing, has been relegated to the statistical appendices. There are 28 statistical appendices, which contain basic data on the five countries.

Where the tabulated information given on different nations is not directly comparable, footnotes sometimes explain the difference. In some cases, however, the sources of data fail to describe what these differences may be, and there is no option in these cases but to remember that compilation methods for national accounts statistics generally differ slightly in practice. Data references are usually quoted with sufficient accuracy to enable the interested reader to find the data in the original source document, except when the data source or reference is so relevant in its entirety that a broad citation is appropriate.

The authors of this book could be described as managers or administrators rather than academics. We have privately studied this subject for over five years. The bias of this book is toward a practical understanding of economic forces rather than the construction of a theoretical edifice, which may possibly follow later. Our major emphasis is on the evidence, and on the conclusions which seem to follow naturally from it.

The chapters of this book could be encapsulated as follows: first, a short statement of the purpose, plan and summary argument of the book is presented; second, the relative economic decline of the UK, and the solutions so far suggested to ameliorate or reverse that decline are reviewed; third, the central contribution of capital investment to producing rapid economic growth is reviewed in theory and calculated (for five nations) in practice, with special attention to the UK's capital productivity; fourth, a review of investment-funding procedures, and a summary of the different relationships between industrial and financial sectors, is produced for five nations; fifth, a short examination is made of the theory and practice of capital gearing; an estimate is provided of the costs and profits of capital arising from different investment-financing traditions in five nations, emphasising the result that where the cash-flow cost of capital is low, liquidity is less threatened, and therefore investment is higher; sixth, real standards of living, the levels of net household saving, the possible relationship between inflation and economic growth, and the linkage between investment and employment, are discussed; and finally, in the seventh chapter, three choices for Britain (continuing as at present; a socialist solution, or an improved flow of funds for private investment) are outlined, and a preferred set of policies, aimed at reversing the UK's relative economic decline in the longer term, is put forward.

The outline of the chapters in the above paragraph may be too compressed; this book is sufficiently complex in structure and scope to warrant a plan, which may serve to render reference easier while also providing a summary of the argument and a short note on the main purposes of each chapter.

1.2 PLAN

CHAPTER 2

The purpose of Chapter 2 is to set the scene for the book by describing the relative economic decline of the UK and critically examining some of the policies which various sources have suggested may assist in producing higher economic growth in Britain.

Section 2.1

It begins with a brief review of some of the statistics which illustrate the relative decline of the United Kingdom. Economic comparisons are made throughout this book between Britain and four other developed countries — France, Japan, West Germany and the USA — and some reasons are advanced for selecting these nations as comparators. The sizes of these five economies are assessed as percentages of the free world economy, and annual incomes per head in US dollars (converted at exchange rate values) are quoted and briefly discussed. Production and output in a number of industries are quoted for the five nations; in virtually every case, Britain has grown most slowly.

Section 2.2

Having described the recent economic history of the UK, we then review the proposed solutions to Britain's economic difficulties. We classify these solutions as usually falling into one of three categories; the suggested solutions of the Right, which have as their cornerstone the actions of government in distorting or dominating one or several aspects of the free market economy; the proposed solutions of the Left, which imply that more and not less government involvement in the economy is required; and the solutions by imitation of foreign practice, which argue or imply that the problem arises because the British do not behave, socially or industrially, as do economically successful overseas nations. Classifying suggested solutions as economically right- or left-wing, or as originating from overseas studies does not imply any value judgment on our part, but merely acts as a useful classification system.

Perhaps the most brilliant exponent of the right-wing is Professor Milton Friedman, who argues that there is a strong correlation between inflation and the money supply, and that government control of the money-printing presses is at the root of the inflationary process. However, Friedman's economics has little to contribute to the discussion of investment finance or economic growth problems. Bacon and Eltis believe that Britain's failure to grow is due to the actions of the government in preferring public investment and expenditure to the group of producers who provide marketed output. Their argument has won considerable numbers of converts and we will accordingly allocate discussion to a section of its own (section 2.4). A further right-wing economic argument is that the stop-go cycle of the British economy has worsened growth prospects and weakened industry; this view is also briefly discussed. The opinion that higher profits would radically improve British growth prospects is put into perspective.

The solutions of the Left are discussed. There seem to be two such solutions; first, limitation of overseas competition by the adoption of import controls; and second, the nationalisation of major UK companies and/or financial institutions. (These policies may not be alternatives; all could conceivably be implemented simultaneously.) Strong academic support for import controls, rather than devaluation, is given by the Cambridge School. While import controls may be preferable to devaluation in some respects, these policies are proposed adjustments to the reality of the UK decline, rather than holding out hope of reversing that decline. Nationalisation of parts of UK industry seems to have several problems associated with it; first, the costs of compensation would be large; second, the political involvement created by nationalisation seems to produce lower returns on assets in the nationalised sector; and third, the companies and managements which are proposed for nationalisation are not volunteers for that solution. Similar problems would be met with if government proceeded with the Labour Party's National Executive Committee's proposal to nationalise banking and insurance. There are therefore hindrances to nationalisation, not least of which is low public approval of such a policy.

One solution from overseas—the Hudson Institute's *The U.K. in 1980*—is critically reviewed, and found wanting, for the proposals it puts forward have either been tried previously or are not apparently based on a sound economic understanding of Britain's situation.

Section 2.4

The Bacon-Eltis hypothesis, that the relative decline of the UK economy may be partially due to the large size of the non-market sector in the UK, is summarised and discussed. Some of the suggestions of Bacon and

Eltis — that Britain has too few producers in the sense of employees in the market sector, and that a profits squeeze has reduced fixed-interest debt — do not seem to be borne out by other data. NEDO studies, for example, suggest that there may be too many industrial employees per machine in the UK compared with overseas, and fixed-interest debt in the UK shows no long-run tendency to decline. But the basic case of Bacon and Eltis, that the government and non-market sector share of the economy has increased, and ought to be diminished in the interests of providing resources for improving industrial production, seems substantially justified. The measures proposed by Bacon and Eltis, however, appear to do little more than set the clock back to about 1960 by reversing the deterioration of recent years. It seems unlikely that this will produce adequate economic growth in Britain, if the aim is to match the growth rates of (say) France or West Germany. An examination of capital-output ratios and the investment-financing procedures abroad may help to demonstrate this.

CHAPTER 3

The purpose of Chapter 3 is to argue that the rate of capital investment, may, under appropriate circumstances, be a crucial factor in determining the rate of economic growth experienced by an economy. To do this, it is necessary to examine the theory of economic growth, critically comment upon Denison's work in this area, and calculate the capital-output ratios of the five nations. The output and employment which may result from investment in different economic sectors in the UK is also discussed, and finally some conclusions on the relative importance of capital investment in producing economic growth are suggested.

Section 3.1

The chapter begins with an outline of the classical position on capital formation, as one of several factors in the economic growth process. Although the situation is complex, a number of operationally useful generalisations can be made. It is clear that observers of the Industrial Revolution saw the changeover from hand-work done at home, to machine-work done in factories, as one of its most significant aspects. One author defines the Industrial Revolution in these terms, while another suggests that possibly the greatest factor in the making of the revolution may have been the invention of machine tools. Other significant variables such as resource discovery, population growth and technological progress, are highlighted, although the way in which the factors generally affect output through induced, autonomous or more productive investment is also indicated. Most economists give rapid capital accumulation pride of place in producing a high rate of economic growth. General agreement on this topic, however, produces no specific, agreed prescriptions on the relative importance of factor inputs to the production process.

Section 3.2

One man who has adopted a mathematical, almost arithmetical, approach to the problem of economic growth is Edward Denison of the Brookings Institution. In *Why Growth Rates Differ* Denison assigns values to the relative proportions of manpower and capital inputs in nine developed economies. He adds to these inputs by several special factors, modifies the values of these inputs by special qualitative changes, and calculates the supposed improvement in the productive use of resources, to arrive at estimates 'explaining' much of the economic growth rates of the nine nations for the period 1952–65. The work of Denison, however, may be doubtful for several reasons. First, his central assumption, in distributing input shares, is that enterprises will combine factors of production in cost-minimising proportions, and that earnings per factor of production therefore reflect relative contributions to output. This is an assumption perhaps justified in a purely capitalist economy, but seems less relevant to the post-Keynesian world, where the earnings of labour are increased by the deliberate action of governments. Government actions transfer income from enterprises and workers to the unemployed, to pensioners and to welfare benefits, and this results in a re-distribution in the earnings of income and capital, undermining Denison's central assumption.

The earnings of labour and capital may be determined more by bargaining power and political forces than by logical economic criteria. Capital earnings in recent years have also been squeezed due to government price controls, which have been a feature of nearly all western economies. Both these factors would tend to understate the output-assisting contribution of capital while overstating the labour contribution, even if we accept the basic principle that income shares reflect marginal product. Second, Denison seems to confuse the earnings of capital with its share of national income; the two are not the same, for in some nations (as we will show later in this book) a saving-to-investment transformation process increases the income share of capital. Third, Denison generates more explanations than the number of independent observations; 22 factors are used to explain 18 independent growth estimates. This may meet the demands of logical plausibility but fails any test of statistical proof; it can in fact be shown that the solution of the weights of some of the factor contributions can be set almost arbitrarily. For all that, Denison's book is a great attempt to deal with the problem of assessing the contributions of various factor inputs to economic growth. Yet the marginal theory is subject to so many qualifications that there must be extreme doubt whether Denison's work is rooted in economic realities.

Section 3.3
The capital-output ratios of the five nations are calculated and compared in section 3.3. This is done by a number of methods, and all of these involve some difficulties in the relative comparability of the statistics calculated. It is virtually impossible to calculate the overall capital-output ratio for all the five economies, for perpetual-inventory estimates of the capital stock are not available in all cases. Marginal cumulative capital-output ratios for a number of years can however be calculated, and these can be stabilised by examining real cumulative increases in output with real cumulative gross and net capital investment during the period 1961–71 for the five nations. There are three results which follow from an examination of these capital-output ratios; first, they seem to be falling in each of the five nations; second, there are great discrepancies between these ratios in different nations; and third, the make-up of the investment, e.g. the proportions spent on productive machinery and the proportions of gross investment which is net new investment, are different for the five nations. The capital-output ratios based upon the rate of equipment investment for the period 1956–63 are then presented and discussed for a number of nations.

Section 3.4
The sectoral allocation of fixed assets in the UK — between households, companies, public corporations, local authorities and central government — is discussed. It seems that the low returns in UK public corporations and the nearly nil returns on social overhead capital are concealing a tolerably adequate capital-output ratio in the UK companies sector.

Section 3.5
Tentative conclusions about the role of capital formation in assisting rapid economic growth are then proposed. It seems that low capital investment in the UK may be one of the significant factors limiting a

higher rate of economic development. Indeed, it could be suggested that while low economic growth may not always be attributable to a low rate of net capital formation, there are no developed nations which appear to combine high economic growth with low rates of capital investment. High capital investment is obviously an essential, but not a sufficient, condition for rapid economic growth. It is not enough to have a high investment rate; the sectoral allocation of that investment is a crucial factor in determining the overall productivity of investments. That sectoral allocation is decided partly by market forces, and partly by deliberate government policy, as the next chapter shows.

CHAPTER 4

Different nations have various institutions to collect liquid savings, transform them from short- to long-term use if necessary, and advance these as loans to final users. Chapter 4 outlines and qualifies the relative importance of various financial institutions and the net effect and overall efficiency of national procedures in the saving-to-investment transformation process. The different degrees of integration of the financial and industrial structures are also commented upon.

Section 4.1
International comparisons can be facilitated by outlining, for the five nations, the amounts advanced from sources of saving to the end-users of the loans. The history and socio-political background to the national financial institutions will be disregarded in favour of analysing how the procedures operate. In each of the sections 4.2 to 4.6 the different national procedures for financing capital investment from external sources are described. All of these summaries follow the same general outline — a brief note on the nature of banking in the country, comment on the relative importance of various sources of saving, a discussion of the tabulated savings-to-investment transformation process (usually from 1970 to 1974) and a conclusion about the investment priorities of the system. However, within each nation there are some unique characteristics which affect the pattern of investment finance; these are commented upon in the text. Many items of detail are covered in these sections which cannot be adequately summarised here.

Section 4.2
The transformation of saving to investment in France for the period 1970–73 is discussed. The sources of funds, and the sizes of these sources

10   *Financing Industrial Investment*

as percentages of GDP, the institutions used to canalise these funds from savers to investors and the extent of the transformation of resources from short- to medium- and long-term funds is discussed. The major difference between the French system of financing capital investment (in comparison with the other four nations) is the large role of French public and para-public banking, in taking the risk of transforming short-term saving to medium- and long-term loans. The French economy benefits from this process.

Section 4.3
Japanese procedures for funding capital investment from savings are outlined and put into perspective. Bank debt as a source of new investment capital is paramount and the canalisation of saving to investment via various financial intermediaries is diagrammed and analysed. One unique aspect of the Japanese system is the overloan procedure, which permits major banks to advance more money as investment loans than the banks' deposit base. The Japanese government assists the banking system to give loan priority to the private sector.

Section 4.4
West German saving-to-investment conversion procedures are summarised for the period 1970–74. The role of private banks in the conversion of short-term assets to long-term resources is outlined, and the efficiency of the conversion process estimated. The unusual aspect of the West German economy is the willingness of private banks to take the risk (without any government support) in converting short-term saving to long-term loans.

Section 4.5
The sources and uses of saving in the UK during the period 1970–74 are tabulated and discussed. Special reference is made to the 'Heath boom' of 1973, when banks were requested to give industrial lenders a high priority. Reasons for the failure of this initiative are suggested. The relative sizes of UK sources of new external capital for industrial and commercial companies is assessed for the period 1963–75. One notable aspect of the UK economy is the low level of long-term bank debt for financing private sector industrial investment. The greatest beneficiary of UK capital loans in recent years is the public sector.

Section 4.6

The advancement of loans from savings in the USA during the period 1965–73 is tabulated and discussed. The United States seem to possess very laissez-faire capital markets, but these have not produced comparatively high rates of capital investment in productive enterprises.

Section 4.7

The priorities of the saving-to-investment transformation process, its major national purpose (in terms of the economic sectors which benefit from that transformation) and its structure in terms of the capital market and the role of the banking sector, all vary considerably within the five nations. In France, where para-public banking, supported by the state, provides funds for companies whose aims coincide with the National Plan, bank lending of capital funds to enterprises considerably exceeds funds raised on the capital market; the money markets are managed by the public and para-public banks to favour public enterprises and the ends of the state. In Japan, there is a highly efficient savings-to-investment transformation process, assisted by government, in which banks are used to advance large-scale capital to private enterprises. The stock and bond markets are sizeable but have a small role in comparison with the capital funding functions of banks. Banks and business are often very integrated. In West Germany, money from the capital markets and loans to enterprises are generally provided by the banks, without the assistance of government; the saving-to-investment process is highly efficient, with private enterprises as the major beneficiaries. In the United Kingdom, private enterprises rely upon long-term external capital advanced from new stock issues, debentures, and bonds. Banks provide some medium- and long-term capital to private enterprises, but advance a great deal of saving to public corporations, local authorities and the state. The UK financial and industrial sectors are almost entirely distinct, in two completely separate economic compartments. In the USA new issues of equities and bonds form the most significant source of new external capital funds for enterprises, but there are some medium- and long-term bank loans to enterprises.

The personal savings of households, which are principally canalised to support investment in Japan and West Germany, are partially loaned back to households as consumer and mortgage credit in France, the UK and the USA. This factor explains one difference in the availability of savings for investment loans; the net savings of households are less (as a percentage of GDP) where consumer or mortgage financial systems are highly developed.

The UK and the USA — the economic growth laggards, in the post-war period — rely more upon capital markets to provide enterprise capital. In France, West Germany and Japan, the banking system also provides enterprises with medium- and long-term capital. The net results of these national systems are different costs and profits of capital, as Chapter 5 makes clear.

CHAPTER 5

The purpose of Chapter 5 is to discuss the theory of capital gearing and the costs and profits of capital in the five nations. However, the theory of capital gearing is largely Anglo-Saxon, and may partially explain why debt-equity ratios are lower in the USA and the UK than elsewhere. Interest rates and the resulting costs of capital in most nations have varied so widely in recent years that the comparative discussion is perhaps best made in approximate terms.

Section 5.1
This section deals with the Anglo-Saxon theory of capital gearing, which alleges that there is a minimum weighted-average cost of capital where debt is about one-third of long-term capital resources. This allegation rests upon the argument that low-cost fixed-interest debt can be advanced, secured by the fixed assets of the company, and this will help gear upward the rewards of shareholders, up to a point. If debts are advanced beyond about a third of the capital structure, however, the risk of the debt is increased because there may be no fixed assets to act as a security for the loan, while large debts could significantly reduce profits in bad years, making the share price less stable. Furthermore, unsecured loans would, beyond a certain point, act as if they were equity, bearing high risks which would command a higher interest rate. This theory is interesting and plausible, but reality is much more variable, and causes certain difficulties for the theory. First, Japanese companies have about 85 % debt (in 1975 — the percentage is steadily increasing) in their capital structure, and the Tokyo stock exchange has signally failed to collapse or become unstable. (West German and French companies also have loans which are more than one-third of their capital structure).

Second, the theory has no basis in observed statistical fact, despite various attempts (notably by Modigliani and Miller) to prove it. Third, the theory tends to be an analysis of the theoretical position of long-term debt in the capital structure of a company, and short-term debt generally poses a greater threat to cash flow and earnings. However, the theory is useful as a rationalisation of Anglo-Saxon practice. If the theory is used as a guide to practice then it becomes a self-fulfilling prophecy; if companies which have over one-third debt in their capital structure are considered to be risky ventures, then bankers may deny them loans, thereby making these companies risky ventures. If France, Japan and West Germany had restricted themselves to the rule of thumb that debt should not exceed about one-third of a company's capital structure, then the quoted companies in their economies would be much smaller than their present sizes.

Section 5.2
This section deals with the apparent costs of stock-market capital in the five nations. It begins by drawing attention to some of the difficulties involved in estimating the costs of equity. The dividends to shareholders are not an adequate indication of the cost of equity. In theory it is possible to estimate the yield of stocks, assess the capital value trend of stocks, take taxation into account, and assess the costs of capital to pre-tax profits. In practice, it is much more difficult. Interaction between stock markets tends to equalise equity yields, in the absence of capital controls; but some capital controls are widespread. An appreciating currency creates a gain in earnings to the foreign investor; to what extent should this be taken into account? As Keynes remarked, share prices fall when interest rates rise and equity yields in recent years have often been below interest rates.

Furthermore, the yields calculated for national stock markets are not directly comparable as they differ in coverage; the French yields are based on a sample of 295 companies, with average yields per industry scaled-up in the proportions of those industries' total quotations on the stock market; the Japanese yields are arithmetical averages of yields on all shares quoted in the First Section of the Tokyo stock exchange; West German share yields are total dividends divided by total market value; UK yields are based on the prices of 500 industrial shares; while USA yields rest upon 500 common stocks selected by Standard and Poor and representing about 90 % of the total market value of all common stocks quoted on the NYSE. If, despite these and other differences, we are prepared to assume that the yields quoted reflect average market yields, then a crude estimate of the cost of equity can be made. This shows great instability over the 1970–75 period due to the oil crisis and the subsequent world depression. Finally the size of secondary equity markets, relative to GDP, is mentioned.

Section 5.3

The purpose of this section is to summarise the costs of new investment capital in the five nations. There are three aspects to the section; first, the calculation of investment capital sources as percentages of GDP; second, the tabulation of interest rates of loans in the five nations; and third, a nation-by-nation summary of capital schedules and costs. The sources of new investment capital — internally from business savings and depreciation, and externally from the stock market and the banking system — are summarised as percentages of GDP. This procedure enables us to see where the finance for capital investment originates. Incidentally, we note the high propensity of British and US companies to declare high profits and pay higher taxes; the tendency of loan finance to generate depreciation to protect profits is outlined, with special reference to the special depreciation allowances of Japan. During the 1960s, UK corporate savings declined steadily; USA corporate savings were proportionately lower (as a percentage of GDP) than the French and West German equivalents. Depreciation in corporations in the UK and the USA also ran at a lower level relative to GDP than in France or West Germany. External sources of capital funds ranged from $5-7\frac{1}{2}\%$ of GDP in the USA to $12\frac{1}{2}-22\%$ of GDP in Japan. The sum of internal and external medium- and long-term finance made available to enterprises ranged from 10% in the UK and the USA to about 30% in Japan.

The interest rate costs of loans are tabulated and discussed for the five nations. Capital schedules, giving the amounts of capital available to enterprises as percentages of GDP and the estimated costs of each source, are then summarised in subsections 5.3.1 to 5.3.5 (France 5.3.1; Japan 5.3.2; West Germany 5.3.3; UK 5.3.4; USA 5.3.5).

Section 5.4

This section outlines a procedure for calculating the return on investment from the capital-output ratio. This is done by adding the stock and inventory investment to the fixed capital investment required to receive total investment, and by deducting the costs of output from the value of output to receive net output due to the investment; net output divided by total investment gives the gross return on the investment. It is suggested that investments can be regarded as profitable if they fund their own cash flow repayment costs of capital, i.e. an investment is regarded as profitable if it is an asset to cash flow. This definition of profitability leads directly to an emphasis on the repayment costs of loan capital, in which the term of a loan is shown to be more significant to the repayment costs than the interest rate. Repayment costs for profitable companies (which can set both interest and capital repayments as a cost against pre-tax profits) are tabulated. The rate of return on average existing investments in UK industry in 1970 is assessed and the procedure for calculating rates of return on net investments is outlined.

Section 5.5

This section contrasts the effects of the two different industrial traditions of financing investment — the Anglo-Saxon tradition, where there are high equity ratios in the capital structure and depreciation and business savings fund most new investments, and the alternative tradition, as practised in Japan and West Germany, where external bank loans are a major source of new investment capital. The basic reason why the banking system is more efficient at providing new external investment capital is that the banks can tap great proportions of the available savings in the economy, advancing it to all credit-worthy companies, while stock markets rely on the willingness of investors to buy new issues and the willingness of quoted corporations to issue new shares and bonds. Banks can transform more saving, advancing it cheaply to virtually all of the economy, placing the loans wherever they will earn a return; the stock market helps only quoted companies and the costs of initial flotation are comparatively high. Perhaps one reason why banks are highly efficient at advancing loan capital to companies is that credit creation within the banking system increases the ability of that system to advance further loans every time more credit is created. A banking system advancing investment credit to business is demonstrably an efficient method of financing capital investment.

In the nations where there are large-scale external sources of loan capital from banks, the cost of that external capital is low, due to the long-term nature of the debt. Profitability is therefore more assured because of the lower repayment rates. The external capital, once provided, creates depreciation funds, and protects profits from taxation, while increasing business savings and industrial capacity. This may be the key to the virtuous cycle of savings generating higher investment, which generates still higher savings.

CHAPTER 6

The purpose of this chapter is to outline the linkages between welfare objectives — high real private consumption, high personal savings, high living standards for households, and full employment; and economic growth.

Section 6.1

Because Britain's trading position has been weak, the implied comparative standard of living in the UK, in terms of dollars per head, is lower than the real private consumption level. Data about the level of real private consumption in five countries in 1960 and extrapolations to 1970 are tabulated. Considered in these terms, Britain seems to have had a trading problem rather than a living standards problem, although failure to solve the former could lead to the latter. Some economists would argue that it already has.

Section 6.2

Household savings are the major source of uncommitted resources which can be applied to increase investment credit. The use made of these savings — the extent to which households borrow their savings — differs in various countries, as published data demonstrates. There seem to be several phenomena which are related to increased personal savings (limitation of hire purchase debt, inflation, periodic bonuses as part of income increases, time deposits in the banking system, and pension savings). Several of these factors could, under the appropriate circumstances, be manipulated by governments wishing to increase household savings and possibly consequently investment, if there is a savings-to-investment transformation process to provide that function.

Section 6.3

The greatest gains from higher economic growth are made by households. The savings of these households are also reduced in purchasing power by inflation. Some nations seem to prosper on relatively high rates of growth and inflation; this observation raises the question of the relationship between past saving, present consumption, and saving for the future in an inflationary world. A trade off can be calculated between the increased real income of households due to economic growth and the reduced purchasing power of savings. Under particular circumstances where credit is being created to fund increased investment, a certain amount of inflation may be the price of some economic growth. Whether this is regarded as worthwhile is a political judgment.

Section 6.4

This section deals with investment and employment, and contrasts British economic philosophy with that of Japan. It is a contrast between the management of demand (increased public investments with a low continuing income and employment component) and the management of supply (increased private investments and industrial capacity with a high continuing employment component). The comparison is the more stark because high UK savings are not adequately transformed into investments. A Japanese-style rate of development, aiming at headlong economic growth, is not advocated for Britain, but higher UK economic growth and more private investment seems to be widely held out as a desirable aim. Finally, the ironic observation that an emphasis on employment and welfare in the UK has resulted in unemployment and a slowly improving welfare is contrasted with the Japanese situation, where 'Economic Growth First' has resulted in virtually full employment (although this is partly culturally caused, due to the lifetime employment bargain between employee and employer in Japan) and rapidly improving welfare.

CHAPTER 7

The purpose of this chapter is first, to discuss the possible methods which could increase the flow of investment finance and second, to outline a set of policies which, in the opinion of the authors, might hold out a reasonable chance of successfully financing more British industrial investment, and possibly a subsequent economic revival.

Section 7.1

There are three possible options for the UK, as far as investment finance is concerned. First, no action may be taken, in which case the UK will probably continue on its current trajectory of economic decline, increasing unemployment and relative eclipse in western Europe. Second, the left-wing solutions of the Labour Party—the nationalisation of the banks and much of the economy—could occur. Third, steps could be taken to assist banks to advance long-term capital loans to industry, as happens abroad. Each of these options is discussed in turn, and we conclude that the third option—the voluntary transformation of banks from within—holds out the best hope of future prosperity.

Section 7.2
This section summarises what may need to be done to produce higher industrial investment in the UK. The size of the problem — the gap between UK enterprise investment and that abroad — is assessed. The need to reduce the Public Sector Borrowing Requirement and ensure that funds released go to private investment is touched upon. The required policy of more term deposits in UK banks, and proposals to increase personal saving are discussed. The suggestion is made that UK banks should voluntarily take the risks involved in transforming short-term saving to long-term resources. The role of government — in restricting consumer credit, assisting higher savings, legislating investment credit bonds, providing higher depreciation allowances for plant and machinery, and releasing some bank deposits from the Bank of England — is outlined. Higher productive industrial investment in the UK is not a panacea. It will not produce an economic miracle unless constructive co-operation is established between workers, managers, banks and government. However, higher productive investment makes UK economic success more likely; it improves the probabilities, in conditions where other factors are right. No nation succeeds economically without adequate investment.

Section 7.3
Finally, we conclude that although the difficulties of the programme we outline are considerable, there may be a fair chance of reversing Britain's relative economic decline, through an improved procedure for financing industrial investment.

2 Britain in the Industrial World

2.1 BRITAIN'S ECONOMIC DECLINE

Britain's economic performance during the post-war period has been poor in comparison with that of other developed countries. There are many illustrations of this. An economic survey of the United Kingdom, published by the OECD in 1962, showed that Britain's growth during the 1950s was lower than that of any other member country.[1] A Brookings Institution study of Britain, published in 1968, remarked in the introduction that the casual observer often treats Britain as burnt-out, by comparison with her North Atlantic neighbours.[2] More recently, the Hudson Institute, Europe has produced a popular book indicating at some length the extent of the relative economic decline of the United Kingdom.[3] Virtually every recent book about the British economy touches upon Britain's decline at some stage, while many newspaper articles also discuss Britain's waning economic power. Perhaps the one point of general agreement among economists is the reality of Britain's relative economic decline.

It is not that Britain has been doing badly in terms of its historical growth record; it has been growing relatively rapidly by that standard.[4] Indeed, Denison has remarked that there is little doubt that the British people would have regarded post-war economic growth as highly satisfactory, if the United Kingdom were an isolated state.[5] However, Britain is far from isolated from the rest of the world; and other developed countries during the post-war period have been growing more rapidly.

Table 2.1 shows the economic performance of 17 developed countries, ranked in terms of their growth of GDP. Britain is at the bottom of the league, with the lowest annual rate of real GDP growth, during the 1961–72 period whether measured in absolute or per capita rates of growth. In the 1961–74 period, Britain's share of world trade fell from 12.1 % of the total exports of developed countries, to 7.0 %, an absolute

TABLE 2.1   The economic performance of 17 developed countries

Country	Annual growth rate of real GDP 1961–72	Annual growth rate of real GDP per capita 1961–72	Share of total exports of developed countries in 1961	Share of total exports of developed countries in 1974	Change in share of exports between 1961 and 1974	Annual growth rate of exports by volume 1961–72
Japan	10.1	8.9	4.6	10.1	+ 5.5	15.3
Spain	6.9	5.7	0.8	1.3	+ 0.5	12.6
France	5.8	4.7	7.9	8.4	+ 0.5	10.3
Netherlands	5.6	4.4	4.7	5.9	+ 1.2	10.1
Canada	5.5	3.8	6.6	6.2	− 0.4	8.9
Australia	5.4	3.4	2.6	2.0	− 0.6	7.4
Austria	5.0	4.4	1.3	1.3	0.0	8.8
Finland	4.9	4.5	1.2	1.0	− 0.2	7.5
Belgium	4.8	4.3	4.3	5.1	+ 0.8	8.9
Italy	4.8	4.1	6.4	5.5	− 0.9	10.8
Denmark	4.7	4.0	1.7	1.4	− 0.3	7.4
West Germany	4.5	3.6	13.8	16.1	+ 2.3	8.9
USA	4.4	3.2	23.0	17.8	− 5.2	6.4
Switzerland	4.1	2.8	2.2	2.2	0.0	7.6
Ireland	4.0	3.4	0.6	0.5	− 0.1	6.5
Sweden	3.7	3.0	3.0	2.9	− 0.1	7.3
UK	2.5	2.0	12.1	7.0	− 5.1	4.9

Source: Quoted in 'Public Consumption and Economic Performance' by David Smith, *National Westminster Bank Review*, Nov. 1975. (Ultimate source: *IMF International Financial Statistics* and *OECD National Accounts 1961–71*.)

loss of 5.1 % of export share. Only the USA lost as much as this, but since its share fell from 23.0 % to 17.8 %, the loss was proportionately less; that is, Britain lost 42.1 % of its previous share, while the USA lost 21.8 %.

No matter which statistics are chosen, the reality of the relative economic decline of Britain is abundantly clear. For the purposes of further comparison we will from now on usually confine our comments to the position of the United Kingdom relative to four other developed countries — France, Japan, West Germany and the United States. There are several reasons for the choice of these nations for the drawing of economic parallels. The predominant reason is the range of different institutions and procedures used within these countries to finance industrial investment; but there are other justifications. France and

West Germany have internal markets and populations similar in size to those of the UK, while the international markets of all three nations are superficially similar, in that all three are inside the tariff structure of the European Economic Community. The United States shares with Britain a common Anglo-Saxon heritage, up to a point, in its attitudes and forms of business, although beyond that, similarities may end, for the USA is the world's largest economy. Japan is included as the fastest-growing major economy.

The purpose of this book is to compare the various national traditions of financing industrial investment, demonstrating that investment may be central to the process of economic growth, highlighting differences in national attitudes to investment, calculating the approximate costs and profits of capital investment in each country and finally drawing out lessons for the UK from that analysis. To satisfy these purposes, it is necessary to perform a cross-sectional analysis of the economic experience of a number of nations. To discuss more than half a dozen nations could become unmanageable; to discuss less than five would run the risk of failing to examine a wide enough range of circumstances.

It is as well to begin by estimating the economic sizes of these five nations as percentages of the total free world economy. The economists of the United Nations calculated that the absolute size of the market economies of the world (excluding the planned economies of the Soviet and Chinese blocs) was about one and one-eighth trillion dollars in 1960. ('Trillion' is here defined as in American usage, i.e. 10^{12}.) By 1970, the total output of the free world economies had grown and inflated to almost two and a half trillion dollars (Table 2.2). The developing market economies failed to grow as rapidly as those of the developed economies, with the result that the developed economies (at 84.4 % of the free world economy) were in 1970 more than half a percent larger as a proportion of the free world economy than ten years previously. The poor had indeed grown relatively poorer.

In absolute terms the poor are probably even poorer than Table 2.2 suggests. Nearly all developing countries have non-convertible currencies, and their exchange rates are determined by their governments rather than by market forces. Yet there is always a market in currencies, suppress it how governments will; and an exchange value is put on the foreign currency of most developing countries by Swiss banks (although there is often no market in the higher denomination notes). For most developing countries, the market value of their currency, as decided by Swiss bankers, is less than the official rate; hence the poor are probably poorer than the UN calculate. The yen, the French franc, the

TABLE 2.2　Size of five developed economies, 1960 and 1970

Area	Absolute size* ($m.)		Relative size (% of free world economy)	
	1960	1970	1960	1970
Market economies of the world	1125700	2485300	100.0	100.0
Developing market economies	181900	386900	16.2	15.6
Developed market economies	943800	2098400	83.8	84.4
France	61041	144734	5.4	5.8
Japan	43097	196917	3.8	7.9
West Germany	72036	187694	6.4	7.6
UK	71244	119811	6.3	4.8
USA	509030	983237	45.2	39.6

* Absolute sizes are converted to US dollars at official exchange rates.
Source: *United Nations Statistical Yearbook, 1974*, Table 189, pp. 650–2. Copyright, United Nations 1975. Reproduced by permission.

deutschmark, sterling, and the US dollar are all hard currencies in the sense that at any one time there are only fractional bankers' margins in their interrelating exchange values throughout the world; they are all convertible currencies. Hence, although there may be an overstatement of the real income of the developing market economies in Table 2.2, the comparisons between the five countries are more realistic.

Within the five developed economies which are our chosen field of examination, Japan had greatly increased its share of the free world economy, growing from less than 4 % in 1960 to almost 8 % in 1970, while France and West Germany also became relatively larger. The economies of the United States and the United Kingdom both grew more slowly between 1960 and 1970 than the world average and that of the developed world, and both consequently lost ground as a percentage of the free world economy. From 1960 to 1970 the USA became about one-eighth smaller, relatively speaking, while the decline of the UK was about twice that amount.

Incidentally, although we are discussing only five major economies, these represent in total about two-thirds of the free world economy, and possess over three-quarters of the industrial output of the developed western world. If we further examine the annual income in dollars per head for each of these five countries in 1960 and 1970, (Table 2.3) it is clear that while both France and West Germany were slightly below UK levels in 1960, by 1970 both had considerably surpassed the UK;

Japan—which had a per capita income of about one-third of the UK in 1960—was by 1970 approaching UK levels. Japan passed UK levels in 1973. Meanwhile, the poor of the world in the developing nations lost ground between 1960 and 1970: they recorded increases in incomes per head of about 60 %, while in the developed world, incomes per capita nearly doubled in the same period. (However, such comparisons rest upon exchange rates—see the note to Table 2.3.)

TABLE 2.3   Annual income per head in US dollars

Area	*1960*	*1970*	*% increases 1960/70*
World (developed market economies)	550	980	78.2
Developing market economies	130	210	61.5
Developed market economies	1500	2980	98.7
France	1336	2851	133.4
Japan	458	1887	312.0
West Germany	1323	3095	133.9
UK	1355	2162	59.6
USA	2817	4799	70.4

Source: *United Nations Statistical Yearbook, 1974*, Table 189.
Note: Incomes per head have been calculated by converting to a common currency at exchange-rate values. For some international comparisons of real private consumption per head (which is a better measure of comparative living standards) see Chapter 6.

The relative decline of the United Kingdom was principally due to the poor performance of its industrial sector during the post-war period. Between 1960 and 1973, Japanese industrial production multiplied by over four times, French and West German industrial output doubled; United States real industrial growth was nearly 90 %; British industry grew by less than 50 %[6].

Table 2.4 shows the trend rates of growth of output, employment and productivity between 1953 and 1972 for the five countries. It is interesting to note that agricultural output in the UK has been increasing as rapidly as Japan's. Agricultural productivity has been increasing at about 5–6 % in all of the five countries, but growth rates of productivity per man in industry and the services is comparatively low in both Britain and the USA. It is clear that higher economic growth in Japan, France and West Germany has been due to higher growth rates in services and in industrial production. British economic decline is largely due to low growth rates of industrial output.

TABLE 2.4   Growth rates in five nations, 1953–72

Country	Trend rates of growth (annual average percentages)			
	Total	Agriculture	Industry[1]	Services
Output[2]				
Japan	9.7	2.5	12.5	9.6
France	5.5	2.0	6.4	4.8
West Germany	5.2	1.7	6.0	4.7
UK	2.6	2.5	2.9	2.4
USA	3.7	1.9	3.6	4.1
Employment				
Japan	1.4	− 3.6	3.7	3.0
France	0.5	− 3.7	1.0	2.2
West Germany	0.5	− 4.4	1.0	1.6
UK	0.4	− 2.9	0.0	1.1
USA	1.6	− 3.8	0.9	2.6
Productivity[3]				
Japan	8.3	6.1	8.9	6.5
France	4.9	5.7	5.4	2.6
West Germany	4.7	6.1	5.0	3.1
UK	2.2	5.4	3.0	1.4
USA	2.2	5.7	2.7	1.5

Notes:
1 Defined as mining, manufacturing, construction and public utilities.
2 GDP at constant prices.
3 Output per person employed.
Source: Andrea Boltho, *Japan: An Economic Survey 1953–73*, Oxford University Press, 1975.

It hardly seems to matter which British industries are examined, as almost all illustrate the relative decline of the UK productive base. In 1964, Britain was making nearly 1.9 million passenger cars; nine years later in the boom year of 1973, Britain produced over 100,000 less. Japanese production of passenger cars grew from less than 600,000 in 1964 to nearly 4.5 million in 1973; during the same period West German passenger car production increased from 2.6 to 3.6 millions; French passenger car production more than doubled, from 1.35 to 3.2 millions.[7] Now that a large section of Britain's car industry is nationalised, that could conceivably help provide investment capital; could the steel industry which was re-nationalised in 1967, provide a pointer on this? Production of crude steel in Britain in 1973 was 26.65 million metric tons—almost identical to production in 1963. During the same period of 1963 to 1974, Japanese crude steel production trebled (from 39.8 to 119.3 million metric tons); equivalent French production increased by over a quarter (19.8 to 25.3 million metric tons) and United States production of crude steel rose by almost 20 % (115.3 to 136.8 million metric tons). Only Britain stood still in crude steel production. [8]

There are a few exceptions (such as the production of primary aluminium, where Britain's growth of output in recent years has been very high − +535 % between 1970 and 1973, for example) and doubtless the production of North Sea oil in the last few years is similarly exceptional, but the general picture is of the relative economic decline of whole industrial sectors of the United Kingdom — in textiles, chemicals, plastics, cement, metals, electronics, shipping and motor vehicles. Individual firms within these industries may have been able to do well, but the living standards of the British have been based upon their ability to trade successfully in the world at large. That capability, and hence those living standards, are now in question. So much for the situation; but what solutions are presently suggested to reverse Britain's decline?

2.2 SOME SUGGESTED SOLUTIONS

The relative decline of the industrial and exporting base of the UK economy has given rise to a number of reports and some of these have suggested solutions. Solutions which have been put forward have generally fallen into three categories. First, there have been the solutions of the Right — solutions of the classical economist's laissez-faire school, who have maintained that the reason for UK decline lies in increasing government interference in or domination of one aspect or another of the market economy. Among these right-wing solutions are such diverse opinions as those held by Friedman, who has stressed the role of governments, in printing money, as generators of inflation; Bacon and Eltis who have pointed to the growth in the UK public sector, which has limited the resources available for productive investment in the private sector; and many others, who have suggested that lack of investment in the company (due to price controls) or lack of incentives to the individual (due to high taxation) or the 'ham-stringing of capitalism in the name of welfare', as Schumpeter predicted, could lie at the root of the UK's failure to grow adequately.

A second set of solutions has been put forward by various left-wing politicians and trade unionists and sometimes their ideas have been supported by economists. Their argument has been that the market economy has failed in Britain, and that the solution is not less socialism, but more; socialism to compel industrial investment where market forces seem to have failed. These policies may also propose protectionism against foreign competition, and have many of the hallmarks of a siege economy, which, it is said, might offer better employment prospects for more people. (The Cambridge School have calculated in the *Cambridge Economic Policy Review* of March 1976 that trade protectionism in the form of UK import controls is preferable to devaluation, but this conclusion is a preferred choice between two possible policy options, not a possible solution to low UK growth.)

A third set of solutions has been suggested by those who have looked at certain aspects of growth in a selected overseas economy, and believe that Britain could gain by imitating those solutions which seem to have worked overseas. The report of the Hudson Institute, Europe, entitled 'The United Kingdom in 1980', which grew out of their report on the French economy 'L'Envol de France,' is a good example of this. This kind of response also seems endemic in letters to the press, which often allege (with very little or no objective evidence) that the British do not work as hard as certain foreigners or that Britain (compared with other countries) has insurmountable class warfare, a Luddite workforce, and incompetent management. Such letters suggest that some social factors in the UK are responsible for economic failure. This argument may be no more valid today than it was in the 1930s; economic problems frequently have economic solutions; national cultures, while undoubtedly relevant in the broadest sense to the determination of the rate of economic growth, cannot be held responsible for British economic failure. Britain is culturally similar, in such respects as educational standards, technological levels, unionisation etc., to many successful economies. The solution to the problem of low UK growth should surely be sought in an area where Britain is definitely deficient (such as the productive investment level). To say that everything is wrong is another way of saying that the pattern of causation of a phenomenon is not well understood. To explain low economic growth by reference to every apparent defect of British life is to sin against Occam's razor by multiplying causes unnecessarily.

Before World War II, most western governments did not generally interfere with market forces during peacetime and hence it was relatively difficult to pin responsibility for the failure of any part of the economic engine upon governments. Distressing economic consequences such as inflation (if it happened) or scale unemployment, when that occurred, were held to be the result of market forces for which governments could, and frequently did, disclaim responsibility. The dramatic post-war success of Keynesian economics, in keeping unemployment down, may have perhaps caused the pendulum to swing to the opposite extreme, creating a situation in which many right-wing economists may take the view that governments are causally responsible for most aspects of national economic performance.

Friedman, for example, firmly and brilliantly argues that national inflation rates are a direct consequence of government control of the printing of money. Many other economists admit the correlation between money supply and inflation, but question the direction of causation, disputing which comes first.[9] Friedman's work, however, relates largely to inflation and the money supply, and he has very little to say on the subjects of investment and economic growth, which are our primary concern in this book.

The most formidable intellectual argument of the economists we have classified as right-wing is perhaps that advanced by Bacon and Eltis. It could be questioned whether their arguments are proper to be classified as right-wing. Although Bacon and Eltis do not commit themselves to any line of action, the thrust of their arguments and the way they are delivered tends to support a pro-market line. We discuss their arguments in detail in the next section of this chapter.

Some economists have also noted a correlation between government inspired increases in demand management and the worsening of the trade balance. In their view, higher demand results in imports being sucked in to the British economy, and hence a high pressure of demand seems to give little benefit to British industry. Walter Eltis in particular has pointed out the conflict of the UK government policy objectives[10]; on the one hand, there has been political exhortation that faster economic growth can lead to more rapidly-growing exports, and an export-led boom could lead to an improved balance of payments position; while on the other hand, lower growth reduces the demand for imports, and British governments have acted to reduce growth and imports and hence improve the balance of payments (Table 2.5).

The suggested solutions Eltis proposes include a programme of import substitution, higher investment, and high-capacity working in UK industry, possibly by utilising a combination of taxation and depreciation incentives for new investments. However, the position with regard to the relationship between the value of exports and imports and economic growth seems more doubtful and is complicated by devaluations.[11]

TABLE 2.5   UK economic expansion and stagnation

Period	Annual growth rate of UK industrial production	Annual growth in exports (volume)	Annual growth in imports (volume)
Expansion periods (1953–55, 1958–60, 1962–64)	5.8 %	4.9 %	7.9 %
Stagnation periods (1955–58, 1960–62, 1964–66)	0.9 %	2.7 %	1.3 %

Source: W. A. Eltis, 'Economic Growth and the British Balance of Payments', op. cit.

Some business economists, seeing the erosion of company profits due to price controls, have sometimes suggested that higher profits will provide faster UK growth. Some relief along these lines is obviously essential, for the replacement cost rate of return (after deducting stock-appreciation) on capital employed in British industry fell from 13 % in 1960 to less than 4 % in 1975.[12] The contribution which could be made to investment by higher profits is, however, strictly limited. Higher retained earnings during the next few years following the partial or full adoption of inflation accounting, are at best only due to restore the position of UK companies to that which prevailed in the early 1960s. This will obviously be an improvement on the present position, but it will not produce a British economic miracle. Indeed, a cynic might be forgiven for observing that the reliefs allowed might marginally assist growth but in many cases might merely prevent the shut down of some medium-sized businesses due to capital transfer tax. Before profits could make a sizeable impact on increasing the investment rate, they would need to be increased very substantially indeed. The charges against profits — principally taxes, but also dividends — would erode the final residual which could be used for new fixed investments. Prices would need to rise disproportionately due to the larger mark-up required for higher investment; British goods would become less competitive; exports could be lost; the value of the pound could fall. At current rates of corporation tax (52.5 %) and if retained profits alone had to finance the expansion of industrial investment, then for an investment rate in private industry equal to that of Japan, retained profits would need to rise by about 15 % of GDP, and pre-tax profits by over 22 % of GDP. We do not believe this is even remotely politically feasible, as the implied price explosion would approach hyperinflation levels. There are other and better ways to finance some industrial investment.

On the other hand, the Left frequently suggest that nationalisation may be a cure to the problem of investment in industry. That comment reflects a lack of understanding of the situation; as we, shall show, British industry may not be investing enough because it does not have access to the low-cost external funds made available abroad, not because of any proven lack of desire to invest. But, to place that observation on one side, the costs of any large-scale programme of UK nationalisation seem very daunting.

In the recent past the UK government has had some difficulty in trying to finance its short-term needs, without embarking on a major programme of purchasing industrial assets, so that any nationalisation programme the UK could afford would offer no solution, barring a policy of nationalisation without compensation unknown outside the communist countries. Furthermore, even if a much larger section of the economy were nationalised, this might provide no solution to the problem of UK growth, because the return on investment in public sector industries is relatively low.[13]

The reasons for low returns in the public sector are not hard to find, because industries, once nationalised, are obliged to adopt some politically-determined social policies — such as maintaining uneconomic steel plants in small communities, or holding down politically sensitive gas or electricity prices in pre-election years — and so-called investment money is canalised to these ends. It is recognised in the various nationalisation Acts that the public sector industries have social obligations in addition to their commercial principles. The 1947 Electricity Act, for example, requires the industry to extend supply to rural areas, so far as practicable. But the involvement of governments in the decisions of nationalised industries goes far beyond these laid-down social obligations, for all nationalisation Acts have a clause which requires the industry to do as the Minister instructs. This results in more day-to-day direction than the overall legislation may intend. At the time of writing, the CEGB is not being allowed to decide whether the new generating station, Drax B, is economically justified; political needs, including the requirement to generate some short-term employment, seem to be deciding the issue. At the other end of the scale, British Rail's decision to quit the carriage of pigeons has been politically reversed, following public objections.

It is conceivable, of course, that British governments could cease their involvement in the decision-making of nationalised industries, allowing these to be run as commercial concerns, and governments need not, for example, instruct nationalised industries to hold their prices down in pre-election years. However, there is no sign of any lack of political desire to control nationalised industries, which have sometimes been nationalised to avoid the rapid run-down which commercial considerations would dictate; if nationalised industries where possible (e.g. in steel, gas and electricity) were to raise their own capital requirements through higher prices, these prices might well be so politically unacceptable that some political interference may be inevitable. Nationalisation seems to involve an almost unavoidable usage of capital for social or political purposes, and public savings are not so adequate that the UK can afford to scale up that kind of policy.

It is perhaps no accident that one of the first calculated risks taken by British Leyland, following nationalisation, was the use of the first tranche of investment capital to pay wages. Additionally, wholesale nationalisation still would not help the majority of small- to medium-sized firms. There is much talent and many people involved in small-scale industries, which are a precious asset no policy-maker should ignore. Government simply cannot involve enough investors in its planning; only the push of market forces produces fast and efficient growth. We shall later argue that given the necessary investment resources, bankers and industrialists, in their thousands, can do what is required; government and nationalised industries cannot get everyone involved on the scale required. Finally, nationalisation smacks of a command economy, and a policy of wholesale nationalisation and massive government involvement in the economy is not compatible in the longer run with the British tradition of a mixed economy state. For essential services and for certain public utilities, nationalisation is necessary; but for goods-producing industries it seems to be a last resort, not a panacea for the UK's problems.

If few economic solutions seem available from the political Right and Left, where could Britain seek solutions? It could look abroad, to see if the seeds of economic success can be analysed and transplanted. There are, however, certain dangers in doing this, and paramount among these may be the possibility that one may see and select the accidental, rather than the relevant, factors of success. Perhaps the report of the Hudson Institute, Europe ('The United Kingdom in 1980') illustrates that danger, for this report was produced upon the heels of a report on the French economy for the French government.

The report describes, in dramatically-worded journalese (two of the chapter headings—'Some stark truths for Britain', and 'The myths of salvation' — give the tenor) the relative weakness of British economic performance, and forecasts the probable future course of that continuing decline, pointing out some of the consequent social and political implications of these projections. The facts of the past and, to some extent, their forecasting by trend extrapolation to 1980, are unexceptional.

The Hudson Report is a fair description of the UK's economic decline, but falls far short of any explanation of that reality. First of all, it alleges that Britain's crisis is unique, despite the fact that relatively low industrial growth is common to virtually all Anglo-Saxon economies. Indeed, the report lists, but fails to highlight, the relatively low investment and growth rates of the USA compared with the nations of continental Europe or Japan. Furthermore, the recent response of the Anglo-Saxon economies to that low industrial growth has been broadly similar, and has resulted in the discovery and sometimes development of new primary resource bases in the Anglo-Saxon economies, almost always in energy or metals—iron ore in northern Australia; new oilfields in the North Sea, northern Alaska, the Mackenzie river basin in Canada and the western and eastern continental shelves of the USA; fresh commercial coalfields and metal ore deposits in Britain and in the mid-west of the USA and so on. The development of these new resource bases may be a myth of salvation but it should at least help lessen one possible constraint on future economic growth.

When it comes to suggesting remedies to Britain's economic problems, the report's suggestions approach the banal. A national development plan is suggested — as if the UK had not had plan after plan in the fifties and sixties—plus a National Investment and Development Corporation, which is proposed to be a non-political NEB: and a National Administration College,[14] along the lines of the French Ecole Nationale d'Administration, as if London or Manchester Business Schools were inadequate as centres of excellence. Finally, increased controls on capital outflows are proposed, and even a change in the make-up of the hereditary peerage is put forward. All of these suggestions, taken together, do not approach an understanding of the basic problems of financing industrial investment in Britain.

In conclusion, the Hudson Report describes the UK's decline without understanding it; rationalises and justifies the reality of decline rather than explaining it; and suggests one solution which has been tried and found wanting previously (the National Plan) along with other sociological, symbolic and almost-magical acts such as the imitation of some French institutions (which are largely irrelevant to France's growth rate) and the alteration of national 'style', psychology, and perhaps the House of Lords.

The Hudson Report, however, may be the victim of its origin in a report on the French economy in which Britain was defined in terms of not being France. Herman Kahn, the founder of the original Hudson Institute, remarks in an aside in his book *The Emerging Japanese Superstate*,[15] that the 13 additional reasons he suggests for the continued growth of the Japanese economy are, by and large, also reasons why the UK will continue to decline. We see, however, certain difficulties in trying to understand any economic situation in terms of what it is not; to paraphrase Auden:

How reliable can any prescription be which is got
By simply observing what's good, and then just inserting a not?

Not good, we suggest. The Hudson Report offers no practical solutions which hold out hope of reversing the UK's relative economic decline. Comparisons of Britain's declining industry with those which flourish overseas can be usefully made, provided these comparisons are based upon relevant data which provides pointers on how to improve the performance of British industry. This is something which the Hudson Report fails to do.

A more solid, though perhaps turgid, piece of work has recently emerged from NEDO on the financing of UK industrial investment.[16] As one would perhaps expect, the document is largely a description of how UK industry is currently financed, although in one chapter there is an international comparison of how industry is financed.[17]

Other studies produced for NEDO deal with the higher levels of manning in British industry compared with overseas — indeed, in some cases, identical machinery is being used in the USA, where the output per man-hour is much higher due to lower manning levels. Yet no-one should look at these comparisons without contemplating the results which might have followed if British industry had the same manning levels as overseas. The USA and West Germany have had a great number of new industrial investments which have resulted (until relatively recently) in the unemployed finding jobs elsewhere.[18] In Britain, if industrial machine manning were as low as in the USA or West Germany, the dole queue would probably be several millions larger. To say this, is not to justify over-manning in the UK, but it does to some extent explain it. Furthermore, to point out that the machinery in use is identical in no way accounts for the different age structure of the capital machinery; there may be a system of productivity decay whereby new machinery is introduced with relatively few workers, and additional employees are involved in the work as restrictive practices develop. It certainly seems to be the case that the introduction of new machinery imposes its own operational logic, cutting across existing work patterns, creating new and more efficient working practices in young companies and forcing productivity increases (or bankruptcy) in older competing companies. There can hardly have been a great deal of this in the UK, as the level of new machinery investment has been so low; it is notable that the comparisons are made of UK firms with those overseas, not highly efficient UK firms with less efficient ones.

Perhaps it could be asked, with some justice, why UK firms have not responded to an international threat, as they might have done to one from a nearby competitor. The principal reason may be that most UK firms do not appear to react strongly to the loss of their export markets, as most of their production is for the home market. A domestic company, however, which increased productivity greatly, would not only threaten a competing firm's exports, but also the very survival of the company. The extent to which works managers in the same industry tend to keep a watchful eye on what the opposition is up to also helps to explain why productivity gains either seem to occur as ripple effects across many sectors of an industry, or not at all. Sometimes not at all, perhaps because consolidated unions across an industry may unilaterally decide upon those technologies which they will not agree to introduce. Language and cultural barriers (or, in the case of the USA, three thousand miles of ocean) prevent these managerial or union effects from happening to the same extent on an international scale. Additionally, even foreign competition seems to be feared only when it attacks British firms on their own ground, in the domestic UK market; many companies have responded by asking for protection from such foreign competition (which has not, in most cases, been granted). An alternative strategy of asking UK governments for a similar access as abroad to cheap large-scale investment funds for UK industry has not yet been tried by British managers, but might have a greater chance of ultimate political and economic success.

2.3 THE BACON-ELTIS HYPOTHESIS

Robert Bacon and Walter Eltis, two Oxford economists, have recently published an analysis of Britain's economic development since 1961[19].

To use their own term they are structuralists in their approach to what needs to be done to improve Britain's economic position. By this they mean that adjustments in the exchange rate or the money supply will not be enough to put Britain right. These have been the policies adopted by the tinkerers —again to use their term— who have dominated economic thinking in Britain from, say, 1961 up to the time of their writing. Treasury civil servants they class as tinkerers. Structuralists believe that tinkering will achieve nothing if the underlying structure of the economy is wrong.

To support their view they produce some interesting insights into the way the British economy has developed. For example, while the rate of increase in industrial production declined over the period 1955–75, going from an increase of 35 % in the decade 1955–65 to an increase of 15 % between 1965 and 1975, they show that output per man hour in manufacturing industry rose by 3 % p.a. over the period 1955–65 and by 4 % p.a. between 1965–74. Moreover, by 1971 the service life and average age of British machine tools were almost exactly the same in the USA as in the UK over a wide range of categories and user industries. Why the decline in the absolute rate of increase in output? The potential boost to output was lost, say Bacon and Eltis, because fewer were employed in manufacturing and hours worked were substantially less. A big shift in employment took place from production industries into the public sector, and this was not paralleled in any other major western developed country. In fact, between 1961 and 1974 over one-third of those employed in industry moved into other sectors. This was partly due to government stimulating the economy in time of depression via public spending. Initially the extra labour taken on had been relatively cheap but the wages spiral between 1972 and 1975 made these employees much more expensive and a considerable burden on the state and consequently the taxpayer.

There seems to be a clash of evidence between the Bacon and Eltis conclusion that there are too few producers in Britain, and the NEDO studies which demonstrate that the manpower used for similar (and sometimes identical) industrial machinery in Britain is higher than overseas. The proposition that there is too little employment in the British industries may not sit easily with the conclusion that some of British industry is over-manned. It could be that Bacon and Eltis are correct in general, while the NEDO results pertain only to the industries they studied, but this seems unlikely. It is possible to integrate these conclusions into one general observation, that British industry may be contracting because it has low productivity due to low capital investment per head, and that a lot more manpower may still have to be shaken out unless more investment capital becomes available.

However, let us continue to outline the arguments of Bacon and Eltis, who say that the massive recent increase in public sector employment has placed a considerable extra burden on industrial production which is competing for resources with the now bigger non-industrial sector. In 1961, 59 % of total industrial sales was consumed and invested outside industry; by 1974 this was up to 72 % — leaving 28 % for industry itself and the balance of payments. Exports of industrial production between 1961 and 1974 fell from $15\frac{1}{2}$ % to $6\frac{1}{2}$ % and the proportion that was invested in industry, net of capital consumption, fell to 6.0 % of industrial production in 1974 from 8 % in 1961. Industrial investment was therefore not capable of meeting increased demand during 'go' periods and this resulted in increased imports. Perhaps the most disquieting result has been the growth in some structural unemployment—a symptom of an underdeveloped economy. This is because increased manpower efficiency has led to unemployment, and there has been insufficient capital to create more industrial jobs.

Profits in manufacturing industry fell from 17 % of manufacturing output in 1964 to 7 % during 1970–72 and 3 % in 1973. Thus profit margins in Britain therefore have been much more determined by government price policies, by Trade Unions and by foreign competition than by the saving to investment mechanism that is crucial to the Cambridge theory.[20] New investment has not however meant higher employment rates because labour is not cheap. A kind of vicious circle seems to have developed and a situation has arisen where only government has been able to afford to create extra employment.

Bacon and Eltis go on to develop the production versus non-production approach to economic analysis. The division between employments is not as clear as between those who produce and those who do not. Invisible exports such as insurance or tourism benefit the economy and a definition was clearly needed to cover such sectors, as well as the non-production infrastructure like distribution. To this end, they developed an alternative hypothesis first outlined by Professor J. Johnson of Manchester University in an article on inflation in the June 1975 edition of the *Economic Journal*. He observed that instead of dividing economic activities into industrial and non-industrial, they can be divided instead between those who produce marketed outputs and those that do not.[21] A country has to live on the total of its marketed output and the balance between marketed and non-market sectors, conclude Bacon and Eltis, has gone wrong over the period 1961–75.

Bacon and Eltis cover in some detail the history of Britain's various 'stop' and 'go' economic measures from 1961 to 1975 to emphasise the strength of their diagnosis. They also examine some of the views which have been put forward as a means of re-vitalising the economy. In examining various philosophies they state as a note of caution:

> Both a Left and a pro-market sector government must achieve two objectives. They must solve the problem of high unemployment which represents obvious waste — and damages the economy and society. In addition, they must do this in ways which increase the economy's long-term capacity to provide jobs. The mistake has been made repeatedly of solving short-term problems by weakening the economy's ability to produce and employ in the long-term, and it could be fatal if this error was repeated once more. In contrast, policies to achieve a distant Utopia which ignore the need to solve immediate problems will not do. The British people will hardly tolerate deterioration for several years with little to show for it.[22]

Both the Left and pro-market sector philosophies run into the same problem — how to finance the massive investment required to re-juvenate the economy against the present pattern of heavy taxation to support a large public sector. The successful policy will have to find a way of funding investment and maintaining the social fabric provided by a large public sector. Thus: 'The world's viable economies are those which have solved the problem of providing adequate resources from their productive sectors for both non-marketed expenditure and investment.'[23] It is in this critical area that we feel our analysis has something to offer for Britain, as we shall endeavour to show later in this book.

Bacon and Eltis go on to examine the British problem in great depth. To reinforce their earlier analysis they show that between 1964 and 1974 the combined spending of central governnment and local authorities (including transfer payments) rose from 40.6 % to 52.5 % of GNP. The claims on marketed output from outside the market sector increased from 41.4 % in 1961 to 60.3 % in 1974. They also examine one particularly crucial element in investment financing (resulting from economic tinkering during the period) which is interesting against the economic analysis which we shall later develop. There is the risk that there may be a twofold effect on investment if profits are cut. First, retained profits will be smaller and thus the amount available for new investment will be reduced. Second, the amount of fixed investment borrowing will be affected; in fact, this may be affected most. As profits fall the amount of cover available for fixed interest investment will fall and the amount taken up will be reduced or eliminated leaving the brunt of new investment to be borne by retained profits. Thus aggregate investment as a share of marketed output will fall. This argument is not fully borne out by the statistics for the UK. New bank borrowing has continued to rise despite falling profits.

Statistical analysis has however shown that increases in public expenditure leading to a higher tax burden has adversely affected private sector investment. Here Bacon and Eltis quote, as corroboration of their own findings, the work of another economist, David Smith, who has examined investment, public spending, inflation and growth in 19 countries over the period 1961—72. In an article published in November 1975, Smith gave as a rule of thumb guide that 'each increase in the narrow definition of state consumption of 1 % of NDI (net domestic incomes) produces a 0.94 % drop in the ratio of investment to the NDI'.[24] This reflects the classic Harrod-Domar rubric that a country's long-term share of investment must equal the rate of growth times the capital needed to produce a unit of output. Thus if the aim is to increase output by 5 % p.a. and £2 of capital is needed to produce £1 of output, then 10 % of output must be invested each year. If investment is cut back and manpower productivity is rising more quickly than output then under-employment will occur or employees move to the non-marketed sector. Both these seem to have happened in Britain since 1961.

The danger which exists, and which Britain seems to be moving toward, is that a self-generating vicious circle will arise. As the public sector grows, this leads to increased taxation and less investment, and company profits fall as taxes are increased and sectoral unemployment/underemployment takes place and those displaced are taken up in the public sector. There are of course a few ramifications on this fundamental interaction. Because capital is not available to soak up those who could be displaced by new plant investment, there is no incentive for the work force to participate in increasing labour productivity. In a stagnant society, growth in productivity is not rewarded.

Having considered the basic economic situation and the problems attendant upon any policy aimed at breaking the vicious circle, Bacon and Eltis are clear that the need to rejuvenate the British economy requires structural changes, not more economic tinkering.

They do not, however, commit themselves to the kind of structural change required. They observe:

So these economists, and they are numerous, must choose. They can support the allocation of investment resources through the market, or they can support Left policies for higher public expenditure, but they cannot have both.

And the British people must decide, either to strengthen the market sector so that it can function effectively, or to support the Left. Once the choice is made, it is crucial that the policies chosen be continued long enough to allow the balance of the economy to be restored.[25]

But before any such decision could be taken, it is necessary to examine the returns on capital investment in public corporations and companies. This is done in the next chapter, where the place of capital in assisting economic growth, and the capital-output ratios in several nations, are considered and discussed.

3 The Contribution of Capital to Economic Growth

3.1 CAPITAL FORMATION IN ECONOMIC THEORY

The role of capital formation in assisting economic development is so much a part of the natural background to the modern economy, that it seems quite possible to under-rate its relative importance. One author, in a basic textbook on economics, reminds us that:

> . . . the Industrial Revolution was a change in industrial method, from hand-work to work done by machines driven by power, and in industrial organisation, from work at home to work in factories[1].

There are three striking aspects of this definition. First, it points out the change in the nature of the motive force — from human muscles to other power sources (water power in the first instance, steam power later and electricity later still). Second, it draws our attention to the shift from cottage industries to factories. But third, and possibly above all, it is a definition which could mean nothing in the absence of capital investment; without capital for the machinery and the factories, the Industrial Revolution would have been still-born. It is possible to describe the changing development of entire industries largely in terms of their altering machine-technologies,[2] but such outlines sometimes fail to satisfy. Why did the Industrial Revolution not simply change from a relatively static system of handiwork to a static system of machine work? Why did the change go on, and on, up until the present day, and doubtless will continue. What factor produced this ceaseless change? Another author, John Hicks, answers this by saying:

> It is science, especially physical science, which has opened up such seemingly illimitable prospects for industry. This is a connection

39

which, as time goes on, has become increasingly apparent. It was less obvious at the start, but one does not have to go far beyond the start to find it. [3]

Hicks goes on to illustrate this by the example of the steam engine, and to suggest that the invention of machine-tools may have been *the* essential part of the Industrial Revolution; for, prior to the invention of machine-tools, machinery could not have moving parts which fitted together accurately and reliably. It was machine-tools which bred the improved machines.

There is no reason to believe that these driving forces which produced the unparalleled development of the Industrial Revolution are different in nature today from what they were then. The nub of rapid economic development was then, and probably still is, the advance of science and its effective application to the productive processes, usually through the means of new investment in improved plant and machinery. This phenomenon of continual improvement of plant and machinery due to improving technology is so usual that there is a special term for it — the 'embodied technological progress' in new plant and machinery.

Samuelson's basic economic textbook, in a chapter about the price functioning of a mixed capitalistic enterprise system, points to three important features (capital, division of labour and money) of modern industrial society, and summarises the feature of capital as:

> Modern advanced industrial society rests upon the use of vast amounts of capital: elaborate machinery, large-scale factories and plants, stores and stocks of finished and unfinished goods. [4]

The place of capital in contributing to increased output is established, but the relative importance of capital investment in producing growth is sometimes not agreed upon. Different economists have stressed the contributions of different factors in the process of economic growth. Limits of space prevent us from detailed coverage of the position taken up by major economists on economic growth; instead, a few sentences about their opinions follows, and the interested reader is invited to pursue the issue from the references.

Adam Smith saw the benefits of the division of labour and specialism of task, and he devoted the first chapter of his book to a discussion of this topic, describing the specialist methods involved in pin making. [5] Smith also dealt with agricultural developments and the inter-relationship between land and population, which loomed large in his ideas of economic growth. Nonetheless Smith also saw the accumulation of capital and technical progress as the principal agents of economic growth. Additionally, he clearly implied a relation between advancing science and improving technology:

> All the improvements in machinery, however, have by no means been the inventions of those who had occasion to use the machines. Many improvements have been made by the ingenuity of the makers of the machines, when to make them became the business of a particular trade; and some by that of those who are called philosophers or men of speculation, whose trade is not to do anything, but to observe everything; and who, upon this account, are often capable of combining together the powers of the most distant and dissimilar objects. [6]

Malthus discussed economic development primarily in terms of land and labour, and pointed to the impossibility of indefinite agricultural growth, since land was limited and at best could grow arithmetically by addition of previously uncultivated areas, while population and the labour force could grow exponentially. [7] Malthus's contribution to economic thought has produced a controversy which, in its modern form of exponential economic growth in a finite world, is raging still. [8]

Marx predicted the increasing impoverishment of the workforce, despite rising real wealth; 'The worker becomes the poorer the more wealth he produces, the more his production increases in power and size.' [9]

However, Marx was writing in the Britain of the 1840s, and one of the most notable factors about the beginning of the Industrial Revolution was that the standard of living of the great mass of the British people did not improve by much between about 1780 and 1840. Marx was writing about a historical reality—that wages did not rise in real terms until several generations after the Industrial Revolution was well under way—and he was forecasting the future from his knowledge of the historical experience of the UK economy, predicting that real wages would not rise in the longer term. The same kind of lag in real wage rates following industrialisation can sometimes be seen in the developing countries of the present day (in Kenya, for example) and the possible reasons for the lag are not hard to find. Hicks, for example, suggests that part of the reason for this lag, in Britain at least, was the abundant supply of labour, [10] and it seems likely that the very high unemployment rates of some developing countries would suggest that similar factors are operating today However, the power of capital investment in producing much higher output from fewer men may also have been contributory. The same author goes on to cite the well-documented case of Maudsley's block making machinery,[11] which in 1801 was introduced to Portsmouth dockyard, and enabled the work of 110 skilled men to be done by 10 unskilled men. This example illustrates in a nutshell three of the possible effects of new capital machinery — first, labour may be assisted because output per man can become much higher; second, labour may be displaced because one man is enabled to do the work of many; and third, the quality of the labour required may change. In a situation where labour is abundant, the introduction of capital machinery can obviously lead to very high profits indeed, at least until further growth improves the bargaining position of labour by creating a relative labour shortage. However, the point is that Marx recognised the importance of capital accumulation, involving improving technology, as vital to the process of economic growth, although he was more concerned on occasions with the moral arguments about the distribution of income between labour and capital than the dynamics of the growth process.

J. B. Clark, Marshall and Jevons, writing later in the 19th century, saw the distribution of incomes between labour and capital as dependent upon the marginal product produced by each. Labour, according to the 'marginal revolution' would be employed up to the point where its marginal output equalled its marginal cost. Capital, and all other factors of production, would be in the same position. This analysis gives a justification in economic terms for the income shares of capital and labour, for the income share acquired by each can be said to be earned by its contribution to output. However, this classical theory of the shares of income earned by the factors of production is an extrapolation of the marginal-product theories between land and labour in agriculture (where it may apply due to the comparatively homogeneous nature of land as capital) to the economy as a whole, where capital is much less homogeneous. (We will return to this problem in the next section, for Denison has used the marginal theory in his study of 'Why Growth Rates Differ'.)

In order to attack the classical economists' position, Keynes criticised two of the fundamental pillars of their theories. The first was Say's Law[12] — that supply would create its own demand — and Keynes, in his 'Law of Effective Demand' went to the opposite extreme by postulating that demand would create its own supply. The second principle Keynes attacked was the alleged identity, in classical theory, between investment and saving; Keynes argued that these were different activities 'often carried out by different people for different reasons'.[13] Keynes, by simplifying the issues to their starkest form, succeeded in demolishing part of the fort of classical orthodoxy. Yet Keynes certainly knew that demand would not always create its own supply[14]; it would only tend to do so in an economy with spare capacity, and there was much of this in the 1930s at the time Keynes was writing[15]. Keynes also was well aware that sometimes the savers and investors in an economy are the same organisations and individuals; sometimes the saving of households does provide some new industrial capital; and sometimes saving is available but loans are not advanced. (We shall be examining these issues in later chapters.) To mount an assault on the classical system, Keynes sought to prove that things were not always as the classical economists claimed; that was all that was necessary in the end, to produce a change in government policies.

R. F. Harrod, in a series of lectures in 1947, established the basic foundation for modern economic growth theory.[16] (E. D. Domar, writing in the USA at about the same time, independently produced similar work,[17] so that some economic growth models are described as 'Harrod-Domar'.) The starting points of these models is that it is capital accumulation which is particularly important in producing economic growth. At full employment, with a constant labour force, output per head is likely to increase due to the further accumulation of capital, which results in more capital assets per person employed. Harrod further discriminated between three different growth rates. First, there was the warranted rate of growth (Gw) which would occur if the out-turn growth was just equal to what entrepreneurs wanted, which is equal to the savings in an economy (S) divided by the actual marginal capital-output ratio (Vr) (We can write $Gw = \frac{S}{Vr}$, which is sometimes called the 'Harrod-Domar equation'). This warranted rate of growth depends upon investors borrowing and investing all the available saving; if they do not do so, then the actual rate of growth will fall below that warranted.

Second, Harrod outlined a 'natural' rate of growth (or Gn) which relates to the physically-possible rate of growth in an economy given by population increase and technical progress. This is equal to the rate of work-force increase (e) plus the rate of increase in productivity caused by additional capital assets per head (t). We can write $Gn = e + t$ for this. Because all the saving in an economy may not be borrowed and transformed into capital investment, the capacity rate of growth (due to increases in the work-force plus technical progress in productivity) may be less than that warranted. The third rate of growth — the actual rate of growth, Gy — may be higher or lower than the other two, depending on whether the economy is depressed or booming, or moving from depression to boom conditions, or vice versa.

Harrod's equations provide useful analytic tools for the understanding of economic growth. The warranted rate of growth depends on the supply of saving. The natural rate of growth depends on the availability of that saving for investment and the willingness of entrepreneurs to invest. The actual rate of growth, and the extent to which the economy falls below its potential output, may depend partly on the pressure of demand and government policy. In the analysis which follows in section 3.3 we can only assess the out-turn capital-output ratios of various economies, or the investment-output ratios, by dividing measured capital investment by increases in output. Hence an incremental capital-output ratio of 4 would mean that, for every £4m. pounds invested in an economy, £1m. worth of additional output has been produced. The average aggregate capital full-capacity output ratios, which entrepreneurs may plan, is only knowable between full production peaks.

To sum up: economists are largely agreed that without capital formation, resource discovery, population growth or technological progress, increases in output are severely limited. However, resources generally require capital investment to exploit them; many under-developed nations have large resources of mineral wealth but lack the capital to develop them. Moreover, the combination of the factors of production is a very important element in furthering growth—this is the question of productivity in which the degree of capitalisation plays an important part. It could thus be repeated that breakthroughs in technology and their effective application are central to the experience of sustained economic growth, and to foster an environment in which these breakthroughs are more likely to occur, capital accumulation plays a key role.

Capital accumulation requires investment which traditionally would require increased savings—induced, if necessary, by increased taxation, or by borrowing from abroad. The emphasis has been upon the quantity of saving available. In a non-Communist society there must be some inducement to invest—the profit motive; while Schumpeter has emphasised the point that neither capital accumulation nor technical progress will reach high levels through private initiative unless the social, political and economic climate is one conducive to the appearance of a large and growing supply of entrepreneurs.[18] While other elements can in principle be quantified, the area of cultural acceptance of growth which Schumpeter stressed remains the most nebulous one, and consequently the one most open for debate.

However, in the light of economic theory, there is a deceptive simplicity in the advice of economists to governments desiring a policy assisting economic growth. Such a policy should seek to:

(a) Ensure that government investment is held at a level at which opportunities for private investment are maximised. The methods of financing government investment should not discourage (indeed should if possible positively encourage) private investment and should not result in a less effective use of existing capital.

(b) Increase the rate of resource discovery and technological progress while encouraging a high level of private investment by inducing business confidence in long run economic prospects.

(c) Lower the capital-output ratio, possibly by providing advice to industry on improving industrial methods.

Such is the prescription. Having come so far economists have sometimes resorted to comments like:

. . . theories that enable us to do this sort of planning are very helpful. Just as clearly, however, these theories do not tell us how to turn a poor and stagnant economy into an expanding one with hope of becoming truly prosperous.[19]

Nonetheless, the theory does provide a valuable logic for the analysis of the capital-output ratio of Britain and other nations. But before we proceed with that analysis, it is necessary to note that one author has produced a massive economic study on the reasons for differing economic growth rates, and that author has assessed that low capital formation may not, in his submission, have contributed greatly to Britain's low economic growth.

3.2 DENISON'S ASSESSMENT OF WHY GROWTH RATES DIFFER

Edward F. Denison, assisted by Jean-Pierre Poullier, produced a monumental study in 1967 about the factors which may have been responsible for differences in some post-war economic growth rates.[20] The nine nations he selected were West Germany, Italy, France, the

Netherlands, Norway, Denmark, the United States, Belgium, and the United Kingdom (quoted in descending order of post-war economic growth). Denison's method was to explain economic growth rates in terms of an input model. Among the inputs, he lists and adds contributions from four labour factors (employment, hours of work, age-sex composition, and education) and five capital factors (non-residential structures and equipment, inventories, dwellings, international assets and land input). He then adjusts these totals by four special sources (irregularities in demand pressure, irregularities of farm output, balancing of the capital stock and deflation procedures) to arrive at adjusted output per unit of input.

These adjusted totals are modified in turn by a calculated improved allocation of resources (consisting of the contraction of agriculture, the contraction of non-farm self-employment, and the reduction of international trade barriers) plus economies of scale (comprising those associated with the national market, income elasticities and independent growth of local markets), advances of knowledge, and the change in lag in application of knowledge and errors and omissions (composed of reduction in age of capital, and other). In total, these factors explain the growth rate of each nation divided into the three periods 1950–62, 1950–55, and 1955–62. To say that Denison's procedures and propositions are complex is an understatement.

However, his work seems doubtful for a number of reasons. In order to weight the various contributions of labour, capital and land to national income, Denison finds it necessary to make some assumption connecting the growth rate of the resource with the growth rate of total input. The assumption he chooses to make is derived from neoclassical marginal theory, which states that for optimum factor utilisation, different factors should be used in production up to the point at which their price equals their contribution to output. Denison interprets this to mean that the weightings of factor inputs are related to their shares of national income, i.e. if labour has earned 70 % of national income, then a 1 % increase in labour used would produce, all other things being equal, an 0.7 % increase in total input and hence, if there were no improvements in output per unit of input, this would result in an 0.7 % increase in output. (This seems to be a method used first, in the context of a national economy, by Kendrick.[21]) This assumption is justified by arguing that it is a necessary conclusion of the proposition that enterprises will seek to combine factors in optimal cost-minimising proportions, and hence earnings per unit of the various factors of production are proportional to their marginal products. This is a crucial assumption which underlies all Denison's work; it is therefore a pity that there is no evidence (beyond a few pages of discussion) for the assumption,[22] which is tantamount to the setting out of an assumed economic model. This model assumes many of the answers it purports to prove. If one is trying objectively to assess the relative contributions of labour and capital to economic growth, to assume their contributions are proportional to their income shares is to assume much of the result.

There is a great problem here, for increases in output are the joint product of labour and capital. Labour is always a flow—it cannot be saved—and capital is always a stock, but is cumulatively added to, and capital is therefore at least partially a flow also. To propose that capital is only worth its earnings is to assume that investment only produces investment incomes, i.e. new investment (in Denison's model) does not necessarily produce increases in output which are shared between labour and capital. This is contrary to much of economic theory. To propose that productive capital and labour in each year produces output in proportions relative to their total value is to count the total value of capital in the outputs of every year. The problem apparently cannot be solved either by making capital a theoretical flow nor labour a theoretical annual stock. Where theory fails, recourse to further research seems indicated.

The choice facing those enterprises in possession of funds may be whether to employ additional employees or to purchase additional capital machinery; the outcome of this choice may depend on whether the return is greater to the enterprise through the employment of more men or more machinery. One could therefore go to the opposite extreme to the one taken by Denison, by assuming that because the choice facing enterprises is to employ additional men or machinery, then the marginal product per pound of capital invested in any year may be equal to the marginal product per pound of labour employed. In 1970, the UK used £180.2bn. of capital and £42,925m. of labour to produce a GDP of £43,303m. If the marginal product per pound of capital employed is equal to the marginal product per pound spent on labour, then over 80% of the output of the UK economy may be due to the capital employed. This is vastly different from Denison's estimate of 12%, and demonstrates the extent to which the results of abstract economic thinking depends upon the assumptions made. As Maurice Dobb has observed vis-à-vis the income share of capital and labour:

> The truth is that if a number of factors are jointly necessary to a given result, there is as little meaning in comparing the degree of necessity of

these factors in the creation of wealth as is asking whether the male or the female is the more necessary in the creation of a child[23].

In the real world, however, the distribution of national income between capital (in various forms) and labour may relate to the outcome of wage bargaining processes and the labour price of co-operation in the introduction of new capital machinery. Also, in most modern economies during the post-war period, there have been successful government policies of low unemployment. This has increased the labour share of income due to deliberate government actions. Hence, even if there were a granting of Denison's assumption that income shares reflect marginal contributions to input, the labour share would be different from that which would have been decided by free market forces. The income shares calculated may therefore not reflect the results of enterprises minimising the costs of output through appropriate combinations of capital and labour.

Denison has assessed the earnings of capital from its share of national income, or more accurately, from the residual which is not the labour share. It is a commonplace observation that capital earnings in the UK have been partially determined by political forces such as price freezes, which have depressed profits considerably, pushing them down to very low levels in recent years. In the view of many economists, low profits would lead to low investment and growth; in Denison's model the causation is reversed — low income shares of capital leads to low additions to output due to capital; this may be strong in arithmetic but seems weak in logic. This also produces a logically circular argument; growth is geared highest where capital earnings are high, not through the means of the capital-output ratio, but because non-labour investment income is a high proportion of the demand side of national income. This says little or nothing about the contribution of capital to producing economic growth; it only says something about the distribution of purchasing power between labour and capital. Furthermore, as an assessment of capital earnings, the share taken by non-labour income is a very bad guide. This is because in France and Germany (as we will see in Chapter 4) capital earnings are augmented by savings canalised to investment by the banking system. These are in no way the earnings of capital; they are additions to the income share of capital. However, Denison's assessment of the labour share of income is in any case derived, for most countries, from heroic assumptions involving the apportionment of 63 percent of proprietors' income plus employees' compensation to labour.[24]

Denison has explained a system of 27 numbers (a 3 × 9 matrix of 3 periods of nine nations) by reference to 22 different factors. In fact, it seems that there are less than 27 numbers, for the growth periods selected — 1950/62, 1955/62 and 1950/55 — are related, for the addition of the second and third periods produces the growth rate of the first. If about 18 numbers are being explained by 22 factors, this may meet the demands of Denison's logic, but generates more explanations than the number of independent periods observed. Mathematically, it can be shown that if there are more variable factors than observations, then the weightings assigned to each factor have many solutions. Denison cannot therefore be refuted; but neither can his results be proved. No doubt many of the factors cited are relevant; but Denison's book fails the test of replication; no-one given the same data would be likely to produce a remotely similar book. To our eyes, Denison seems to have used a large system of Euclidean circles when a Copernican system, which placed relevant matters centrally, might explain more, using less variables.

For all that, Denison's book is a heroic attempt to delineate the reasons why growth rates may differ in nine western nations. There can be little doubt that many of the factors Denison cites are involved, to some degree or another, in producing economic growth. Yet there is room for considerable doubt as to whether these factors produce growth in the relative proportions which Denison has assigned.

As two other authors remark, vis-à-vis Denison's study:[25]

> The technique of apportioning growth between factor inputs and the residual may well understate the contribution of capital, if, as is often the case, technical advances are embodied in investment, part of which comprises the replacement of assets . . .
>
> Moreover, it is quite probable that improvements in many of the other residual items are dependent on capital accumulation to some degree. In so far as this is the case, then there is an inherent danger in underestimating the role of capital in any attempts at measuring the sources of economic growth in the manner described above.[26]

Denison's study is crucially dependent upon the theory of marginal productivity of labour and capital, for he uses this theory to determine the weightings of factor inputs. This theory is by no means universally accepted; many of the assumptions underlying it have been criticised, especially in the area of neo-neo-classical capital theory where homogeneous capital is assumed. These criticisms throw useful light upon Denison's basic assumptions.

Joan Robinson, for example has criticised the neo-neo-classical distribution theory of income shares.[27] She has pointed out that real capital is not expansible, i.e. it does not expand to provide every man with his share of capital equipment to work with. As this is the case, the marginal output of an additional man depends upon whether equipment is working at full capacity (when the additional employee will contribute nothing to output, and hence his marginal product is zero) or whether equipment is working below capacity, when the marginal product of an additional man will depend on the average output minus certain overhead costs (including profits). The marginal product of labour becomes indeterminate unless capacity considerations are taken into account. The neo-neo-classicists (as Joan Robinson calls them) could not accept this demolition of their theory. Professor Samuelson 'retreated behind a surrogate production function.'[28]

As Joan Robinson points out, the neo-neo-classical concept of capital, called 'leets' in honour of Meade,[29] is capable of being expanded so every worker can have his leets per head to work with. She goes on to add that many economists have questioned the value of this doctrinal dispute:

> 'What does it matter?' they are inclined to say. 'Let him have his leets; what harm does it do?' But the harm which the neo-neo-classicists have done is to block off economic theory from any consideration of practical questions.[30]

Joan Robinson goes on to observe that with leets, there is no distinction between the long- and short-term problems; no such phenomenon as under-capacity working; no room for imperfect competition; no problem of unemployment; no place for technical progress. In short, an ideal world with little relation to the real one; the kind of ideal world Keynes demolished. She observes: 'The main function of leets is to provide a theory of the distribution of the product of industry between labour and capital.'[31]

Leets is therefore an updated neo-neo-classical version of the theory of marginal products, for it assumes labour and capital are each paid depending on their marginal productivity; as J. B. Clark put it: 'What a social class gets is, under natural law, what it contributes to the general output of industry.'[32]

The neo-neo-classical concept of leets is intended to be a parable. But as Professor Ferguson argues, the question is whether an analysis of the real system can establish neo-classical results.[33] Denison does not question whether the neo-classical theory of income shares is valid; he assumes it is.

What fraction of the increase in real national income that would result from a 1 % increase in all factors of production is obtained from 1 % increase in one factor or group of factors? . . . The question cannot be answered with absolute precision, but an approximation that is sufficiently accurate for the purposes of this study can be obtained: the fraction is the same as the fraction of total national income that is earned by the factor or group of factors that increases.[34]

This is an arithmetical version of Clark's principle, quoted above. But what evidence is there for it? Some economists do not seem to need any: 'Professor Ferguson asserts that belief in the neo-classical system is a matter of faith.'[35] Joan Robinson observes that Professor Ferguson has declared: 'Personally I have faith.'[36]

So what it comes down to is whether one believes in Denison's results. On the one hand we have the tradition of observation and history, with its concomitant economic growth theory stressing capital formation, and culminating in the Harrod-Domar model; on the other hand, there is Denison's work, a monument to the theory of marginal productivity, which places capital in a subsidiary role as a relatively minor factor assisting economic growth. Personally, we have more faith in the historical tradition which tends to emphasise the place of capital formation in producing economic growth; we believe the marginal products theory is less firmly grounded. The contribution of capital to economic growth is founded on observation; the same cannot be said for the theory of marginal productivity.

If such a book as Denison's were to be produced nowadays, it would be more likely to add energy and raw materials as basic inputs to the process of economic growth, in addition to Denison's categories of labour, capital and land. As the relative emphasis placed upon one productive factor or another changes through time, different views can be taken of the importance of various essential inputs to the joint product of economic output. In these circumstances, the economic understandings least liable to change are likely to be those based upon the firm foundations of checkable, observed economic realities. For unprovable abstract argument based on an input analysis is no substitute for the intellectual challenge involved in trying to understand, from the first principles, why some economies invested more in productive industry and hence grew more rapidly. Growth rates differ because inputs differ; and why did capital inputs differ so much? This is a question to which Denison provides no adequate answer.

3.3 SOME CAPITAL-OUTPUT RATIOS

The calculation of capital-output ratios obviously depends upon the definition of the concepts of capital and output adopted. A number of different definitions of these concepts is possible, and each may be appropriate to the calculation of capital-output ratios, depending upon the objectives of the analysis. It should be noted from the outset that our objective is to calculate the ratio between the fixed productive assets of the economy and the output which they help produce. Land, stocks, working capital and financial assets will not be included in the estimates of capital.

One financial measure of the capital stock is derived from the sum of historic prices of fixed assets. This definition, however, while it may meet the technical requirements of the capital account, is no reflection of the present or productive value of the capital assets, nor is it an assessment of the real purchasing power or previous capital expenditure. Capital-output ratios based upon the capital stock at prices paid would be misleadingly low, and would largely reflect the inflation in the prices of recent output compared with the original costs of the capital stock.

Another, better concept of capital is the gross fixed capital stock at constant prices; this is calculated by converting the financial amounts of the capital investments of a long period of years into the prices of one year, and adding. The gross fixed capital stock at constant prices is therefore the real value of the sum total of previous investment. If this definition of gross capital stock is adopted, then the capital-output ratio will reflect the real previous average financial investment which was required to produce 1 % increase of output (however defined). This concept is principally a financial indication of the real value of past investments; however, it does not relate to the amount of fixed capital stock in use in any one year, for it includes the cost of plant and machinery which has been withdrawn from use.

A more useful concept than the gross capital stock is the net capital stock at constant prices, which is equal to the gross capital stock minus known plant and machinery withdrawals. The net capital stock is also equal to an estimate of the real price of the total capital assets currently in use in the economy, and hence is an assessment of the constant-prices value of the prices paid in purchasing all capital assets in use. The net capital stock is therefore a concept which can be checked, by estimating and converting to constant-prices the prices paid for the total plant and machinery still in use in the economy and this estimate can be kept up to date by using perpetual-inventory methods to keep track of new capital investment and withdrawals. Capital-output ratios based upon the net capital stock have the advantage of being an assessment (in real prices) of the relationship between output and the total capital stock in use to produce that output.

An estimate of the net capital stock in constant prices derived from past prices paid, is, however, sometimes inadequate. If the existing net capital stock were to be replaced, the cost of replacing the plant and machinery would be different from the historic price of existing assets converted to present prices. An estimate can be made of the replacement cost of the net capital stock at current prices. There are difficulties in calculating replacement costs; for existing plant and machinery may be obsolete, and its replacement by new equipment generally increases output. The replacement costs therefore do not mean the replacement by equipment of similar capacity; only the cost of replacement by machinery of similar type. A capital-output ratio in current prices between the replacement cost of the net capital stock and current output estimates that percentage of output which, if new investments had the same efficiency as existing capital, would raise output by 1 %. However, caution must be exercised in interpreting such a capital-output ratio, for if the prices of replacement capital goods fall, relative to the rate of inflation, the capital-output ratio can improve, not necessarily because the capital is being used more efficiently, but simply because replacement costs have fallen. Capital-output ratios based upon current prices of output and current replacement costs of capital reflect movements in both price and productivity.

Whatever definition of capital stock is adopted, there is a rising trend of capital stock in all developed countries. It can therefore be argued that the output of an economy is dependent upon the mid-year value of the capital stock. However, the guide to the UK National Accounts assesses the reliability of the estimates of total capital stock as within plus or minus 20 % of the correct figures, although investments in recent years or particular industries are often much more reliable.[37] The reliability of capital stock statistics available for other developed nations is likely to be broadly similar. To average the capital stock values, when the accuracy may be in question to a greater extent than the proposed correction, seems unjustifiable.

The observations made in the previous paragraphs about the estimates of the gross and net stock apply with equal force to estimates of gross and net investment. In some of the accompanying tables the incremental capital-output ratio (or the investment-output ratio) is calculated, and to stabilise this estimate it is cumulatively derived, (e.g. constant prices of total investment, 1961–70, divided by real output increases 1961–70). If investment-output ratios are calculated on the gross investment, then the ratio is probably understated for some gross investment replaces worn-out assets. Gross investment-output ratios do not allow for the decline in output due to capital withdrawals; on the other hand, gross investment does include all new investment, hence the effect of technological progress (in making new machinery more productive) is taken into account. Some authors claim that, due to the existence of embodied technological progress, the gross investment rate may matter more than the net investment level[38]. Net investment-output ratios may overestimate the contribution of new net investments, for some output (which is possibly being produced due to the replacement of old machinery by new) is being ascribed to the net investments. Some economists attempt to solve this problem by making some arbitrary assumption — Denison, for example, averages the growth rates of gross and net investments[39] — but these assumptions are equivalent to an assessment of the output-increasing effect of replacing old capital stock with new. To average gross and net investments, in order to take account of the embodied technological progress involved in replacing old by new capital, is to assume that the output-increasing effect of technological improvements is given by an amount of net capital equal to half the difference between the gross and net investment level. This seems an arbitrary process, for if six years old intensively-used machinery is being replaced by new equipment the improvement due to technological progress may not be great, while if 20 year old machinery is replaced, the improvements may be considerable.

Furthermore, some replacement investments, such as a road widening scheme, may have no measurable effect on marketed output whatsoever, while others, such as replacement investments in automatic electrical machinery, can have very large effects. The sectoral allocation of new investment is therefore crucial. It is also sometimes difficult to assess net investments, for the assessment of capital consumption is not on the same basis in different countries. The British National Income and Expenditure Accounts assess capital consumption directly, by estimating the value of plant and machinery withdrawals.[40] Many other nations have a column for capital consumption in (for example) the OECD national accounts; these can be used to assess net capital investment. Depreciation estimates cannot be used for this purpose, because depreciation provisions are considerably larger than capital withdrawals; there is a great deal of capital investment which is, for accounting purposes, fully depreciated but still in productive use. This can be shown by considering depreciation allowances with estimates of real capital consumption in UK companies; in 1965, capital consumption by companies was assessed as £1181m.; depreciation allowances were £2161m.[41] In 1972, the relevant figures were: companies' capital consumption £2309m.; depreciation allowed, £4282m.[42] Any attempt to use depreciation as an estimate of capital consumption would be subject to considerable risks.

The only fairly reliable investment statistics, available on approximately the same basis for the five nations which are our chosen area of interest, are the gross and net investment levels,[43] and their components (e.g. plant and machinery, residential dwellings and business structures, government investment). It is therefore proposed to use gross and net investment (or its components) at constant prices as the best measure of capital formation.

There are many measures of national output which could conceivably be used to calculate the capital-output ratio. One important consideration in this matter is consistency — for example, if the earnings from overseas foreign investments are to be included in output, then these investments should also be included in capital. The definition of the output therefore follows (for the most part) from the definition of the capital base, given that it is proposed to compare the ratio of the capital used with the resultant output.

The capital base (or investments made) will in all cases concern the national territory of a country. The GDP of that country will therefore be the most appropriate measure of the output produced from that capital base. Foreign investments will not be included in the capital base; remitted earnings will be excluded from national output. It could be argued that the net national product, or GDP minus capital consumption, should be used as the most appropriate index of output, for some capital goods are used up every year, and this capital consumption can be seen as a charge against output. However, capital consumption is perhaps more appropriately set against gross capital investment.

It is proposed, therefore to set 1960 as an arbitrary base year, and calculate cumulative capital-output ratios by the formula

Increase in GDP over 1960 level (at 1970 prices)

Increase in gross (or net) capital stock over 1960 level (at 1970 prices)

In the first year, this calculation gives an incremental capital-output ratio (or an investment-output ratio); in later years, this index gives a more valid capital-output ratio. As we will later see in the case of Japan, over 72 % of Japan's real 1975 GDP was due to growth between 1960 and 1975; capital-output ratios spanning 1960–75 may be a reflection of over 72 % of the 1975 GDP divided by the increased gross (or net) capital stock during that period. We shall call these calculations 'cumulative incremental capital-output ratios' but it should be remembered that they relate to a cumulatively greater degree of investment and output as the span of years increases.

These resulting cumulative incremental capital-output ratios or gross investment-output ratios, are composite indices which take account of a number of different effects. First, the effect of capital consumption between economies may not be equal. Economies which invest relatively low proportions of their output (such as the USA and the UK) tend to have an older age structure of existing capital investments,[44] and hence when obsolete machinery is replaced, the output-increasing effect of embodied technological progress is much larger. On the other hand, a low proportion of that older machinery is replaced (and much new investment covers replacement of existing assets) and there may be some reductions in the operating efficiency of existing capital stock due to older age structure and the higher proportion of time taken by maintenance, and these reductions may be masked by the introduction of some new machinery. High-investment economies, such as Germany or Japan, have productive plant and machines which are only about 4–8 years old on average, and hence a low proportion of new investment replaces younger machinery (most of it is not replaced) and the gains of embodied technological progress may be less, because the efficiency of existing capital stock may be higher due to its relative youth.

Second, gross investment includes investment in social overhead capital—on items such as dwellings, roads, hospitals, schools, public buildings and all the improvements in social infrastructure—and these can be quite different proportions within national gross investment. Third, the proportions of investment in plant and machinery taken up by government departments (which sometimes include telecommunications), nationalised industries and private industry vary considerably between nations, depending upon whether governments have structured the capital market to favour the public sector (as in the UK), or the public sector first and the private sector second (as in France), or the private sector first (as in Japan). Finally, if investment occurs at a high rate, the size and efficiency of the investments may produce great economies of scale, so capital-output ratios between nations may not be comparable unless full account is taken of the absolute rate of investment, as well as its sectoral allocation and net productive capital effects.

Despite these failings of the marginal capital-output ratios, the calculation of the percentage of national income which is apparently required as investment to raise production by 1 % is interesting in itself. If we invert the capital-output ratios, we can calculate a percentage rate of return on new national investments, but that percentage rate of return will not be the rate of return found by the industrialist or entrepreneur, for his returns are calculated after all charges of the costs of capital and additional labour are deducted. The rate of return given by the inverse of the capital-output ratio is the gross percentage return in real terms to all the economy, without specification how the value of that increased output is distributed. In other words if the capital-output ratio is 4 and the rate of return 25 %, we are assessing that 4 % of GDP needs to be invested, on average, to produce 1 % real growth, and that this is a 25 % return on investment to the whole economy. (How that return is distributed will be our concern in Chapter 5, when we consider the costs and profits of capital.)

Finally, it is reasonable to assume that, due to some deficiencies in annual demand and the time taken to place new investment in operation, the investments made in any single year are not necessarily reflected in increased output that year. Economic instability and the time taken for new investments to come on stream can make assessments of annual capital-output ratios relatively unstable. Investments and economic growth tend to fluctuate cyclically — a kind of stop-go cycle is obvious in many economies[45] — and it may be that only at economic peaks is productive capacity fully utilised. During economic depressions, investments generally reduce but continue in the expectation of better years to come. Capital-output ratios calculated during individual years of depression are no real reflection of underlying increase in the productive strength of the economy, which may be operating below capacity due to low demand. The calculation of cumulative capital-output ratios over a period of years avoids the instability associated with any individual year (excepting the first year, which is an annual capital-output ratio, and hence may provide a poor estimate).

There is always some difficulty in establishing valid, internationally comparable data on any subject. In our tables, different definitions of the constitution of the gross and net capital investment and GDP do exist. The basic difference in the tables is that both West Germany and Japan still use a former system of national accounting in their reports to the OECD: France (after 1960) the UK and the USA use a 'present SNA' (System of National Accounting). The interested reader is advised to consult Appendix B1 where these differences are outlined.

In all the tables which follow, the capital-output ratios are calculated up to 1975. However, the effects of the oil price rises in November 1973 are obvious in these tables; many economies had not recovered by 1975 from the depression which followed the 1973 boom and the oil price hike. It is therefore prudent to examine the 1961–71 period rather than the abnormal boom of 1973 (when virtually all major economies expanded simultaneously) and the subsequent depression, which caused widespread over-capacity.

Table 3.1 shows the estimated cumulative incremental gross capital-output ratios for France. It seems that, over period 1961–71, France had to invest over 4 % of GDP for every 1 % of economic growth. However, as the French economy was increasing its investment rate from less than 20 % in 1960 to more than 26 % in the early 70s,[46] the underlying growth rate should have accelerated, had there not been a compensating fall in the return on new investments. Table 3.1 understates the fall in the marginal return on new investments, due to averaging of early years with late; if increases in GDP are divided by increases in gross investments (to calculate the incremental capital-output ratio) higher investment-output ratios can be derived. These are shown in Table 3.1 as gross incremental capital-output ratios (ICORs): they are somewhat unstable estimates, as the output increases from year to year may reflect the level of demand rather than the growth in the economic capacity of the country.

The demands of French government expenditure over the period fell from over 14 % of GDP in 1960 to about 11 % of GDP by 1971; annual investment in new productive plant and machinery, in the economic engine of France, grew from less than 7 % to nearly 10 % of GDP. Consequently, the percentage share of plant and machinery investment in gross domestic capital formation grew slightly from 34 % in 1960 to 37 % in 1971, and most of that new productive plant was in industry.[47] Consumers had about 60 % of France's GDP expenditures throughout the period 1961–71.

It is possible to calculate the cumulative incremental net capital-output ratios for France during the period 1961–75. This can be done by

TABLE 3.1   Cumulative incremental gross capital-output ratios for France, 1960–75

Year	Increase in GDP over 1960 level*	Increase in gross fixed capital stock over 1960 level*	Cumulative investment-output ratio	% rate of return	Incremental capital-output ratio (gross)
1961	29.83	96.10	3.22	31.0	3.26
1962	61.15	198.24	3.24	30.8	3.26
1963	84.95	307.88	3.62	27.6	4.61
1964	106.71	427.59	4.01	25.0	5.50
1965	140.16	555.35	3.96	25.2	3.82
1966	178.29	693.73	3.89	25.7	3.63
1967	200.68	839.43	4.18	23.9	6.51
1968	230.62	993.37	4.31	23.2	5.14
1969	280.90	1161.59	4.14	24.2	3.35
1970	332.55	1344.63	4.04	24.7	3.54
1971	374.0	1540.62	4.12	24.3	4.73
1972	421.44	1750.54	4.15	24.1	4.42
1973	467.92	1974.63	4.22	23.7	4.82
1974	494.35	2201.63	4.45	22.5	8.59
1975	484.68	2418.66	4.99	20.0	NA

* in Frs bn., 1970 prices
Source: Calculated from *National Accounts of OECD Countries, 1960–75*, OECD, 1975, Vol. 1, pp. 62, 63.

calculating net capital investments from the ratio of capital consumptions to fixed capital formation in current prices, then reducing the constant-price estimate of gross fixed capital investment by the proportion of capital which replaces capital consumed. The resulting estimates of additions to net capital can then be compared with output. The dangers of this procedure, in imputing the increased output possibly due to the replacement of old equipment by new, have already been touched upon.

The cumulative incremental net capital-output ratios for France are shown in Table 3.2. It would seem that the productivity of new French net investments is falling, for the cumulative capital-output ratios rise; hence investment-output ratios based on single years (incremental capital output ratios, or ICORs) show some tendency to rise, but with much variability in the estimates for single years.

France's GDP in 1970 was Frs 782.56bn., hence during the period 1960–70 France invested, in gross terms, an amount equal to one and

TABLE 3.2 Cumulative incremental net capital-output ratios for France, 1960–75

Year	Increase in GDP over 1960 level*	Increase in net fixed capital over 1960 level*	Cumulative net capital-output ratio	% rate of return	ICOR (net)
1961	29.83	51.17	1.72	58.3	1.72
1962	61.15	104.45	1.71	58.5	1.70
1963	84.95	164.45	1.94	51.7	2.52
1964	106.71	230.45	2.16	46.3	3.03
1965	140.16	301.00	2.15	46.6	2.11
1966	178.29	378.25	2.12	47.1	2.03
1967	200.68	458.70	2.29	43.7	3.59
1968	230.62	542.34	2.35	42.5	2.79
1969	280.90	634.60	2.26	44.3	1.83
1970	332.55	732.95	2.20	45.4	1.90
1971	374.0	838.39	2.24	44.6	2.54
1972	421.44	952.20	2.26	44.3	2.40
1973	467.92	1074.76	2.30	43.5	2.64
1974	494.35	1197.48	2.42	41.3	4.64
1975	484.68	1307.70	2.70	37.1	NA

* in Frs bn., 1970 prices
Source: Derived from the same table of OECD data as Table 3.1.

three quarters of its 1970 GDP, while the net investments over the 1960–70 period were less than its 1970 GDP. By 1970, France's output was some 74 % higher than 10 years earlier — a growth rate of almost 5.7 % p.a. — or, to put it slightly differently, 42.5 % of France's GDP was an increase over the 1960 output level. If the existing stock of capital did not become more productive, then the cumulative capital-output ratios calculated for the period 1961–71 reflect the relationship between capital and output in some 42.5 % of the economy.

Japanese marginal (and cumulative) capital-output ratios are estimated in Table 3.3. The rate of return on new investments in Japan has been apparently falling rapidly, but the capital-output ratio has been very low by world standards, for in the 1960s Japan had needed to invest only about 2–3 % of GDP, on average, to produce 1 % growth. There are several possible reasons for the high returns on new Japanese investments; first, Japan has consistently invested over 15 % of its GDP in plant and machinery; second, the size of these investments has produced great economies of scale; third, the increase in capital stock

TABLE 3.3 Cumulative incremental gross capital-output ratios for Japan, 1960–75

Year	Increase in GDP over 1960 level*	Increase in gross fixed capital formation over 1960 level*	Investment-output ratio	% rate of return	ICOR (gross)
1961	3704	7841	2.12	47.2	2.12
1962	5761	16569	2.88	34.8	4.24
1963	9038	26206	2.90	34.5	2.94
1964	13594	37455	2.76	36.3	2.47
1965	15598	49065	3.15	31.8	5.79
1966	19610	62024	3.16	31.6	3.23
1967	25435	77367	3.04	32.9	2.63
1968	32288	96054	2.97	33.6	2.73
1969	38468	117896	3.06	32.6	3.53
1970	45427	142667	3.14	31.8	3.56
1971	50601	169758	3.35	29.8	5.24
1972	57361	199729	3.48	28.7	4.43
1973	65483	233578	3.57	28.0	4.17
1974	64491	263990	4.09	24.4	NA
1975	66615	293541	4.41	22.7	NA

* in ¥bn., 1970 prices
Source: Calculated from *National Accounts of OECD Countries, 1975*, pp. 34, 35.

referred to in Table 3.3 is largely industrial investment,[48] due to Japanese government policy of putting economic growth first. As Erik Lundberg has written vis-à-vis Japan's low capital-output ratios during the 1950s and early 1960s:

> The main explanation must, however, be the unusual domination of relatively short-term investment in machinery and equipment — and the extremely low share of residential and also public infrastructure investments.[49]

The observed fall in the capital-output ratio seems to be partially due to the increase in infrastructure investments in industry, but this could be a short-term effect.

Bieda has pointed out that in many Japanese industries there are industrial councils which decide on the current optimum size for a plant, and the government sanctions such recommendations; an example of this is that: 'In the petro-chemical industry the minimum permitted capacity for a plant is 300,000 tons output p.a.'[50]

The relative newness of the capital machinery also produces highly productive investments. That the plant and machinery is relatively new can hardly be doubted:

> It was estimated that in the mid-60s, two-thirds of the capital in manufacturing and over half of the total private capital stock, excluding housing were less than five years old.[51]

Japanese government expenditure demands upon the economy lay between 16 and 20 % of GNP, and consumers' expenditure accounted for about 54.60 % of GNP, during the 1961–71 period.[52]

If we calculate the capital-output ratio from net capital, taking scrapping and equipment withdrawals away from gross fixed investments, the cumulative capital-output ratio in Japan falls below 2 for the 1960s period, as shown in Table 3.4.

TABLE 3.4   Cumulative incremental net capital-output ratios for Japan, 1960–75

Year	Increase in GDP over 1960 level*	Increase in net fixed capital over 1960 level*	Net capital-output ratio	% rate of return	ICOR (net)
1961	3704	5334	1.44	69.4	1.44
1962	5761	11112	1.92	51.8	2.94
1963	9638	17260	1.91	52.4	1.55
1964	13594	24278	1.79	56.0	1.77
1965	15598	31044	1.99	50.2	3.38
1966	19610	38564	1.97	50.9	1.87
1967	25435	47859	1.88	53.1	1.60
1968	32288	59355	1.84	54.4	1.68
1969	38468	72741	1.89	52.9	2.17
1970	45427	88026	1.94	51.6	2.20
1971	50601	104538	2.07	48.4	3.19
1972	57361	122658	2.14	46.8	2.68
1973	65483	144184	2.20	45.4	2.65
1974	64491	163010	2.53	39.6	NA
1975	66615	180540	2.71	36.9	NA

* in ¥ bn., 1970 prices
Source: Calculated from the same data source as Table 3.3.

To put these ratios into perspective, we should note that Japan invested over twice her 1970 GDP (of ¥70868bn.) in gross capital, and about one and a quarter times her 1970 GDP in net capital, during the period 1960–70. Growth between 1960 and 1970 accounted for some 64 % of the 1970 GDP, so the cumulative capital-output ratios for 1960 to 1970 do not reflect only marginal rates, but the capital-output ratio for about two-thirds of the economy.

The cumulative incremental gross capital-output ratios for West Germany are shown in Table 3.5. It would seem that West Germany required an investment of an additonal 5–6 % of GDP for every 1 % of economic growth during the period 1961–71. West Germany's total investment rates were between 24–27 % of GDP during this period. Government expenditure, at about 14 % of GDP, showed no long-run tendency to increase, and consumer expenditure averaged about 56 % of GDP. Machinery and equipment investment, which in 1960 was less than 8 % of GDP and about a third of total capital formation, grew to almost 10.4 % of GDP and approached 40 % of capital formation in

TABLE 3.5 Cumulative incremental gross capital-output ratios for West Germany, 1960–75

Year	Increase in GDP over 1960 level*	Increase in gross fixed capital over 1960 level*	Investment-output ratio	% rate of return	ICOR (gross)
1961	23.98	115.15	4.80	20.8	4.80
1962	42.05	236.63	5.63	17.8	6.72
1963	58.68	361.06	6.22	16.1	7.76
1964	90.83	500.24	5.51	18.2	4.25
1965	119.92	645.81	5.39	18.6	5.00
1966	135.58	792.75	5.85	17.1	9.38
1967	134.18	927.37	6.91	14.5 ⎫	7.31
1968	173.88	1072.64	6.17	16.2 ⎭	
1969	222.82	1235.24	5.54	18.0	3.32
1970	261.40	1416.32	5.42	18.5	4.69
1971	281.35	1605.60	5.71	17.5	9.49
1972	305.05	1800.12	5.90	17.0	8.21
1973	342.15	1995.77	5.83	17.1	5.27
1974	347.49	2175.51	6.26	16.0	NA
1975	322.98	2347.62	7.27	13.8	NA

* in DM bn., 1970 prices
Source: Calculated from *National Accounts of OECD Countries, 1960–75*, OECD, 1975, vol. 1, pp. 66–7.

1971.[53] The higher proportion of new productive plant was, however, apparently compensated for by a slightly higher capital-output ratio (possibly caused by deficient demand during the late 60s). Net capital-output ratios for West Germany are much lower, implying 3–4 % of GDP is required as net investment for 1 % more output (Table 3.6). Incremental capital-output ratios are once again more variable, and cannot be calculated where investment sends capacity up but demand is deficient (e.g. during the depression years 1966–67, and 1973–75).

TABLE 3.6 Cumulative incremental net capital-output ratios for West Germany, 1960–75

Year	Increase in GDP over 1960 level*	Increase in net fixed capital over 1960 level*	Net capital-output ratio	% rate of return	ICOR (net)
1961	23.98	75.1	3.13	31.9	3.13
1962	42.05	153.2	3.64	27.5	4.32
1963	58.08	230.9	3.98	25.2	4.85
1964	90.83	319.6	3.52	28.4	2.71
1965	119.92	410.1	3.42	29.2	3.11
1966	135.58	498.1	3.67	27.2	5.62
1967	134.18	569.4	4.24	23.6 ⎫	3.91
1968	173.88	647.9	3.73	26.8 ⎭	
1969	222.82	739.3	3.32	30.1	1.87
1970	261.40	845.6	3.24	30.9	2.76
1971	281.35	955.6	3.40	29.4	5.51
1972	305.05	1066.4	3.50	28.6	4.68
1973	342.15	1173.9	3.43	29.1	2.90
1974	347.49	1260.7	3.63	27.6	NA
1975	322.98	1334.5	4.13	24.2	NA

* in DM bn., 1970 prices
Source: Calculated from same source as Table 3.5.

DM 261.4bn. in 1970 prices (or 38 % of West Germany's 1970 GDP of nearly DM 687bn.) represents growth of 4.9 % p.a. over the 1960–70 period. Cumulative capital-output ratios spanning 1960–70 refer to the output and investment in nearly two-fifths of the West German economy.[54] West Germany invested an amount equal to twice its 1970 GDP in gross terms, and one and a quarter of its 1970 GDP in net terms, over the period 1961–70.

In Table 3.7 the cumulative gross capital-output ratios of the UK are

TABLE 3.7   Cumulative incremental gross capital-output ratios for the UK, 1960–75

Year	Increase in GDP over 1960 level*	Increase in gross fixed capital stock over 1960 level*	Cumulative investment-output ratio	% rate of return	ICOR (gross)
1961	1276	6368	4.99	20.0	4.99
1962	1622	12745	7.86	12.7	18.43
1963	3219	19202	5.97	16.8	4.04
1964	5662	26751	4.72	21.2	3.09
1965	6574	34656	5.27	19.0	8.67
1966	7462	42757	5.73	17.5	9.12
1967	8682	51538	5.94	16.8	7.20
1968	10322	60720	5.88	17.0	5.60
1969	10979	69941	6.37	15.7	14.04
1970	12130	79404	6.55	15.3	8.22
1971	13413	89114	6.64	15.1	7.57
1972	14752	99028	6.71	14.9	7.40
1973	17929	109342	6.10	16.4	3.25
1974	18076	119411	6.61	15.1	NA
1975	17340	129350	7.46	13.4	NA

* in £m., 1970 prices

Source: Calculated from *National Accounts of OECD Countries, 1960–75*, OECD, 1975, pp. 118, 119.

calculated from 1961–75. It would appear from this table that the United Kingdom would need to invest about $6\frac{1}{2}\%$ of GDP to acquire 1% of real economic growth. However, not only did Britain invest relatively less than most other comparable nations — about 18–21 % of GDP, as opposed to 20–26 % in France, 33–41 % in Japan and 24–27 % in West Germany — but also, of that lower investment, a greater proportion was in the public sector and much less (only about 4–5 % of GDP) was equipment investment in manufacturing industry. Investment in the production of marketable goods was only about 20–25 % of total capital formation, and the average age of plant and machinery in industry meant that much of the new capital went to replace worn-out machinery.

The change in the percentage allocation of total gross fixed capital formation is particularly revealing.

Investments in public services rose dramatically over the period, while manufacturing industry investments were on a declining trend (although one needs to look at the whole post-war period clearly to see the decline,

TABLE 3.8   Percentage allocation of UK gross domestic capital formation

Year	Public service	Dwellings	Manufacturing	Other
1960	9.5	18.9	25.3	46.3
1965	12.7	20.1	22.3	44.9
1970	16.4	16.8	23.7	43.1

Source: *The British Economy, Key Statistics, 1900–70*, published for the London and Cambridge Economic Service, by Times Newspapers Ltd: Table J.

for manufacturing investment within each investment cycle has peaked at a lower proportion of total investment than it did in the previous cycle[55]). The increasing capital-output ratio of the UK economy seems to be partly due to the decreasing proportion of capital investment in manufacturing, contrary to the trend in France, Japan, West Germany and the USA. (See Table 3.8.)

If we examine net capital-output ratios, then the British economy does not seem to be doing so very badly — some 3.5 % of GDP was required

TABLE 3.9   Cumulative incremental net capital-output ratios for the UK, 1960–75

Year	Increase in GDP over 1960 level*	Increase in net fixed capital over 1960 level*	Net capital-output ratio	% rate of return	ICOR (net)
1961	1276	3392	2.66	37.6	2.66
1962	1622	6688	4.12	24.3	9.52
1963	3219	9969	3.10	32.3	2.05
1964	5662	14185	2.51	39.9	1.73
1965	6574	18605	2.83	35.3	4.85
1966	7462	23071	3.09	32.3	5.03
1967	8682	28016	3.23	31.0	4.05
1968	10322	33179	3.21	31.1	3.15
1969	10979	38208	3.48	28.7	7.65
1970	12130	43226	3.56	28.1	4.36
1971	13413	48247	3.60	27.8	3.91
1972	14752	53238	3.61	27.7	3.73
1973	17929	58540	3.27	30.6	1.67
1974	18076	63521	3.51	28.5	NA
1975	17340	68162	3.93	25.4	NA

* in £m., 1970 prices
Source: Calculated from same data source as Table 3.7.

as net investment during the 1960s to produce 1 % more output (Table 3.9). Much of the apparently poor productivity of gross investment could be due to high scrapping rates resulting from obsolete equipment.[56]

During the 1960–70 period, Britain invested in gross fixed capital an amount equal to 1.57 times its 1970 GDP, but capital withdrawals reduced this to 0.83 times the 1970 GDP. Economic growth between 1960 and 1970 was about 2.8 %—the 1970 UK economy was 31.4 % larger than it was in 1960, or almost 24 % of the output of the 1970 economy was additional to the 1960 one. Cumulative capital-output ratios for the period 1960–70 therefore refer at best to one quarter of the economy.

Cumulative and incremental gross capital-output ratios for the USA are shown in Table 3.10. It would seem that the USA needed to invest about 5 % of its GDP during the 1960s to acquire a 1 % growth of output. Total US gross domestic capital formation has been between 13

TABLE 3.10 Cumulative incremental gross capital-output ratios for the USA, 1960–75

Year	Increase in GDP over 1960 level*	Increase in gross fixed capital stock over 1960 level*	Investment-output ratio	% rate of return	ICOR (gross)
1961	15.6	117.4	7.53	13.3	7.53
1962	54.2	243.9	4.50	22.2	3.28
1963	83.7	379.9	4.54	22.0	4.61
1964	122.4	525.5	4.29	23.3	3.76
1965	170.1	686.1	4.03	24.8	3.37
1966	220.9	854.0	3.87	25.9	3.31
1967	244.7	1018.8	4.16	24.0	6.92
1968	285.7	1193.5	4.18	23.9	4.26
1969	310.4	1372.1	4.42	22.6	7.23
1970	309.0	1542.4	4.99	20.0 ⎫	6.27
1971	337.5	1721.0	5.10	19.6 ⎭	
1972	395.5	1915.6	4.84	20.6	4.31
1973	453.4	2121.4	4.68	21.4	3.55
1974	435.7	2311.6	5.31	18.8	NA
1975	418.0	2478.6	5.93	16.9	NA

* in $bn., 1970 prices
Source: Calculated from *National Accounts of OECD Countries, 1960–75*, OECD, 1975, pp. 30, 31.

and 16 % of GNP; investment in plant and machinery has been 5–7 % of GNP. Plant and machinery investment has grown faster than the economy as a whole and during the early 1970s was taking $1-1\frac{1}{2}$ % more of GNP than a decade earlier. Government expenditure tended to decrease by a few percent of GNP from 23–25 % in the mid-60s to 20–22 % of GNP in the 1970s.[57]

Economic growth in the USA was about 3.85 % during the period 1960–70; the 1970 economy was almost 46 % bigger than it had been in 1960. The gross investment required to produce that result was about 1.57 times the 1970 GDP and the additional output produced by 1970 compared with 1960 was 31.5 % of the 1970 GDP. The 1960–70 cumulative gross (and net) capital-output ratios refer to about a third of the output of the economy.

The fixed capital scrapping rates in the USA are abnormally high — equal to nearly 58 % of gross investments between 1960 and 1970 — and hence the net capital-output ratios of the USA approach Japanese levels, indicating that only some 2 % of the GDP in the 1970s was required to produce 1 % more output (Table 3.11).

TABLE 3.11 Cumulative incremental net capital-output ratios for the USA, 1960–75

Year	Increase in GDP over 1960 level*	Increase in net fixed capital over 1960 level*	Net capital-output ratio	% rate of return	ICOR (net)
1961	15.6	41.3	2.65	37.8	2.65
1962	54.2	90.1	1.66	60.2	1.26
1963	83.7	146.2	1.75	57.3	1.90
1964	122.4	209.3	1.71	58.5	1.63
1965	170.1	284.4	1.67	59.8	1.57
1966	220.9	363.3	1.64	60.8	1.55
1967	244.7	434.8	1.78	56.3	3.00
1968	285.7	511.3	1.79	55.9	1.87
1969	310.4	586.6	1.89	52.9	3.05
1970	309.0	648.9	2.10	47.6 ⎫	
1971	337.5	716.1	2.12	47.1 ⎭	4.78
1972	395.5	796.7	2.01	49.6	1.39
1973	453.4	882.8	1.95	51.4	1.49
1974	435.7	947.6	2.17	46.0	NA
1975	418.0	984.2	2.35	42.5	NA

* in $bn., 1970 prices
Source: Calculated from the same source as Table 3.10.

Total net investments in the 1960–70 period were about 66 % of the 1970 GDP of the USA, which was $981.2bn. Despite the low net investment level, the efficiency of net investment has led to relatively high growth.

TABLE 3.12 Growth and investment statistics of five nations, 1960–70, and 1960–75

| Country and period | Real GDP growth p.a. | Fixed capital formation (% of GDP) | | Capital-output ratios | | Capital consumption |
		gross	net	gross	net	(%)
France						
1960–70	5.69	23.0	12.5	4.04	2.20	45.5
1960–75	4.99	24.9	13.5	4.99	2.70	45.9
Japan						
1960–70	9.29	29.2	18.0	3.14	1.94	38.2
1960–75	7.97	35.1	21.6	4.41	2.71	38.5
West Germany						
1960–70	4.90	26.6	15.9	5.42	3.24	40.2
1960–75	3.84	27.9	15.9	7.27	4.13	43.2
UK						
1960–70	2.77	18.1	9.9	6.55	3.56	45.7
1960–75	2.50	18.7	9.8	7.46	3.93	47.3
USA						
1960–70	3.62	18.1	7.6	4.99	2.10	57.9
1960–75	3.12	18.5	7.3	5.93	2.35	60.5

Sources: Calculated from *National Accounts of OECD Countries, 1960–75* and Tables 3.1–3.11.

In Table 3.12 the growth and investment statistics of the five nations are summarised to facilitate comparison.[58] The summary deals with both the 1960–70 and 1960–75 periods; the decade of the 1960s has been quoted because all of the five economies in Table 3.11 were operating considerably below capacity in 1975, hence the capital-output ratios for the 1960–75 period are understated and do not reflect the growth of economic capacity between 1960 and 1975. The United Kingdom is once again at the bottom of the economic growth league — despite the fact that the UK invested (as % of GDP) as much as the USA. However, the capital-output ratios were higher, and the productivity of the investment was therefore lower in the UK than in the USA. Britain's capital-output ratios seem similar to West Germany's, but that country invested nearly 28 % of its GDP over the 1960–75 period, while Britain invested less than 19 %. West Germany in the 1960s therefore illustrates that high capital-output ratios need not mean low growth if the investment level is high enough. France occupies an investment position intermediate between Britain and West Germany, investing more than the UK and less than West Germany. Yet France grew faster than West Germany over both 1960–70 and 1960–75, because the productivity of French capital investment was relatively high. Japan, with low capital-output ratios and high investment rates, grew very rapidly. It is interesting to note that capital consumption, as a proportion of gross investment, is highest in the USA and the UK, where (because investment rates are lower) productive plant and equipment is generally older; while Japan is at the opposite extreme, with not only a high gross investment level but a low rate of capital consumption due to younger plant and machinery, and hence a high rate of net fixed capital formation.

Table 3.12 also shows gross capital-output ratios for the 1960–70 period which vary from a little over three (in the case of Japan) to over six and a half (for the UK). Net capital-output ratios range from less than two to over three and a half, for the same nations and the same period. One factor which may be responsible for part of this difference in the productivity of investment is the extent to which new investment is placed in plant and machinery in industry, where high investment can lead to high rates of growth of output.

Table 3.13 gives some evidence for this view. Japan's gross capital stock has been growing at about 10 % p.a., with economic growth occurring at about the same rate. Yet the gross capital stock has not grown equally rapidly over all economic sectors; Japanese industrial investment has grown very rapidly, investment in services at slightly below the national average rate, and agricultural investments have grown relatively slowly. Inequalities in the growth rates of the gross

TABLE 3.13   Growth rates of gross capital stock

Average annual percentages	Total	Agriculture	Industry	Services
Japan (1954–71)	10.1	5.6	12.5	9.6
France (1953–70)	5.3	4.3	5.8	4.7
West Germany (1952–71)	6.4	3.4	6.9	
UK (1954–72)	3.8	2.7	4.2	3.6
USA (1953–70)	3.6	1.9	3.3	3.9

Source: Andrea Boltho, *Japan: An Economic Survey 1953–73*, Oxford University Press, 1975.

capital stock seem less well marked in France. Growth of the gross capital stock in industry and services in West Germany has been at over twice the rate of growth of agricultural investments. The UK follows the French and Japanese pattern, in that the growth of industrial gross capital stock is higher than that of service industries, which in turn is higher than that of agriculture. The USA seems unusual in that the growth of the gross capital stock of service industries is higher than that of industry; this may be a natural consequence of a very high level of economic development.

If the productivity of investment were similar in the economic sectors of agriculture, industry and services, the sectoral allocation of investment capital would not greatly affect increases in output. But as Table 3.14 indicates there is evidence that investments in industry are more productive (in the sense that they add more to output) than investments elsewhere. The incremental capital-output ratios of industry are dramatically better than those in agriculture or services. Furthermore, the incremental capital-output ratios in industry are also lower where the growth of gross capital stock is high, indicating that the economies of large-scale industrial investment can produce better returns per unit of investment. From the data given in Table 3.14 it does not seem that Japanese industry is much more productive (with an incremental capital-output ratio of 2.0) than French or West German industries (where the equivalent capital-output ratios are 2.4 and 2.5). British industry's performance does seem to be markedly poorer, with a gross capital-output ratio equal to over twice those elsewhere, but the relatively low rates of UK industrial investment could partially explain this. Much of Britain's gross industrial investment is placed in public corporations, where returns may be lower.

TABLE 3.14   Incremental gross capital-output ratios

Country and period	Total	Agriculture	Industry	Services
Japan (1954–71)	2.8	7.0	2.0	3.4
France (1953–70)	3.8	7.7	2.4	6.4
West Germany (1952–71)	4.6	15.7	2.5	7.5
UK (1956–73)	6.1	6.5	4.9	9.0
USA (1956–73)	4.4	NA	NA	NA

Source: Andrea Boltho, *op. cit.*

Nonetheless, Tables 3.13 and 3.14 give a better picture of the relationship between increases in gross productive investments and output increases than average capital-output ratios over the whole economy. But there is another sectoral allocation of investments which is possible. Fixed capital formation includes government investments in the social infrastructure, public and private housing, investments by public corporations, and investments in the private sector. The different proportions of these kinds of investment, some of which do not add significantly to output, could explain a great deal. Suppose, for example, we were to assume that the only output-increasing investment is investment in plant and equipment, which adds directly to labour

TABLE 3.15   Capital accumulation rate (equipment investment) and rate of GDP growth, 1956–63

Country	(1) Rate of investment (equipment investment) as a % of GDP	(2) % rate of GDP growth	(3) Marginal capital coefficient (equipment investment)
Japan	21.4	10.4	2.1
West Germany	14.7(a)	6.4	2.3
Italy	13.7	6.0	2.3
France	12.3	4.9	2.5
Austria	14.8	4.6	3.2
Denmark	10.6	4.6	2.3
Norway	22.5	3.9	5.8
Netherlands	16.1	3.8	4.2
Canada	15.2(b)	3.8	4.0
Sweden	12.8	3.7	3.5
USA	9.7	2.8	3.5
UK	6.9	2.6	2.7

Notes:

1 Column (1) divided by col. (2) the growth rate of real GDP gives col. (3).

2 Equipment investment was computed by deducting the investment in building houses and general government fixed investment from the gross fixed capital formation. Consequently, the government investment in building houses was taken away twice.

3 The equipment investment for Japan was given by adding real equipment investment of private enterprises indicated in the statistics on national accounts and the equipment investment of government enterprises actualised, for convenience, by the same implicit deflator.

(a) Investment in building houses and general government fixed investment were given in ratio of value of money.

(b) General government fixed investment was given in ratio of value of money.

Source: *Economic Survey of Japan (1965–66)* Table 5, Economic Planning Authority, Tokyo, 1968.

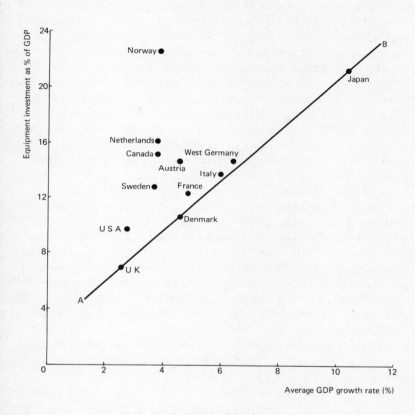

FIGURE 3.1   Equipment investment and GDP growth for 12 countries, 1956–63

productivity and to industrial capacity. What kind of results would that assumption produce?

The Japanese Economic Planning Agency made just such an assumption to derive the figures shown in Table 3.15 and Figure 1. Before any comment is offered on this table and figure it should be noted that the original source of this data commented that 'the UK should not be compared with other countries, because the figures do not include investments of public corporations and government enterprises'.[59] However, by co-incidence, the procedure used by the constructors of this table happens to arrive at about the same result, for the percentage of GDP expended in investment in plant and machinery in the UK during 1956–63 was 6.9 %[60]. The procedure of taking government investment plus housing investment away from total investment may, however, result only in an estimate of equipment investment insofar as the double-counting of government investment in building houses compensates for, and cancels out, investments in the building of business structures. If government did not invest in housing, then the equipment investment resulting from this procedure would be plant, equipment, vehicles and business structures; if government investment in housing equals business investment in building structures, then (and only then) is an assessment of equipment investment derived. Table 3.15 and Figure 3.1 therefore reflect the results of a curious short-cut in calculation. Suspending disbelief for the moment, several observations arise.

First, there are many nations which have relatively high equipment investment rates together with a low productivity (or a high capital-output ratio) of that investment. Assuming this result is not a consequence of the method of calculation, this can be readily explained, for equipment investment (like any other investment) can be wasted for prestige, political, or social purposes. Large-scale steel industries, which are uneconomic in small countries, can be justified on strategic rather than economic grounds. The political direction of investment to particular areas of the country, justified by a need to generate employment in remote areas, may produce lower returns than basing investment in its natural market area. High investment rates do not therefore guarantee high growth rates.

Second, there is no nation represented in the table or figure which has both high economic growth with low rates of equipment investment. Such a condition is feasible — it could exist for oil-producing states for example — but for modern industrial economies, it is apparently impossible for a nation to have high economic growth in the absence of high levels of equipment investment.

Third, no country occupies a position to the right of the trend line AB. It is interesting to note (even if we ignore the position of the UK on this graph) that a few percent of equipment investment may be required to maintain GDP, let alone increase it, for trend line AB intersects the y-axis, implying that about 2 % of GDP equipment investment may be associated with zero growth of GDP. However, given the doubts about the method of derivation of this data, this could hardly be more than speculation.

No matter how the capital-output ratios for the UK are calculated, the results imply a lower productivity of investment capital in the UK than in most other nations.[61] A closer examination of the pattern of UK investments seems indicated.

3.4 CAPITAL INVESTMENT IN THE UK

What factors might explain the UK's comparatively high gross capital-output ratio? One major factor is obviously the relative age of British capital investments, which has meant that nearly half of annual gross capital formation in the UK has been taken up by the replacement of worn-out assets (Table 3.16). This position is, as we have seen, no different from that of some other nations; the UK is similar to France in

TABLE 3.16   Capital consumption and gross capital formation in the UK, 1962–72

in £m., 1970 prices	1 Total capital consumption (all industries)	2 Total capital formation	3 Replacement ratio (%)
1962	3101	6344	48.9
1963	3251	6451	50.4
1964	3429	7504	45.7
1965	3560	7807	45.6
1966	3710	7983	46.5
1967	3897	8564	45.5
1968	4087	8951	45.6
1969	4252	9042	47.0
1970	4447	9223	48.2
1971	4618	9269	49.8
1972	4823	9382	51.4

Source: Data in columns 1 and 2: *National Income and Expenditure, 1973*, HMSO, Tables 58 and 55.

the proportion of capital which replaces worn-out assets. Where the UK may differ is in its industry, where the position is more serious, with more than half, and sometimes two-thirds, of new investment capital being absorbed to replace worn-out plant and machinery (Table 3.17). It is perhaps not surprising under these circumstances that the capital-output ratio of the UK is high, for much of the new industrial

TABLE 3.17 Capital formation and consumption in UK manufacturing industry, 1962–72

in £m., 1970 prices	(a) Gross domestic fixed capital formation	(b) Capital consumption in manufacturing industry	(b)/(a)
1962	1575	799	50.7
1963	1391	831	59.7
1964	1569	869	55.4
1965	1732	906	52.3
1966	1780	945	53.1
1967	1735	986	56.8
1968	1798	1028	57.2
1969	2024	1071	52.9
1970	2129	1118	52.5
1971	1968	1160	58.9
1972	1775	1192	67.2

Source: *National Income and Expenditure*, 1973, HMSO, Tables 55 and 59.

investments is not increasing the size of the capital base but only preventing its erosion.

If we calculate the gross capital-output ratio of the whole UK economy, we find that about 4 % more net investment seems to be required to produce 1 % more output (Table 3.18). This kind of result is similar to that found by other authors.[62] The total capital stock, however, includes expenditure on all social overhead capital such as roads, dwellings, public buildings, hospitals and schools. Social overhead capital is obviously necessary to produce a high quality of life. We are all concerned with the quality of public services such as housing, health, public administration and education—but the capital demands of these services must be kept in proportion as one economic good among many. Britain's public service industries do not seem to be inadequate by the standards of the developed world;[63] it is the UK's industrial base which needs much more investment capital. If productive investments in UK industry were to rise considerably, it does not follow that social overhead capital should necessarily increase in proportion. Nor does it follow that social overhead capital investments should be reduced. Indeed, it could well be the case that a higher productivity of UK industry would produce a situation in which the greater absolute investment in social overhead capital could become possible, although it

TABLE 3.18   Gross capital-output ratios for total UK economy, 1962–72

Year	Total gross capital stock (1970 replacement* prices)	GDP of factor cost* (1970 prices)	Capital-output ratio
1962	131.6	34.06	3.86
1963	136.0	35.45	3.84
1964	141.5	37.51	3.77
1965	147.2	38.47	3.83
1966	153.2	39.22	3.91
1967	159.7	40.12	3.98
1968	166.4	41.64	4.00
1969	173.3	42.16	4.11
1970	180.2	42.79	4.21
1971	186.9	43.67	4.28
1972	193.7	44.34	4.37

*   in £000 m.
Source: *National Income and Expenditure, 1973*, Tables 64 and 14.

may become a lower proportion of total national investments if industrial investments increase. The capital-output ratio of the whole economy is therefore no reliable guide to how much additional industrial investment may be required to produce one percent more output.

The UK capital-output ratios indicated by the gross capital stock, are also misleading. The gross capital stock is interesting as an indication of the gross replacement value of capital assets but no longer forms, in any meaningful sense, the capital assets of the country. The capital-output ratio of the net capital stock (or the gross stock minus capital deaths and machinery withdrawals) is more relevant. Table 3.19 shows GDP, net capital stock, the income return from net fixed assets (GDP expressed as a percentage of net capital stock) and the capital-output ratios of the UK from 1962–72. It should be noted that in Table 3.19, net capital stock is in current replacement prices and GDP in current prices. The average capital-output ratios are therefore a ratio between current-prices output and net capital in each year. If the real costs of capital become cheaper, the resulting lowering of the current replacement costs of capital can lower the capital-output ratio and vice versa. If a trend of changing capital-output ratios appears, then this is a composite index involving both capital prices and capital productivities. However, these capital-output ratios are interesting in that they show, in any year, the

TABLE 3.19   Net capital-output ratio for the UK economy, 1962–72

Year	GDP (£m.)	Net capital stock (£000m.)	% income return on all fixed assets	Capital-output ratio
1962	25279	61.2	41.3	2.42
1963	26878	65.4	41.1	2.43
1964	29187	70.7	41.3	2.42
1965	31156	76.8	40.6	2.47
1966	33057	82.6	40.0	2.50
1967	34835	89.0	39.1	2.55
1968	37263	97.0	38.4	2.60
1969	39168	106.4	36.8	2.72
1970	42788	120.2	35.6	2.81
1971	48159	137.1	35.1	2.85
1972	53484	155.9	34.3	2.91

Note: GDP is at current prices and net capital stock at current replacement costs.
Source: *National Income and Expenditure, 1973*, HMSO, Tables 13 and 63.

percentage of current income which, if devoted to purchasing capital at current prices, could produce about 1 % additional GDP if the capital productivity of that additional investment were equal to the average capital productivity of the economy.

It would seem from this table that only some 2.5–3.0 % of GDP is required as net capital investment to produce additional output of about 1 % of GDP. But the capital-output ratio has apparently been steadily falling during the period under consideration. Why should this be? Is more capital being expended in non-productive economic sectors, or as social overhead capital, or is there a decay in productivity in the use of net capital assets in companies? To examine these questions it is necessary to look at the income and net capital assets for different economic sectors.

Table 3.21 gives an analysis of income and total net capital stock in 1970 for the personal sector, companies, public corporations, central government and local authorities. It is necessary to treat the resulting calculations with some caution, for several reasons. Although capital does flow to each of these sectors, a large proportion of these capital assets are not productive assets. Housing, for example — £19.3bn. of the £26.0bn. worth of net assets in the personal sector — is not a productive

TABLE 3.20   Replacement costs of net capital
assets of UK dwellings, 1970

Economic sector	Net capital of dwellings (£000m.)
Personal sector	19.3
Companies	0.7
Public corporations	1.1
Central government	0.4
Local authorities	14.3
Total	35.8

Source: *National Income and Expenditure,
1973*, Table 63.

TABLE 3.21   Income and net capital assets of UK economic sectors, 1970

Economic sector	Income (£m.)	All fixed assets (£000m.)	% income return on assets	Capital-output ratio	Income percent-ages	Asset percent-ages
Personal sector	7946	26.0	30.6	3.27	18.57	21.63
Companies	23304	39.6	78.7	1.27	54.46	32.95
Public corporations	4336	22.0	19.7	5.07	10.13	18.30
Central government	3076	5.8	53.0	1.89	7.19	4.83
Local authorities	4183	26.8	15.6	6.41	9.78	22.30
Residual error	− 57	–	–	–	− 0.13	–
GDP	42788	–	–	–	–	–
Total capital assets	–	120.2	–	–	–	–
Average figures	–	–	35.6	2.81	100.0	100.0

Source: *National Income and Expenditure, 1973*, HMSO, Tables 13 and 63.

asset in that it does not produce, except at the margin, annual flows of
marketable goods and services. An increase in the housing stock does
not result in large direct and continuing increases in employment. On the
other hand, net capital stock in the companies sector does produce
marketable goods and services; factories need to be staffed, and

machinery needs to be manned. Housing provides an invisible flow of services to the occupiers but it does not enter into the productive process so directly as industrial plant and machinery which produces a measurable flow of marketable goods and services. This is not to say that housing, or indeed any other part of social overhead capital, is unnecessary, as the quality and quantity of housing is an essential determinant of the quality of life; but there is a need for a balanced mixture of social overhead capital with productive assets. There is no purpose in providing excellent housing for virtually everyone at the expense of increased unemployment. All economic sectors possess housing assets to some degree, and these are summarised in Table 3.20.

Nearly 30 % of the UK net capital base in 1970 was therefore composed of dwellings. Central government and local authorities do not trade significantly to acquire their income (although the central government does have ordinance factories and local authorities do trade as providers of housing, water supply and passenger transport). Most of the capital listed as 'other buildings and works' of these economic sectors is not, for the most part, productive and can be regarded as principally social overhead capital, such as schools, hospitals, public buildings, roads and sewerage. These capital assets total an additional £16.4bn. at 1970 replacement cost, and this gives an approximate estimate that perhaps £52.2bn., or nearly 42 % of the fixed capital assets of the UK, may be social overhead capital. Actual social overhead capital could be larger than this, for most private vehicles are not used for business purposes, except by the self-employed. To calculate capital-output ratios by removing social overhead capital assets would perhaps give a better estimate of the relationship between productive output and productive assets, but such a calculation could not be reconciled with the overall capital-output ratio, which includes all social overhead capital. In any case, for the major trading sectors—companies and public corporations—it could be argued that the provision of housing is an essential adjunct to business activity, and income may depend upon all assets employed; while for non-trading sectors, income is not so dependent on capital assets but rests largely upon self-employment in the personal sector, and upon taxation in the central and local government sectors.

Bearing these caveats in mind, Table 3.21 leads to some interesting reflections. The income of the personal sector is over 30 % of its fixed assets, including housing; if housing is removed, then the income return on fixed assets in the personal sector leaps to almost 120 %. This partly reflects the fact that some employment in the personal sector is by households employing domestic workers who require virtually no capital assets for their duties; also that self-employed individuals generally do their work (in jobs such as painting, decorating, gardening, electrical wiring and small-scale building etc.) with very little capital; and finally the capital requirements of unincorporated enterprises are also modest. The personal sector, overall, possessed an estimated $22\frac{1}{2}\%$ of the net assets of the country in 1970 while generating about $18\frac{1}{2}\%$ of the income.

The most productive economic sector of the UK, as could perhaps be expected, is private companies; these generated nearly 55 % of national income in 1970 from a capital base of less than a third of the net fixed assets of the nation. Income was produced to a value of almost 80 % of replacement costs of the net capital assets; hence the net capital-output ratio of British industries was 1.27.

Public corporations, on the other hand, possess vast amounts of capital but generate relatively little income (with an income return on net capital assets of 19.7 % and a capital-output ratio of 5.07). Public corporations had over half the net capital base of private companies, but generated less than a fifth of their income.

The income percentages on capital assets and capital-output ratios for local and central government do not mean much, as these sectors do not trade except for small parts of their incomes. As previously mentioned, perhaps some 95 % of their fixed net capital assets (housing plus other buildings and works, equals to £31.1bn. at 1970 replacement prices) is social overhead capital, while the income of government sectors is largely taxation.

Table 3.22 is based upon the income and net capital assets of economic sectors of the UK economy in 1962. This table, together with Table 3.21 lets us see in which economic sectors the capital-output ratios of the UK rose and hence resulted in declining capital productivity in the UK. The net capital productivity, of companies improved by over 12 % (capital-output ratios fell from 1.43 in 1962 to 1.27 in 1970 but see the note to the table); this was more than compensated for by a worsening by almost 25 % in the net capital productivity of public corporations (where capital-output ratios rose from 3.82 to 5.07). The distribution of the net asset base of the economy changed between 1962 and 1970; the proportions of the net asset base of the economy taken by the personal sector and by companies fell (by 2.06 % and 0.87 % respectively) while the share of net capital assets taken by public corporations, central and local government increased, in absolute percentages, by 1.80 %, 0.42 % and 0.73 %.

TABLE 3.22   Income and net capital assets of UK economic sectors, 1962

Sector	Income (£m.)	All fixed assets (£000m.)	% income return on assets	Capital-output ratio	Income shares in GDP	Asset shares in capital base
Personal sector	4479	14.5	30.9	3.24	17.72	23.69
Companies	14489	20.7	70.0	1.43	57.32	33.82
Public corporations	2646	10.1	26.2	3.82	10.47	16.50
Central government	1689	2.7	62.6	1.60	6.68	4.41
Local authorities	1900	13.2	14.4	6.95	7.52	21.57
Residual error	76	–	–	–	0.30	–
GDP	25279	–	–	–	–	–
Total capital assets	–	61.2	–	–	–	–
Average figures	–	–	41.3	2.42	100.0	100.0

Note: This table is not precisely comparable with Table 3.21 because the steel industry transferred its fixed assets from the category 'companies' to 'public corporations' on 1 July 1967.
Source: As Table 3.21.

Some idea of the capital investment priorities in the UK during the period 1962 to 1972 can be assessed by reference to Tables 3.23 and 3.24. These show the gross investments in 1970 prices in each economic sector from 1962–70, and the net capital increases resulting from that gross investment. On average, only about 40 % of the gross and net investment in the UK economy was in companies. Public corporations and local authorities both invested some 20 % each of the gross investments made during 1962–70, although when we look at net investments the picture is somewhat different — public corporations invested less than 15 % of net capital formation, while the share of local authorities in total net investment during the period rose above a quarter. The personal sector and central government taken together also accounted for over 20 % of gross investment and some 17 % of net investment.

Economic success in the industries of Britain depends largely upon the generation of wealth and employment by private companies and public corporations. It is therefore interesting to examine the average efficiency of investment in these sectors. Suppose that say £1,000m. of gross investment capital were invested in both public and private industry in 1970 — what average results might have been produced?

TABLE 3.23 UK gross domestic capital formation by economic sector, 1962–70 in 1970 prices, £m.

Year	Personal sector	Companies	Public corporations	Central govt.	Local authorities	Total
1962	1074	2685	1228	284	1071	6342
1963	1119	2578	1313	291	1132	6433
1964	1174	3076	1484	355	1390	7479
1965	1226	3237	1577	367	1445	7852
1966	1174	3141	1690	390	1564	7959
1967	1303	3080	1909	454	1802	8548
1968	1404	3329	1806	509	1902	8950
1969	1257	3770	1584	517	1869	8997
1970	1219	3905	1650	576	1873	9223
Total	10950	28801	14251	3743	14048	71793
%	15.25	40.12	19.85	5.21	19.57	100.0

TABLE 3.24 UK net domestic capital formation by economic sector, 1962–70 in 1970 prices, £m.

Year	Personal sector	Companies	Public corporations	Central govt.	Local authorities	Total
1962	375	1434	489	191	755	3244
1963	396	1288	540	199	801	3224
1964	411	1726	665	260	1043	4105
1965	444	1796	710	268	1081	4299
1966	386	1651	779	292	1188	4296
1967	472	1547	921	353	1402	4695
1968	536	1739	730	403	1478	4886
1969	378	2090	476	406	1430	4780
1970	304	2114	491	461	1406	4776
Total	3702	15385	5801	2833	10584	38305
%	9.66	40.16	15.14	7.40	27.63	100.00

TABLE 3.25 Average net/gross investment percentages

Personal sector	Companies	Public corporations	Central govt.	Local authorities
33.8	53.4	40.7	75.7	75.3

Sources: Tables 51 and 56 of *National Income and Expenditure, 1973*, inflated by the price indices of fixed assets to 1970 prices.

The gross investment would be discounted three times. First, the gross investment would have been converted to net investment, and on average during the period 1962–70, about £1,000m. in private industry produced a net investment of £534m. In public corporations the resulting net investment was lower — at about £407m. Second, that capital could be expected to produce income according to the net investment multiplied by the ratio of income to net investment. The income generated in private industry would have been about £420m.; in public corporations, about £80m. Third, of that income, a certain proportion would have generated employment. Based on average 1970 values, the employment generated in companies would have been £335m.; that of public corporations, £54m. The results of these calculations are displayed in Tables 3.26 and 3.27. These calculations rest upon the productivity of new net investments being equal to those of existing fixed assets — in practice, the marginal productivity of new net investments may be somewhat higher for companies and perhaps lower for public corporations. Investment in the companies sector seems likely

TABLE 3.26   UK investment average discount factors

Sector	Ratio of net to gross investment*	1970 values Ratio of income to net investment	Ratio of employment to total income
Companies	0.534	0.787	0.797
Public corporations	0.407	0.197	0.678

* These are 1962–70 averages, from Table 3.25. The 1970 figure for companies is 0.541 and for public corporations 0.30.

TABLE 3.27   Average results of company and public corporation investment

(in £m.) Sector	Gross investment provided	Net investment	Income generated	Employment generated
Companies	1000	534	420	335
Public corporations	1000	407	80	54
Multiplier (Companies ÷ public corporations)	1.00	1.31	5.25	6.20

Source: Calculated from Table 3.26.

to generate over 30 % more net investment, over five times as much national income and perhaps six times as much employment as public corporation investments. There is a lesson in this for politicians attempting to stimulate demand via public investment, but we will defer that discussion to Chapter 6. At this point we wish merely to note that Britain seems to have a capital-starved companies sector and a capital-rich public corporations sector. Perhaps the best way of illustrating this is by calculating the net plant and machinery investment per head in public corporations and the private sector; this is done in Table 3.28.

TABLE 3.28   Plant and machinery investment per head, 1970

Sector	Net plant and machinery (£000m.)	Employment (000s)	Plant and machinery per head (£)
Personal sector	2.1		
Companies	19.7		
Total private sector	21.8	18790	1160
Public corporations	12.3	1921	6400

Source: National Income and Expenditure, 1973, Tables 63 and 13.

The private sector, with £21.8bn. worth of plant and machinery investments, employs nearly 19m. people. The plant and machinery investment per head in the private sector was £1,160 in 1970. Public corporations, on the other hand, had £12.3bn. worth of investment and employed less than 2 million people. Public corporation investment per person employed was about £6,400—or five and a half times greater than in the private sector. Now it cannot be doubted that some public corportions, such as British Steel or British Rail, have relatively high capital-output ratios. But all the evidence—indicating capital starvation in private industry where returns are high, and high capital consumption and investment in public corporations where returns are low—points to a massive mis-allocation of capital resources in the UK economy. If public corporations had been obliged to generate their new capital requirements from profits or on the open market, this mis-allocation might not have happened. If private industry had access to the kind of cheap capital which public corporations use, UK economic growth would probably have been higher.

This conclusion leads to speculation about why UK companies do not have access to the kind of cheap investment capital available overseas; and this is the subject of the next chapter.

3.5 SOME CONCLUSIONS

It has long been recognised that one of the principal requirements of high economic growth is a high rate of capital accumulation. Indeed, Maddison goes so far as to say that: 'High investment has, in fact, been the major factor in explaining the acceleration of post-war output in response to high demand.'[64]

Denison, on the other hand, places capital investment in a relatively subsidiary role, but there must be some doubt about the basis of the assumptions made; especially concerning the marginal theory of allocation of the weights of factor inputs. If the field of study included less developed countries, then low plant and machinery investment might not act as a delimiter of economic growth, for the absence of other equally crucial factors, could, in many cases, prove highly significant. However, the question vis-a-vis the UK is: what factor is absent in the UK economy which is present in the success stories of other economies? There are many factors which Britain shares as part of the western heritage with its European and North American neighbours. The most notable difference between Britain and much of the rest of the developed west is the low level of British productive investment, which seems the most obvious limit to UK growth.

Not only have British investment rates been low, but also that investment appears to have been less productive than investment overseas. Yet a closer look at the UK economy suggests that pessimism about some private-sector capital investment returns may be misplaced. It could well be that a better sectoral allocation of investment funds, with more investment in private industry, could produce considerably higher economic growth.

Developed nations which do not invest at an adequate rate are not noted for their high economic growth. It could be suggested that this statement may be as close to an unalterable law as economists may have yet found. High investment does not guarantee rapid growth, but low investment does constitute a bar to rapid economic growth.

Perhaps the pertinent reflection upon this issue could be left to a Japanese Embassy publication, quoted in a letter by Mr Montague Calman:

A professor of industrial analysis, making a detailed comparison of a British Leyland small car company and its counterpart in Japan, found that the Japanese worker could turn out £1000 worth of car in nine days whereas the Leyland worker took 47 days. This was mainly because each Japanese worker had machinery worth £11,780 at his elbow, while the figure for the British worker was £1000.[65]

If we have doubts about the place of capital investment in generating economic growth, then many of the Japanese do not; and perhaps they have more reason, in their recent direct experience, to know.

4 The Transformation of Saving to Investment

4.1 INTRODUCTION

Within the five nations under consideration, there are various financial institutions which attract savings and transform them into short-, medium-, or long-term loans. In this chapter, limits of space compel us to deal with the functions and methods of these financial institutions only in outline, for the history and nature of each country's financial markets could easily fill several volumes.

Nonetheless, despite historical differences, the financial institutions of any nation serve the same basic purposes. Each group of institutions attracts various amounts of new saving, and these can be reduced to the same common and relative denominator as a percentage of each nation's GDP. Each group of institutions characteristically puts different proportions of its funds to various purposes such as new issues of shares, loan stock, short-, medium- and long-term debt, housing finance, or existing stocks and shares. The extent of the transformation process — from predominantly short-term funds, saved largely by individuals, into medium- and long-term productive investments — can be estimated. The degree of support given by various national governments to assist the transformation process and to avoid bank failures, usually caused by lending long while borrowing short, can also be assessed. In short, the many activities of the financial institutions in the five nations can be reduced to two different aspects; first, for each nation the flow of funds from financial institutions to investing organisations can be outlined, and the sources and users of these funds can be summarised; second, a comparative analysis of national savings-to-investment transformation procedures can be attempted.

It must be emphasised that if a complex system is reduced to its skeletal pattern, many details will be omitted which some knowledgeable observers· may consider crucial. Yet there are advantages in this procedure, for it enables the financial backbone of the savings-to-investment transformation mechanisms to be examined. An outline summary of national financial mechanisms and their results may not fully describe the capital markets of a country, any more than a friend could be recognised from an x-ray plate, but this does not deny diagnostic value to either procedure.

It is necessary from the very outset to distinguish between financial and productive investments.

A financial investment is the use of savings (whether by an individual or an institution) to purchase a pre-existing stock, share or loan bond. These financial investments may affect the ownership of a company, or the entitlement to receive dividends or interest payments from that company, but the company is thereby provided with no additional funds for investment. Financial investments release savings for purposes of consumption, much as consumer credit does, for the seller of the stock has an addition to his income. Of course, under some circumstances, the seller may switch into purchasing other stocks, in which case the income gain goes to subsequent sellers of stocks.

A productive investment on the other hand is the use of savings to purchase shares on the new issue market, or to provide new loans to industrial or commercial companies, or to purchase new rights issues. It should be noted that this definition involves a potentially productive use of savings, rather than necessarily providing capital for fixed investment. A company receiving new-issue capital funds does not need to invest all of that risk capital in new buildings, plant and machinery; part of the capital could be used as stock investments, part to improve company liquidity. However, short-term loans may be available for the finance of increased stock-holding and improved liquidity, and a long-term loan improves an organisation's ability to invest by providing additional capital for investment. The long-term capital provided by new issues or long-term loans is more likely to fund long-term fixed capital, although there is no guarantee this will occur; nonetheless, financial prudence usually puts long-term funds to long-term uses. In City parlance, productive investments are purchases in the primary markets — the new issue market and the new loans market — while financial investments are purchases in the secondary market.

All financial markets utilise the savings canalised to them in a mixture of financial and productive investments. The balance between these two types of investment is crucial to the economy, for financial investments generally release savings for consumption while productive investments may increase the capital stock of the country. In the pages which follow, an attempt will be made in some cases to assess financial investments separately from productive ones. Sometimes this is relatively easy to do, where financial companies are recognised as a separate breed who may canalise pension funds into paper investments, or borrow funds to provide consumer credit, or attract small savings to the balanced portfolio of an investment trust. On occasion, however, all financial institutions are lumped together, and as some banks borrow from their customers to lend to industry or to other non-financial final users, there is an inherent danger of over-counting the available savings due to the financial intermediation of the banking system. If we add all assets acquired by both depositors and banks, then we may double-count the onward lending of savings by banks to final users; if we add liabilities acquired by both banks and companies, then the amounts owed to banks by companies is added with the amounts owed by banks to their depositors. There is sometimes therefore a danger of mistaking financial intermediation with financial investment, as the funds advanced to final users are always less than the total flow of funds recorded. Yet this danger cannot be allowed to mask the reality that some conversion of saving to consumption, via genuine financial investment, is actually occurring. In many cases, where the level of consumer credit is assessable, or where financial companies are distinctly listed, a minimum estimate of the degree of financial investment can be made. Yet even where this cannot be assessed, financial investment is obviously extant.

One interesting question which may be asked of the financial systems is: which economic sector gains most from the procedures described? Surprisingly, the answer to this question is not generally doubtful. The major borrowers, in today's inflationary world, are the principal beneficiaries; and the major borrowers may be either government or private or public industry.

Another aspect of the conversion of saving to lending is the extent to which the time structure of funds is altered in the transformation process. Much of saving is short-term; much of the demand for funds is for long-term resources; financial intermediaries, acting at the point where supply meets demand, need to alter what is available to what is wanted. Whether they are willing to perform this transformation, the assistance they receive, and the extent to which they provide funds, is the subject of this chapter.

4.2 TRANSFORMATION OF SAVING TO INVESTMENT IN FRANCE

The first basic principle of double-entry book-keeping is that the assets of the company are equal to its liabilities. The same general observation holds in the transformation of saving to lending — in every individual transaction, the amount of the asset acquired by the lender is equal and opposite to the amount of the liability incurred by the borrower. It is therefore possible to make up a table of the kind of assets and liabilities which are exchanged through the financial system of a country. Eurostat — the Statistical Office of the European Economic Community — make up such tables for EEC countries, and Table 4.1 shows the transformation of saving to lending in France in 1970. The year of 1970 is quoted in Table 4.1 only to illustrate the flow of funds. Other years will also be commented upon later.

It would seem that, during 1970, some Frs 226bn. were exchanged from lender to borrower.[1] This is almost 29 % of France's GDP (which was Frs 782.56bn. in 1970) and involves a great deal of double-counting of the flow of funds from initial saver to final user. The credit institutions (Column S40 of Table 4.1) acquired liabilities of some Frs 91.7bn., largely from their depositors and other sources, and loaned over Frs 101bn. to final and other users. The generic term 'credit institutions' includes all financial intermediaries except the state, the stock market and insurance companies; all kinds of banks — savings banks, those para-public banks which are run as financial corporations distinct from the French state, merchant banks, regional development banks, and equipment credit banks are included — and the banking equivalent of French building societies (which are also banks) are taken in under this heading. These credit institutions will sometimes be called 'banks' in the text which follows, but the broadness of the definition of the functions of these institutions should be kept in mind. The credit institutions were principally engaged in the onward lending of the funds they had raised from their depositors, from bond and share issues, and from borrowing from other financial institutions. Virtually all of the assets acquired and liabilities incurred by these institutions is at least a double-counting of the flow of funds, for the movement of funds from saver to final user involves, at the very minimum, an increase in assets by a saver (e.g. a French household) and a corresponding increase in the liabilities of a bank, followed by onward lending represented by an increase in the assets of a bank and an increase in the liabilities of the

TABLE 4.1   Transformation of saving to lending in France, 1970*

Code	S10	S80	S40	S50	S60	S90	Total
Part I—Assets acquired by each sector (sources)							
F20	12445	7477	7318	213	653	−4237	23869
F30	2869	36099	4928	426	3084	11067	58473
F90	1067	5259	8	–	10	13	6357
F40	−952	–	−451	205	–	25	−173
F50	3244	335	3679	2919	659	1382	11219
F60			3953	1741	4354	4254	18301
F10	–	–	952	–	–	919	1871
F70	6601	60	34266	1504	4534	3405	50350
F80	46020	−60	46430	691	2730	2961	57372
Total	29894	52170	101063	7699	16024	19789	226639
Part II—Liabilities incurred by each sector (borrowers)							
F20	–	–	14964	–	3185	5717	23866
F30	551	–	52072	488	1686	3676	58473
F90	–	–	–	6364	–	–	6364
F40	–	–	721	–	−1894	–	−1173
F50	5474	–	6569	–	−1223	399	11219
F60	9227	–	6682	98	–	2294	18301
F10	–	–	919	–	–	952	1871
F70	32548	8155	2342	254	4097	2954	50350
F80	20642	18446	7413	–	5132	5694	57327
Total	68442	26601	91682	7204	10983	21686	226598

Key

F20 Currency and transferable sight deposits
F30 Other deposits
F90 Insurance technical reserves
F40 Bills and short-term bonds
F50 Long-term bonds
F60 Shares and other equity
F10 SDRs
F70 Short-term loans

F80 Medium- and long-term loans
S10 Non-financial corporate and quasi-corporate enterprises
S80 Households
S40 Credit institutions
S50 Insurance enterprises
S60 General government
S90 Rest of world

* in Frs m.
Source: Eurostat National Accounts, 1976.

final user. In some circumstances, the inter-bank lending could add a further intermediate link in the chain, resulting in some triple-counting of the same flow of fund. Quadruple or quintuple counting is obviously possible. On the other hand, as shown by the fact that French credit institutions as a whole lend more than they borrow, some lending by these institutions is from their own funds, and most of these cases would involve single-counting of the matched pair of entries associated with one transaction—an asset-acquiring bank entry and a liability-incurring other entry. Table 4.1 would lead one to suggest that perhaps about 9.2 % of the loans made by credit institutions in 1970 might have originated from their own funds.

The table shows the flow of funds from source, through the financial channels to final user. The currency and transferable sight deposits of each economic sector (line F20 of part 1) are for the most part the assets of enterprises and households; but they are largely borrowed by credit institutions (line F20 of Part II) for onward lending. Similarly, the other deposits of the banking system are principally household savings (line F30 of Part I) although all economic sectors, including foreign bonds, possess such deposits; however, some 89 % of these funds are the liabilities of the credit institutions, who advance a small percentage of these funds as deposits. Or consider insurance: all economic sectors insure their assets; these assets are canalised to the liabilities of the 'insurance technical reserves' of the insurance companies which lend some of these funds onward, and these then become the assets of the insurance companies. An extended diagram of this procedure is shown in Table 4.2 which shows how insurance funds given in one line in Part I of Table 4.1 are concentrated to a single liability entry in Part II; how these funds are augmented by additional sources of lending; and how these are then loaned in turn to the banks and in the commercial money markets. The insurance sector has been chosen to illustrate the flow of funds, because of the simplicity of the insurance channel; but the principle applies in other cases. In Part II of Table 4.1 we can also compare the issuers of long-term bonds (line F50) and new issues of equity stock (line F60) with the economic sector, which purchased these bonds and shares (lines F50 and F60 of Table 4.1, part I).

The difficulty with Table 4.1, however, is that the information is too compressed to permit easy inspection of the channels by which savings flow to final users.[2] An improvement in clarity can be obtained by concentrating on the function of the banking system, or the credit institutions listed in these tables.

Table 4.3 shows a summary of the activities of credit institutions in France during the years 1970–73. The extent to which these banks advance medium- and and long-term loans (which may be used for investment purposes) is of interest. Borrowings by these banks and loans from them are therefore analysed into two groups — the short-term, and the medium- and long-term. 'Medium-term' in France means 3–7 years; long-term is over 7 years. One fact is immediately obvious—the

TABLE 4.2   Canalisation of funds from insurer to user, in France, 1970*

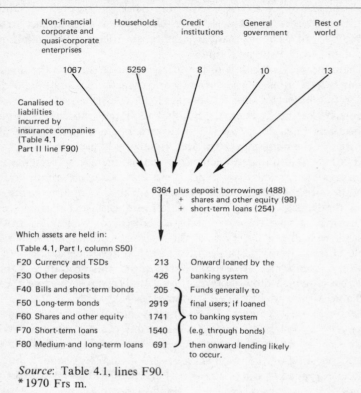

Non-financial corporate and quasi-corporate enterprises	Households	Credit institutions	General government	Rest of world
1067	5259	8	10	13

Canalised to liabilities incurred by insurance companies (Table 4.1 Part II line F90)

6364 plus deposit borrowings (488)
+   shares and other equity (98)
+   short-term loans (254)

Which assets are held in:
(Table 4.1, Part I, column S50)

F20 Currency and TSDs	213	Onward loaned by the
F30 Other deposits	426	banking system
F40 Bills and short-term bonds	205	Funds generally to
F50 Long-term bonds	2919	final users; if loaned
F60 Shares and other equity	1741	to banking system
F70 Short-term loans	1540	(e.g. through bonds)
F80 Medium-and long-term loans	691	then onward lending likely to occur.

Source: Table 4.1, lines F90.
* 1970 Frs m.

liabilities of the banks are largely short-term resources. The reason for this lies in the liquidity preference of French savers: household savings are a major source of uncommitted funds, and as one book has commented vis-à-vis France: '. . . the private saver keeps most of his savings in cash or short-term deposits with the banks and savings institutions.'[3]

It therefore falls to the French banks to convert much of these (and other) short-term funds to longer-term loans. During the years 1970–73, only some 10.8 to 22.8 % of bank borrowings were medium- and long-term, but the onward advances from banks were 42.0 to 54.0 % medium- and long-term. French banks therefore serve as vital financial intermediaries, taking the risks involved in transforming short-term resources to longer-term funds.

Perhaps the best method of putting these funds into perspective is to

TABLE 4.3   Credit institutions in France: transformation of borrowing to lending, 1970–73

in Frs m.	1970	1971	1972	1973
Nature of borrowing				
1 Short-term resources				
(a) Currency and sight deposits	14964	33052	71745	45973
(b) Other deposits	52072	86423	101114	103331
(c) Bills and short-term bonds	721	2187	774	83
(d) Short-term loans	2342	6615	44479	50525
(e) Total short-term	70099	128277	218112	199912
2 Medium-and long-term resources				
(a) Long-term bonds	6569	9741	11117	13832
(b) Shares and other equity	6682	6544	7573	7955
(c) Medium- and long-term loans	7413	7563	7631	10322
(d) Total medium- and long-term	20664	23848	26321	32109
3 Total borrowing	90763	152125	244433	232021
% Short-term	77.2	84.3	89.2	86.2
% Medium- and long-term	22.8	15.7	10.8	13.8
Nature of lending				
1 Short-term lending				
(a) Currency and TSDs	7318	25967	36031	10653
(b) Other deposits	4928	22149	33754	42595
(c) Bills, short-term bonds	−451	−11	−9260	−15336
(d) Short-term loans	34246	39024	83077	96006
(e) Total short-term	46041	87129	143602	133918
2 Medium- and long-term lending				
(a) Long-term bonds	3679	6374	10271	11972
(b) Shares and other equity	3953	3832	6103	7785
(c) Medium- and long-term loans	46430	56840	87519	90837
(d) Total medium- and long-term	54062	67046	103893	110594
3 Total lending	100103	154175	247495	244512
% Short-term	46.0	56.5	58.0	54.8
% Medium- and long-term	54.0	43.5	42.0	45.2

Source: Table 4.1 and appendices A17–A19.
Note: Time deposits and time savings, included in 1(b) and amounting to totals of Frs 28,595m., Frs 42,947m., Frs 55,957m., and Frs 53,425m. in 1970, 1971, 1972 and 1973 respectively, could have been classified as medium-term resources.

express them as percentages of GDP. This is done in Table 4.4. The resources converted by the banks from short- to medium- and long-term have been between 4 and 8 % of GDP—a considerable amount of additional finance, potentially for investment purposes. In the absence of some transformation of funds from short- to longer-term only some

TABLE 4.4 Credit institutions in France: timespan of resources, 1970–73

in Frs m.	1970	1971	1972	1973
1 Medium- and long-term resources borrowed	20664	23848	26321	32109
2 Medium- and long-term resources loaned	54062	67046	103893	110594
3 Resources converted from short- to long-term	33418	43198	77572	78485
4 Gross Domestic Product	782560	872430	981120	1113550
As % of GDP				
5 Medium- and long-term resources loaned	6.91	7.68	10.59	9.93
6 Resources converted from short- to long-term	4.27	4.95	7.91	7.05
7 'Natural level' medium- and long-term resources	2.64	2.73	2.68	2.88

Source: Table 4.3.
Note: If time deposits and time savings were classified as a medium-term resource, then line 6 would be diminished by, and row 7 would be increased by, the following percentages of GDP in 1970 to 1973 respectively: 3.65%, 4.92%, 5.70%, and 4.80%. However, since some time deposits and time savings are at 7 days notice, we consider such an adjustment to be inappropriate. Some adjustment for term deposits or savings, which is at 1 or 2 year terms, may nonetheless be justifiable, but such saving is relatively small.

$2\frac{1}{2}$–3% of GDP would be available from the banking system for medium- and long-term uses; it is the transformation of these funds which permits the banks to advance about 7 to $10\frac{1}{2}$% of GDP as medium- and long-term loans. This fund-transformation activity is therefore a highly significant feature of the French economy, for without such a system, investment in France would undoubtedly run at a significantly lower level. Some of these funds however, are not going to final users; some are used in purchasing the bonds of other financial institutions. On the other hand, the state, insurance companies, and the financial market all advance medium- and long-term funds to non-financial users; a detailed look at the institutions providing all medium- and long-term funds seems warranted.

Table 4.5 shows the transformation of saving to medium- and long-term capital in France in 1973.[4] Part I of the table, dealing with final lending, shows which sector borrowed the money and which financial intermediary provided it, while Part II lists the sources from which each financial institution acquired the funds it loaned.

TABLE 4.5 Medium- and long-term financing, in France 1973 in Frs m., 1973 prices

Lenders / Borrowers	1 Banque de France and Banques	2 Crédit Mutuel Agricole et non-Agricole	3 CDC and savings banks	4 Other credit institutions	5(a) State Loans	5(b) State Grants	6 Insurance	7(a) Financial Market Bonds, debentures etc.	7(b) Financial Market Shares	8 Non-financial domestic agents	9 Rest of world	10 Total
I Uses of funds (Final lending)												
1 Local authorities	3052	935	4922	1633	−24	—	2	599	—	196	—	11271
2 Others (excepting the state)	92	321	761	150	−1	—	—	27	24	68	72	1234
3 Housing												
(a) private households	12851	7087	3797	7961	−729*	—	153	—	—	4932	—	36781
(b) large-scale schemes	423	—	535	10773	—	—	152	4	503	—	524	12177
4 Agriculture	105	3079	—	—	—	—	—	—	—	—	—	3184
5 Industry, services, commerce	10926	3751	1927	8654	455	2236	194	6051	10066	900	1869	47029
6 Rest of world	6585	98	171	1135	843	166	6	632	6765	2875	—	19273
7 Total flow to non-financial sectors	34034	15271	12113	30306	544	2402	503	7265	17358	8832	2321	130949
8 Direct flow to other sectors	−4630	580	5545	33	251	2716	38	23479	6357	300	1759	36428
9 Financial market (subscriptions and new issues)												
(a) bonds, debentures, etc	873	307	8530	2497	—	—	5831	—	—	12580	126	—
(b) shares	3833	102	1058	2152	−66	—	3168	—	—	8484	4984	—
10 Total used in the medium- and long-term	34110	16260	27246	34988	729	5118	9540	—	—	30196	9190	167377
II Sources of funds (Initial and intermediate lending)												
11 Funds received direct from other lenders	2577	−198	40	12824	−8653*	—	2	30744	23715	94450	1876	167377
12 Financial market (new funds)												
(a) bonds, debentures etc	3065	3195	—	12219	5000	—	—	—	—	6633	632	(30744)
(b) shares or bonds	1522	367	—	4380	—	—	88	—	—	10593	6765	(23715)
13 Surplus or shortage of finance	2471	321	499	330	12847	—	1083	—	—	−19407	1856	—
14 Negotiable bonds and re-financing	5175	1229	−1588	10173	−16060*	—	125	—	—	970	−24	—
15 Balance of other employed resources	19300	11346	28295	−4938	12713	—	8242	—	—	−53043	−11915	—
Total resources	34110	16260	27246	34988	729	5118	9540	—	—	30196	9190	167377

* Involving an excess of repayments over and above new loans

Source: *XXI Report du Conseil de Direction du Funds de Développement Économique et Social, June 1976, Ministère de L'Économie et des Finances.*

A few words about each of these financial institutions may help. The Banque de France is in some respects an equivalent of the Bank of England — for example, the Banque is a lender of last resort to the French banking system. The major difference is that the Banque is also associated with three regional and nationalised banks (the Banque Nationale de Paris, the Société Général and the Crédit Lyonnais) which are high street banks with branches throughout France. The Crédit Mutuel Agricole et non-Agricole is a bank which is primarily active in the rural areas of France. The original purpose of the Crédit Mutuel Agricole was to lend development funds to the agricultural sector, which still receives over 95 % of its medium- and long-term loans from the Crédit Mutuel Agricole, but the bank has expanded its lending to private borrowers for housing, and to local, usually rural industries. In addition it provides new funds to local authorities and some overseas investment. The Caisse des Dépôts et de Consignations is an agent of government which canalises much of the money in local savings banks to investments on the financial market.

The heading 'other credit institutions' in Table 4.5 covers the French equivalent of British merchant banks — the banques d'affaires — and a number of other regional development banks. Other headings in Table 4.5 are largely self-explanatory.

Table 4.5 shows the flow of funds from saver to user, but some interpretation of the table is in order. Line 11 shows the 'opening position' of each bank or financial sector.[5] These are the funds each bank, or financial sector, starts with for lending purposes.

'Non-financial domestic agents' — an expression which includes households and industry and commerce, and even agriculture and local authorities — saved a total of over Frs 94bn. (column 8 line 11) out of their own resources. These funds were increased during 1973 by the proceeds of the new borrowings on the financial market by these same sectors,[6] and the re-financing of negotiable bonds also provided a further Frs 970m. The total savings made by non-financial domestic agents (largely made by households) was over Frs 82bn. (column 8, sum of lines 13 and 15). These liquid savings were collected and canalised by the banking system to the major lenders — to the Banque de France, the Crédit Mutuel Agricole, the Caisse des Dépôts and other credit institutions, and to the state. The banking and credit institutions supplemented their funds by issuing bonds and paper on the financial market, and by the re-discounting or re-financing of negotiable bonds by the state. The total funds raised were then transformed to medium- and long-term investment credit, which the banks and institutions advanced to borrowers.

There are several noteworthy features about this process of transforming short-term savings to medium- and long-term debt. Perhaps predominant among these are first, the role of the financial market; second, the different lending priorities of each credit source; third, the relative importance of each source of finance to each non-financial sector of the economy; and fourth, the extent of the transformation process.

The financial markets of any nation are the major mechanisms of inter-bank lending, and France is no exception to this general rule. Table 4.6 summarises the issues and purchases of financial institutions, non-financial domestic agencies and foreign organisations. In 1973 issues of bonds by the Banque de France and banks were slightly less than purchases, or the actions of the Banque were broadly neutral in the capital market. The Crédit Mutuel Agricole on the other hand, issued over Frs 3.5bn. and purchased less than half a billion, using the capital market as a source of funds. The Caisse de Dépôts and the savings banks issued nothing but purchased over Frs 9.5bn. of newly issued stocks, shares and bonds, thereby providing the capital market with funds.

TABLE 4.6   Financial market in France, 1973—issues and purchases (total of bonds plus shares)*

Sector	Issues	%	Purchases	%
1 BDF and banks	4587	8.42	4706	8.62
2 CMA et NA	3562	6.54	409	0.75
3 CDC and savings banks	–	–	9588	17.56
4 Other credit institutions	16599	30.48	4649	8.52
5 State	5000	9.18	66	0.12
6 Insurance	88	0.16	8999	16.48
7 Non-financial domestic agents	17226	31.63	21064	38.59
8 Rest of world	7397	13.59	5110	9.36
9 Totals	54459	99.99	54591	100.00

* in Frs m.
Source: Table 4.5.

Other credit institutions used the financial market as a source of capital, issuing over Frs 16.5bn. of stocks while purchasing less than Frs 4.7bn. The state purchased very little, but raised Frs 5bn; insurance companies, on the contrary, purchased over Frs 9bn. of paper assets and raised very little. Commercial companies received less than a third of the total capital raised, although a closer inspection of Table 4.5 will show that companies received about a fifth of new bonds and debentures, but more than two-fifths of new share capital. Non-financial domestic agents, including companies, local authorities, households, and so on, purchased over Frs 21bn. of new capital issues. Finally, foreign investment in France in 1973 did not balance the capital and loans raised on the financial market by foreign organisations, for nearly Frs 7.4bn. were raised for investment abroad for while foreign investment in France was only Frs 5.1bn. of the new capital raised. Incidentally, the difference between issue and purchase prices seems to have been about 2.4% in 1973, which partly indicates some of the cost (on the capital market only) of raising these funds. The cost to companies of raising the capital is of course much higher — this average cost is obviously greatly affected by the considerable confidence in most new loans raised by the banks.

The general pattern described for 1973 does not seem peculiar to that year. In general, as Table 4.7 shows, from 1970–73 non-financial corporate and quasi-corporate enterprises raised much more in the financial markets than they purchased; households purchased from about 10 to 16% of issues; credit institutions generally used the market as a source of funds, buying more than they issued, but switching funds between themselves to a great extent; insurance companies hardly issued anything, but purchased 16–17% of issues; the French government was a large purchaser of issues from 1970–72, but went to the market for funds in 1973, when it issued over 10% of all bonds, yet bought more than this (12.6% of new financial paper); while foreign investment in French flotations of new commercial paper have generally exceeded foreign capital raised in the French financial market, except during 1973.

The proportions of GDP raised in France by new issues of shares and bonds is relatively high, as Table 4.8 illustrates. Some 4–5 percent of France's GDP is raised in the financial markets annually, about half in bonds and half in shares and other equity.

If we turn to the 1973 priorities assigned by each financial intermediary to the borrowers, we can calculate Table 4.9 which shows the percentage of total funds loaned to particular sectors of the economy in France in 1973. Over 70% of the Banque de France and bank loan funds went to housing and investment in industry. Since the funds placed by the BDF and banks were over 20% of all medium- and long-term loans in 1973, the effect of these priorities was large. The Crédit Mutuel Agricole, with nearly 10% of all medium- and long-term loans, seemed

TABLE 4.7   Financial market in France 1970–3—issues and purchases of bonds plus shares

Year	Non-financial corporate and quasi-corporate enterprises	House-holds	Credit institutions	Insurance companies	Govern-ment	Rest of world	Total
1970							
Issues	14701	–	13251	98	−1223	2693	29520
%	49.8	–	44.9	0.3	−4.1	9.1	100.0
Purchases	3244	3335	7632	4660	5013	5636	29520
%	11.0	11.3	25.9	15.8	17.0	19.0	100.0
1971							
Issues	17310	–	16285	15	−441	3074	36243
%	47.8		44.9	–	−1.2	8.5	100.0
Purchases	4685	4012	10206	5758	6112	5470	36243
%	12.9	11.1	28.2	15.9	16.9	15.1	100.0
1972							
Issues	18117	–	18690	67	963	6394	44231
%	41.0	–	42.3	0.2	2.2	14.5	100.0
Purchases	2358	4099	16374	7661	6479	7260	44231
%	5.3	9.3	37.0	17.3	14.6	16.4	100.0
1973							
Issues	19855	–	21787	88	6042	7563	55335
%	35.9	–	39.4	0.2	10.9	13.7	100.0
Purchases	5137	9075	19757	9157	6950	5263	55339
%	9.4	16.4	35.7	16.5	12.6	9.5	100.0

* in Frs m.
Source: Table 4.3 and appendices A17–A19.

TABLE 4.8   New issues of shares and bonds in France, 1970–73

Year	New issues	Frs m.	% of GDP
1970	Shares and other equity	18301	2.34
	Bonds	11219	1.43
1971	Shares and other equity	16066	1.84
	Bonds	20177	2.31
1972	Shares and other equity	21674	2.21
	Bonds	22557	2.30
1973	Shares and other equity	27178	2.44
	Bonds	28157	2.53

Source: Table 4.1 and appendices A17–A19.

to have private housing as its first priority (43.6%), industries second (23.1%) and agricultural investment credit third (at 18.9%). The Caisse des Dépôts placed over a third of its funds on the financial market, but also provided significant new loans for local authorities.

TABLE 4.9 Distribution of medium- and long-term funds by lenders in France, 1973*

Lender Borrower	BDF and banks	Credit Mutuel Agricole	CDC and savings banks	Other credit insti- tutions	Loans	State Grants	Insu- rance
1 Local authorities	8.9	5.7	18.1	4.7	−3.3	−	−
2 Other (except the state)	0.3	2.0	2.8	0.4	−0.1	−	−
3 Housing (a) Private	37.7	43.6	13.9	22.8	−	−	1.6
(b) Large-scale schemes	1.2	−	2.0	30.8	−100.0	−	1.6
4 Agriculture	0.3	18.9	−	−	−	−	−
5 Industry, service commerce	32.0	23.1	7.1	24.7	62.4	43.7	2.0
6 Rest of world	19.3	0.6	0.6	3.2	115.6	3.3	0.1
7 Direct flow to other sectors	−13.6	3.6	20.3	0.1	34.4	53.0	0.4
8 Financial market (a) Bonds etc.,	2.6	1.9	31.3	7.1	−	−	61.1
(b) Shares	11.2	0.6	3.9	6.2	−9.1	−	33.2
Funds loaned (Frs. m.)	34110	16260	27246	34988	729	5118	9540
As % of total funds of Frs. 167,377m.	20.4	9.7	16.3	20.9	0.4	3.1	5.7

* in percentages.
Source: Calculated from Table 4.5.

Other credit institutions, which includes building societies, naturally loaned out over half their funds for housing, although another quarter of these funds were canalised to industry and commerce. State loans, at less than half a percent of total medium- and long-term funds, were provided to foreign capital, and state grants largely helped industry. Insurance companies purchased shares, debentures and long-term loans on the stock market but provided very little new capital to the non-financial sector.

There is a clear pattern of dependence of some economic sectors upon financial institutions. Local authorities and other administrations received over 75 % of their medium- and long-term funds from the Banque de France, the big three nationalised banks and the Caisse des Dépôts. Housing is funded by virtually all institutions. Agriculture received only medium- and long-term loans from the Crédit Mutuel Agricole and the nationalised banks. Industry, Services and Commerce received financial support from every financial institution, although over a quarter of the funds come from the financial market, and another fifth from the nationalised banks. Investment abroad is shown in the table as largely provided by the financial market and the Banque de France, but was probably largely provided by the Banque Francaise du Commerce Extérieur (a specialised institution operating for the BDF).

Having looked at how funds are canalised from saver to user through financial intermediaries, we can summarise, in a simplified form, how the savings-to-investment transformation process operates in France.

(i) Liquid savings of households and others are collected locally and canalised to the central financial intermediaries — to the public and para-public banks, other credit institutions, and to the state. Insurance companies also collect and centralise savings.

(ii) Interbank lending and new issues partly through the issue and purchase of bonds and loans on the financial market, and partly by private arrangements, alter the distribution of the collected funds in the banks and provides some new capital to final users.

(iii) The public, para-public and private banks then take the risk by transforming some of these short-term assets into medium- and long-term loans which are advanced to final users through the banking system.

Table 4.10 summarises the scale of this process during the years 1973 to 1975. Marketed savings — i.e. savings which were not earmarked for expenditure on investment, as nearly all the savings of companies and government usually are — represents about 11 % of the French GDP. An increasing proportion of this saving is in the form of short-term resources which would not be transformed to long-term loans without some financial intermediation. However, the risks involved in this transformation are principally undertaken by the public and para-public banks. Furthermore, the evidence seems to indicate that the

TABLE 4.10 Summary of French saving-to-investment transformation, 1973–75

in Frs m. at current prices	1973	1974	1975
Medium- and long-term funds to final users	130949	130635	163310
Medium- and long-term funds as % of GDP	11.76	10.64	11.35
Short-term savings transformed to medium and long-term financing	82450	92574	142395
Savings transformed as % of GDP	7.40	7.25	9.89
Medium and long-term funds advanced to industry, services and commerce	47029	53752	84865
Commercial funds as % of GDP	4.22	4.21	5.90

Source: *XXI Report du Conseil de Direction du Fonds de Développement Economique et Social, op. cit.*, pp. 18, 19 and 22.

French financial system may have raised the percentage of short-term savings transformed to medium- and long-term loans over the period 1970–75.

The French system of financing some new investment from saving is largely a state-provided and partially government-controlled means of providing capital for public and social purposes and for those companies whose production aims coincide with those of the National Plan. Banking in France is largely socialised but not nationalised; there is no single monolithic national banking authority, and the large semi-public banks operate with considerable autonomy, and with different objectives. As one book remarks, in the context of France: 'Although in many ways it is as if the Civil Service were to run the City, it is important to realise that just because it is different does not mean it is less effective.'[7]

Indeed, possibly au contraire, for there is much merit in the French approach. A large number of banking institutions with a specified but wide range of objectives seems inherently more likely to meet many more market demands than any nationalised banking system could.

The French system of planning (or the National Plan) is something else again. Private investors are not supposed to find it easy to acquire funds for investment unless their company objectives and production line up with the requirements of the Plan, and inspectors from Paris are employed to audit advances and help ensure some degree of obedience to the Plan's aims. This system seems technically efficient but is perhaps over-centralised; fortunately there are some signs that the final lenders of funds are not over-rigid in their interpretation of which investment projects agree with the aims of the National Plan. At worst, non-specified non-priority industries may find it a little more expensive to raise capital.

No matter what criticisms could be made of the French financial system, one conclusion is indisputable; it cannot reasonably be doubted that the growth rate of France has been increased by the provision of an additional 8% or so of GDP as medium- and long-term investment funds. As Table 4.10 shows, French industrial and commercial companies have received 4–6% of GDP in the form of these funds. If this had not occurred, the French economy would have less productive capacity than it now possesses, and France would not stand where it does, as one of the most rapidly-growing economies in western Europe.

4.3 TRANSFORMATION OF SAVING TO INVESTMENT IN JAPAN

At the end of World War II, Japan's economy lay in ruins. As one author vividly puts it:

> Most of the cities had been devastated by air attack which had destroyed about a quarter of the housing accommodation of the country together with a high proportion of industrial plant and buildings. The amount of physical destruction, it is estimated, was equivalent to about twice the national income of the fiscal year 1948–49.[8]

The Japanese were therefore faced with the need to rebuild their shattered economy, and to adjust it to a peacetime footing. But from where would they get the money to do so? The problem of financing the required re-building of industrial plant and machinery was solved, in the event, by banks lending funds to industry; and the source of much of these funds was banks borrowing money (or discounting the acquired industrial credit bonds) at the Bank of Japan. As Table 4.11 shows, the Bank of Japan's loans and discounts to the banking system were a very potent factor in the increase in the liquidity of the banks during the early post-war years, with about 42, 32 and 22 percent of bank funds having their origin in Bank of Japan loans to the banking system in 1946, 1947 and 1948 respectively. It is fair to remark at this point that, immediately after the defeat of Japan, massive American aid averted widespread Japanese starvation and provided raw materials for industry. Further-

106 *Financing Industrial Investment*

T<small>ABLE</small> 4.11   Credit creation by Japanese banks, 1946–68*

Year	A Bank advances (Other than by Bank of Japan)	B Bank of Japan loans and discounts to the banking system	B/A (%)	Bank of Japan government bond holdings
1946	118.2	49.6	41.96	34.7
1947	136.8	43.9	32.09	145.8
1948	246.2	54.2	22.01	247.7
1949	494.4	77.8	15.74	188.6
1950	820.5	123.3	15.03	136.7
1951	1241.2	179.5	14.46	126.0
1952	1808.1	241.1	7.50	286.1
1953	2391.8	307.5	12.86	314.3
1954	2830.9	365.5	12.91	483.5
1955	3195.8	319.0	9.98	553.6
1956	4066.1	139.9	3.44	586.7
1957	5024.4	551.9	10.98	387.2
1958	5812.9	379.9	6.54	536.0
1959	6802.8	337.9	4.97	644.8
1960	8182.6	500.2	6.11	569.1
1961	9770.1	1284.5	13.15	287.7
1962	11494.6	1285.1	11.18	378.3
1963	14562.6	1155.6	7.94	346.0
1964	16829.7	1100.4	6.54	760.9
1965	19217.9	1627.7	8.47	930.0
1966	22046.0	1741.2	7.90	638.1
1967	25323.0	1515.1	5.98	1144.0
1968	29032.8	1563.2	5.37	1434.1

* in ¥ bn.
Note: Between 1946 and 1954, these are average figures; after 1955, they are end-of year.
Source: Reproduced by permission, from *The Structure and Operation of the Japanese Economy*, by K. Bieda. John Wiley & Sons Australasia Pty Ltd, Sydney, 1970, p. 143.

more, when such aid ended in 1951, it was replaced by an American 'special procurement procedure' which ensured that most goods, required by American forces in the Far East would be purchased from Japan[9]. But having said that, the expansion of bank credit for industrial re-building stands out, as something quite unusual in the world's post-war economies. As another author comments: 'without the vast credit expansion by these banks, the great economic growth would have been hardly conceivable.'[10]

Quite so: and without the Bank of Japan's support of the banking system, the expansion of credit would have been much smaller. The Japanese banking system created credit for the purposes of the expansion of economic and especially industrial capacity; this began during the period of American occupation (1945—51) and has continued up to the present day.

As G. C. Allen writing about the post-war period, says:

At that time, although there was an urgent demand for investment capital, industrial and commercial enterprises were without liquid resources and they were obliged to resort to the commercial banks (especially the city banks) to finance their expansion.[11]

The supportive credit creation by the Bank of Japan almost certainly caused some inflation, but that was part of the price of a rapid increase in industrial capacity, and perhaps in post-war Japan there was no alternative which held out any hope of rapidly rebuilding the economy.

The other main method used by the Bank of Japan to increase the liquidity of financial institutions and to assist industry was through the purchase of bonds. This is also shown in Table 4.11. Japanese procedures of financing the rapid development of industrial capacity of their economy, used first as a response to the destruction of a major war, have continued since, as Table 4.11 demonstrates. The heavy borrowing of other Japanese banks from the Bank of Japan has led to a very centralised control of the level of industrial credit for expansion, for the Bank of Japan can (and has) increased or decreased liquidity by selling or purchasing bonds or by altering the level of the loans and discounts offered. These actions have impinged on a very large and complex financial system.

There are literally thousands of private financial institutions in Japan.[12] The ones which are most active in advancing large-scale loan funds are the so-called 'city banks', whose principal customers (in terms of both deposits and loans) are major businesses. 'Local banks' are much smaller, on average; they principally act as savings banks, and generally have an excess of loanable funds which are canalised (through call money and other markets) to city banks for onward lending. The city banks act as money pumps in the Japanese economy, collecting liquid savings from rural and other sources and advancing loans to industry from these borrowed assets. In 1968, for example the city banks borrowed ¥988bn., or 81.1% of the ¥1,218bn. (or 2.35% of Japanese GDP) offered on the call-money market, and loaned only ¥1bn.; all other institutions were net sources of funds; local banks loaned ¥206bn. and borrowed ¥20bn.; trust banks loaned ¥126bn., and borrowed ¥ 28bn. All other banks (credit associations, savings banks and agricultural co-operates) loaned the residue of ¥757bn. while borrowing ¥ 182bn.[13] However, the city banks are not the only providers of external industrial funds.

In the early 1960s, over 60% of the investment funds of commercial and industrial companies came from external sources, from private and

TABLE 4.12   The increase in the supply of industrial funds in Japan, 1961–75*

Year	Total value of external sources of capital	Stocks and shares	Industrial bonds	Private financial institutions	Loans and discounts, govt. financial institutions	Own capital
1961	41716	9285	3857	26275	1777	26479
1962	42038	7978	1331	29718	2425	28773
1963	57273	5894	1636	46781	2175	31986
1964	50940	7913	1540	37345	3495	39746
1965	49712	2626	2193	40444	3725	40753
1966	56061	3351	2252	45050	4599	51189
1967	70409	3323	2780	58031	5342	65857
1968	74344	4914	1594	59941	6758	82400
1969	103224	7544	2988	83801	7747	98313
1970	126259	10029	3589	102494	9107	NA
1971	173208	8738	6571	145869	10614	NA
1972	200526	11415	3709	173992	10052	NA
1973	217694	11841	7830	180312	15993	NA
1974	166607	8746	5579	133460	16719	NA
1975	195977	12996	13183	146711	20148	NA

* in ¥ 100m.
Source: *Monthly Statistics of Japan*, Oct. 1971 and Dec. 1976, Bureau of Statistics, Office of the Prime Minister, Japan, Table M–4.
Notes:
1 The table reflects total value i.e. equipment funds plus working funds. Note that the table shows increases in the supply of funds, i.e. 'the net increase in outside capital figures of ordinary enterprises except financial institutions.' (Table M–4, *ibid.*)
2 The statistical discrepancies are noted—some small sources of funds have not, we assume, been quoted.
3 The figures for 'own capital' are not published in the source after 1969.

government savings. The financial intermediaries which act as sources of supply of these industrial funds are shown in Table 4.12 and are diagrammed in Table 4.13.

TABLE 4.13   Supply of funds to Japanese business, 1970

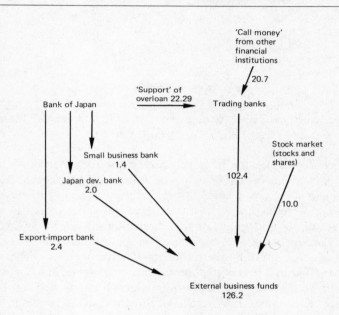

Note: The overloan support and the call money figures have been taken from Table 14–5, p. 111, *Monthly Statistics of Japan*, Bureau of Statistics, Office of the Prime Minister, Oct. 1971.

We can see from these tables that Japanese industry has for the most part been built on borrowed public money—the average capital structure of Japanese corporations has shown an increasing dependence on debt as opposed to equity capital. For industrial and commercial companies, the trend from 1960 to 1965 is shown in Table 4.14.

G. C. Allen comments on the period following 1945:

For the next twenty years the contribution made by the re-investment of profits amounted to only a small proportion of the typical firm's investment. Some 80 percent of the requirements of new capital was

TABLE 4.14   Average debt-equity ratios of industrial and commercial companies in Japan, 1960–65

Year	Borrowed	Owned
1960	77.4	22.6
1961	77.7	22.3
1962	78.0	22.0
1963	79.5	20.5
1964	80.3	19.7
1965	81.0	19.0

Note: Recent figures indicate a 85:15 ratio.

provided from outside the firm and most of this came from the banks and not from the public issue of securities.[14]

This borrowed money has largely been in the form of roll-over loans, which are virtually unknown as a source of finance for capital investment in the UK. These roll-over loans are often negotiable bonds which appear to be short-term interest-bearing capital loans, but which are made on the understanding that the capital will not be repaid at the end of the term of the loan, but the loan will be re-financed at its maturity date at the then-prevailing rate of interest. As Bieda observes: 'In fact it is understood that a very high proportion of short-term loans will be renewed, so that they are de facto long-term loans as well'.[15]

Table 4.13 shows that about one-quarter of Japanese external industrial finance has been provided to industry without any political strings through government support of the city banks and through government banks. This financial support from the Bank of Japan has enabled city banks to loan virtually all their deposits to industry.

Furthermore, a large proportion of the 'own finance' of Japanese corporations is for depreciation, which would not have arisen in the first place if the capital had not been previously advanced through external loans. In 1961, over 61 % of total industrial funds were supplied from outside the company; by 1969 this proportion had fallen 51 %.

One method of placing the vast flows of money listed in Table 4.12 into some perspective is to calculate the sources of supply of industrial funds as percentages of the Japanese GDP. This is done in Table 4.15 which lets us see that Japanese commercial and industrial companies between 1970 and 1975, acquired between 12–22 % of the GDP as industrial funds from external sources. Private investment in Japan, and the resulting Japanese growth rate, would have run at about one-third to one-half of its observed level if there were reliance on internal funds.

It is also possible to calculate, as shown in Table 4.15, that about 40 % of these funds were long-term for they were designated as 'equipment funds'. The year of 1974, which was a slump year over most of the world's economies, due to uncertainties about the future supply and the price of Middle East oil, was exceptional. In normal years, and in fact throughout the 1960s, Japanese industrial and commercial companies were acquiring some 8–10 % of GDP as long-loaned equipment funds.

The procedure for canalising saving to investment is much the same in Japan as in France or West Germany. Savings are collected from a large number of local savings banks and most of these amounts are loaned to city banks for conversion to investment credit.

TABLE 4.15 External supply of industrial funds in Japan, 1970–75

Year	Total funds supplied*	Equipment funds*	Equipment funds as % of total	As % of GDP Total funds	Equipment funds
1970	126259	56614	44.84	17.82	7.99
1971	173208	76610	44.23	21.82	9.65
1972	200562	75496	37.64	22.13	8.33
1973	217694	93923	43.14	19.61	8.46
1974	166607	51302	30.79	12.58	3.87
1975	195977	81285	41.48	13.46	5.58

* ¥ 100 m.
Source: *Monthly Statistics of Japan*, Dec. 1976, Bureau of Statistics Office of the Prime Minister, Table M–4, p. 114.

Table 4.16 shows inter-sectoral flows of finance. The personal sector is, in Japan as in every other developed nation, the prime source of surplus savings, which are relatively high at some 8 to 12 % of GDP. Note that Table 4.16 shows *net* flows of finance between sectors — personal savings which were loaned as consumer credit,[16] corporate business savings which became loans to other businesses, and government loans to public corporations and local authorities, are netted out of this table, despite the probability that such loans may have occurred through financial intermediaries. Clearly the major beneficiary from the transfer of savings to end-users is the corporate business sector, which gained at least some 5–7 % of GDP through the inter-sectoral transfer of resources. The extent to which the Japanese government canalised money to businesses via the Bank of Japan and subsequent financial intermediaries would also be netted out of Table 4.16.

TABLE 4.16   Financial surplus or deficit of non-financial sectors in Japan, 1968–72*

Sector	1968	1969	1970	1971	1972
Personal	4668	5180	5749	7529	10586
Corporate business	−2911	−3457	−4509	−4127	−6181
Governments, public corporations, local authorities	−1380	−960	−531	−1401	−2363
Foreign	−377	−763	−709	−2002	−2042
As % of GDP					
Excess personal saving	9.02	8.66	8.11	9.49	11.68
Corporate business deficit	5.62	5.78	6.36	5.20	6.82

* in ¥ bn.
Source: *Economic Statistics Annual 1970*, Statistics Department of the Bank of Japan, Mar. 1971, Table 166.

Certainly during the 1970–75 period, Japanese industrial and commercial companies acquired from 12–22% of GDP (see Table 4.17) and the single most important source of this finance was those private financial institutions which are principally the Japanese City banks.

The stock market and the industrial bonds market seldom provided over 2% of GDP; government direct support ranged from 1–1½% of

TABLE 4.17   External capital sources for Japanese industrial and commercial companies as percentages of GDP

Year	Total of external capital sources	Stocks and shares	Industrial bonds	Private financial institutions	Government
1970	17.82	1.42	0.51	14.46	1.29
1971	21.82	1.10	0.83	18.38	1.34
1972	22.13	1.26	0.41	19.20	1.11
1973	19.61	1.07	0.71	16.24	1.44
1974	12.58	0.66	0.42	10.07	1.26
1975	13.46	0.89	0.91	10.07	1.38

Note: See notes to Table 4.12: Notes 1 and 2 refer.
Source: As Table 4.12.

GDP. The major role in funding industrial investment is still with the Japanese banks. The value of the loans and discounts made by all Japanese financial institutions rises by sizeable percentages every year. Table 4.18 shows the value of the deposits held and loans and discounts advanced by all Japanese financial institutions, and their ratio with GDP.

TABLE 4.18   Deposits and loans and discounts of all Japanese financial institutions, 1971–75. Values in ¥ Trillion (10^{12})

Year	Deposits of all financial institutions		Loans and discounts of all institutions			
	Value	Ratio of Value/GDP	Value	Ratio of Value/GDP	Loan-deposit %	GDP Value
1971	110.96	1.40	102.19	1.29	92.1	79.37
1972	139.52	1.54	126.01	1.39	90.3	90.63
1973	165.61	1.49	152.72	1.38	92.2	111.00
1974	189.05	1.43	174.89	1.32	92.5	132.49
1975	222.40	1.53	202.71	1.39	91.1	145.62

Sources: For financial institutions' deposits, loans and discounts: Table M – 3 of *Monthly Statistics of Japan, Dec. 1976*. For Japanese GDP: OECD, *National Accounts of OECD Countries, 1975*.

From 1971 to 1975 the deposits of all Japanese financial institutions rose by about 19 % p.a., while their loans and discounts rose by about 18 % p.a. The outstanding value of all loans and discounts to the economy ranged from 1.29 to 1.39 times GDP during the 1971–75 period. Japanese financial institutions were making their money work, lending out over 90 % of their deposits during this period. When this percentage of deposits is loaned, then savings are not financing investments; some circulating credit is financing investment. This happens to some extent in all nations, but nowhere else to the same extent as in Japan.

From a Japanese businessman's or industrialist's point of view, the situation is that if he continues to pay the interest (and none of the capital) on all outstanding loans, he will then get each year on average, some 18 % more external capital than he already has. It is therefore not surprising that Japan is expanding.

Japanese businesses therefore obtain funds from a number of sources: government money (indirectly canalised through Bank of Japan loans to city banks), the saving of private individuals, long-term capital loans directly via government banks, and call money borrowed by city banks from local and often rural savings banks. The Bank of Japan deliberately assists long-term capital formation by permitting city banks to loan more than 100% of their deposits; the city banks had 'overloan', or loan to deposit plus debenture ratios, of 107 in 1957, 105 in 1962 and 104 in 1964; the overloan position during 1956–68 was never less than 90% for all banks, and reached 100% in 1957[17]. The Bank of Japan guarantee — that no major bank would be allowed to collapse because of advancing funds for industrial investment[18] — has obviously released large capital flows which prudence would have kept as reserves.

The Japanese saving-to-investment transformation procedure is probably the most efficient method yet devised of canalising large-scale cheap investment funds to industry. Japanese industrial and commercial companies are receiving capital loans which depend, in volume, not upon the long-term savings made in the economy, but upon the amount of circulating credit in the banking system. When the Japanese banking system as a whole loans out 100% of its funds (as it did in 1957) then the credit extended to the economy must powerfully increase the amounts of money in the banking system. Loans create credit, which in turn creates more loans; but only perhaps in Japan is the procedure of creating investment credit so starkly made obvious for only in Japan are savings in all banks over 90% transformed into short-, medium- and long-term loans.

There are major implications which arise when some capital investment is funded from the quantity of circulating credit, rather than through a capital market which avoids a 'credit-multiplier'. These implications are especially significant for economic growth theory, but these matters are too wide-ranging to be discussed here. Suffice it to say that the Japanese growth miracle depends in no small part upon that nation's very high investment rate, which depends in turn upon an extremely efficient process for canalising saving and bank credit to investment.

4.4 TRANSFORMATION OF SAVING TO INVESTMENT IN WEST GERMANY

The present processes for converting saving to investment in West Germany were developed in response to the economic situation following the end of World War II, although such methods even then had a long history in Germany. The general output level of industrial production in the British and US zones of Germany in 1946 was about one-third of the 1937 level; industrial and economic recovery in West Germany was so swift that 1937 industrial output levels were surpassed in 1950. The procedures used to finance investment were obviously contributory factors in that restoration.

Once again, the tables made up by Eurostat are available to assist the examination of the conversion of saving to lending. Each lending and borrowing transaction is reflected by equal and opposite entries of an asset and a liability, but once more, the flows of finance are often double-counted as they flow from initial saver to final user.

Table 4.19 summarises the assets acquired and liabilities incurred by each of the main economic sectors of the West German economy in 1970. The procedure for transforming saving to investment is similar in West Germany to that of France, with the major difference that the West German credit institutions are major private banks rather than the largely public or para-public banks of France. Although the status of the means of transforming saving to investment differs, the results do not seem so very different.

Table 4.19 summarises the flow of funds from initial saver to final borrower. Part I of the table deals with the total assets acquired by each sector — the savings in currency or other deposits, the purchases of insurance, shares, bills, bonds, or the forwarding of loans by that sector. Part II deals with the liabilities of each sector — the borrowings of currency or other deposits, the acceptance of insurance risks, the issue of shares, stocks, or bonds, and the acceptance of a loan by that sector. As previously remarked in the section on France in this chapter, the information in this table is very compressed. Taking Table 4.19 line by line, and grouping assets and liabilities by their nature, a number of points can be made.

(i) Currency and transferable sight deposits were held by every sector except the financial institutions, who had acquired a debt rather than an asset (line F20, Part I); these assets were increased (line F20, Part II) by foreign borrowing of DM 815m. in 1970, and all of these assets of DM 13799m. became the liabilities of the financial institutions, who used these and other funds to acquire the assets listed in column S40 in Part I.

(ii) 'Other deposits' (line F30 of Part I) were acquired as assets by all economic sectors listed, and 93.4% of these deposits (or DM 50695m.) became the liabilities of the financial institutions, (line F30 of Part II)

TABLE 4.19　Transformation of saving to lending in West Germany, 1970*

Code	S10	S80	S40	S50	S60	S90	Total
Part I—Assets acquired by each sector (sources)							
F20	6622	2572	−892	91	3793	798	12984
F30	2472	32579	3628	1386	3804	10400	54269
F90	430	7559	−	−	−	20	8018
F40	52	−	26700	−	1165	1389	29306
F50	42	10675	621	1735	−208	772	13637
F60	2938	1672	1125	481	309	278	6803
F10	−	−	943	−	−	738	1681
F70	8313	14	12140	−	379	13570	34416
F80	2419	76	49826	4082	2840	5954	65197
Total	23288	55147	93361	7775	12091	33919	225581
Part II — Liabilities incurred by each sector (borrowers)							
F20	−	−	13799	−	−	−815	12984
F30	21	−	50695	−	−	3553	54269
F90	−	−	−	8018	−	−	8018
F40	−237	−	5503	−	−657	24697	29306
F50	1440	−	12212	−	753	−768	13637
F60	3321	−	579	211	−	2692	6803
F10	−	−	738	−	−	943	11681
F70	27214	1101	6198	267	541	−905	34416
F80	47445	2266	8	17	8154	7307	65197
Total	79204	3367	89732	8513	8791	35974	225581

Key

F20 Currency and transferable sight deposits
F30 Other deposits
F90 Insurance technical reserves
F40 Bills and short-term bonds
F50 Long-term bonds
F60 Shares and other equity
F10 SDRs
F70 Short-term loans
F80 Medium- and long-term loans

S10 Non-financial corporate and quasi-corporate enterprises
S80 Households
S40 Credit institutions
S50 Insurance enterprises
S60 General government
S90 Rest of world

Source: Eurostat National Accounts, 1976.
* in DM m.

who again used these funds as part of the asset-base for onward lending.

(iii) Non-financial corporate and quasi-corporate enterprises took out some insurance, but most insurance business came from individuals (DM 7559m. or 94.3% of DM 8018m.) although a small amount was from abroad (line F90, Part I); these insurance funds were entirely the liabilities of insurance companies (line F90, Part II) who increased these funds by issuing DM 211m. of shares and other equity (line F60, Sector S50, Part II) and borrowing short-term loans of DM 267m. and medium- and long-term loans of DM 17m. With acquired and borrowed funds of DM 8513m., insurance companies acquired assets of DM 7775m. in the form listed in column S50 of Part I.

(iv) Line F40 Part I shows that bills and short-term bonds were discounted and purchased principally by financial institutions (which sector acquired DM 26700m. or 91.1 % of total DM 29306m.) while the main beneficiary sector was the rest of the world (which received DM 24697m.) These bills and bonds seem to be principally export credits.

(v) Line F50 of Part I shows how much long-term bonds (in value) were purchased by each sector; issues by sectors are shown in line F50 Part II. Hence the major purchasers of long-term bonds were households, which sector purchased 78.3 % of issues; and their major issuers were credit institutions, which issued 89.6 % of all such bonds in 1970.

(vi) Lines F60, Parts I and II shows values of shares and other equity purchased and issued by sectors. All sectors were active in purchasing equity in 1970, but the new issue market in West Germany seems to be largely a means of supply of funds for enterprises and overseas organisations.

(vii) Lines F10 show special drawing rights.

(viii) Line F70, Part I shows the amounts forwarded by each sector as short-term loans; line F70 Part II shows the sector's acquisition of short-term loan finance.

(ix) The source of medium- and long-term loans advanced from each sector are shown in line F80 of Part I; the acquisition of such loans by each sector is in line F80 Part II.

Tables similar to Table 4.19, covering the transformation of saving to lending in West Germany in 1971 to 1974 are at Tables A20 to A23 in the statistical appendix. It should be noted that these tables include the activities of mortgage banks, and hence assets loaned from the personal sector through building societies as mortgages are in these tables.

It is clear that the credit institutions once again have the principal role as financial intermediaries in transforming saving to lending. Table 4.20 analyses the timespan of borrowing and lending of these institutions for

TABLE 4.20   Credit institutions in West Germany: transformation of borrowing to lending, 1970–73

in DM m.	1970	1971	1972	1973	1974
Nature of borrowing					
1 Short-term resources					
(a) Currency and transferable sight deposits	13799	20504	17718	6717	18882
(b) Other deposits	50695	54562	68097	74648	49899
(c) Bills and short-term bonds	5503	−1055	2012	5392	−990
(d) Short-term loans	6198	3492	3702	1914	1233
(e) Total short-term	76195	77503	91529	88671	69024
2 Medium- and long-term resources					
(a) Long-term bonds	12212	15187	26602	22467	20328
(b) Shares and other equity	579	950	1350	1078	1024
(c) Medium- and long-term loans	8	4	12	115	45
(d) Total medium- and long-term	12799	16141	27964	23660	21397
3 Total borrowing	88994	93644	119493	112331	90421
(a) % short-term	85.62	82.76	76.60	78.94	76.34
(b) % medium- and long-term	14.38	17.24	23.40	21.06	23.66
Nature of lending					
1 Short-term lending					
(a) Currency and TSDs	−892	1159	1873	1527	968
(b) Other deposits	3628	692	106	7574	10407
(c) Bills and short-term bonds	26700	14527	13373	22339	−6325
(d) Short-term loans	12140	18126	24934	15565	14111
(e) Total short-term	41576	34504	40286	47005	19161
2 Medium- and long-term resources					
(a) Long-term bonds	621	5912	7234	3547	18082
(b) Shares and other equity	1125	1042	1472	860	197
(c) Medium- and long-term loans	49826	56934	71065	64421	60095
(d) Total medium- and long-term	51572	63888	79771	68828	78374
3 Total lending	93148	98392	120057	112533	97535
(a) % short-term	44.63	35.07	33.56	40.58	19.65
(b) % medium- and long-term	55.37	64.93	66.44	59.42	80.35

Source: For 1970, Table 4.19: for other years, Tables A20 to A23, in the statistical appendix.

Note: Line 1(b) includes some time savings and time deposits, but the data source does not specify the amounts or terms of such savings.

the period 1970–74. It would seem that while only about a fifth of the funds of credit institutions are in the form of medium- or long-term resources, over half and sometimes two-thirds of lending by these institutions has been medium- or long-term. Credit institutions in West Germany therefore take a considerable risk in transforming short-term resources to longer-term uses; their loans are more illiquid than their sources of funds.

One way to put the extent of this imbalance into proportion is to calculate the amounts involved as percentages of GDP. This is done in Table 4.21, where it is calculated that perhaps 5–6 % of West Germany's GDP has been converted from short- to longer-term by all the financial institutions. In the absence of this risk-taking financial intermediation, only some two to three percent of GDP would be naturally available as medium- and long-term loans (Table 4.21) as opposed to the 1970–74 average of about 8 % of GDP.

TABLE 4.21   Credit institutions in West Germany: timespan of resources, 1970–73

in DM m.	1970	1971	1972	1973
1 Medium- and long-term re-sources borrowed	12799	16141	27964	23660
2 Medium- and long-term re-sources loaned	51572	63888	79771	68828
3 Resources converted from short- to medium- or long-term	38773	47747	51807	45168
4 Gross Domestic Product*	686960	762540	844630	928180
As % of GDP				
5 Medium- and long-term re-sources loaned	7.51	8.38	9.44	7.42
6 Resources converted from short to medium- or long-term	5.64	6.26	6.13	4.87
7 'Natural level' of medium- and long-term resources	1.86	2.12	3.31	2.55

* Last digit not significant.
Sources: Table 4.20, and appendix A28.

Some of the financial institutions in West Germany are integrated with the business community to an extent which is unheard of in English-speaking countries. West German banks can be divided into three broad categories: publicly-owned savings banks, which are usually owned by the local authority to which they provide housing and other social overhead capital; industrially active commercial banks, which are the major shareholders and loan providers to industry and commerce; specialised institutions such as agricultural co-operative banks, building and mortgage banks, insurance companies, etc.

The public savings system is non-profit making and organised by regions, with centralised clearing houses which also provide nationalised industries with some development capital. Mortgages are also offered by these savings banks, which now provide a wide range of banking services to personal customers in competition with commercial banks, but because savings banks are non-profit-making they are much less directly involved with industry.

There are hundreds of commercial banks in West Germany; one recent book assesses the number as 303 commercial banks with about 5000 branches in 1971[19].Three of these banks (the Commerzbank, the Deutsche Bank and the Dresdner Bank) operate on a nationwide basis, while most of the rest are active in a particular region or industry. In the post-war period, there was an unsuccessful attempt to break up the three large private banks:

> After the war, they were split up into thirty institutions, each operating in a federal 'Land' but in 1956 the components were reformed into the three banks . . .[20]

The commercial and financial system in West Germany is so interwoven that any action which affected commercial banks would also affect industry. Banks, through the West German system of depositing shares with banks for safe-keeping, also generally acquire shareholders' voting rights, and may use these rights (in addition to their leverage on companies through the provision of loans) to exercise influence over the policies of companies. As banks also are the main financial intermediaries for the sales of new issues of industrial bonds and shares (which are often not sold through the market, but only via the banks) the power of banks over industry is immense.

Nonetheless, the West German banks are into industry as constructive partners looking for business opportunities, for methods of improving industry and cutting costs. This industry-assisting role of German banks goes back to the mid-19th century. As one author on management puts it, contrasting 19th century capital conditions in the UK with those of Germany:

> In Germany the shortage of capital involved banks not only in

lending, but in supervising the use of funds through positions on the board of directors. The fact that continued credit depended on satisfactory performance resulted in an attention to costs not found in British industry.[21]

This historical observation is almost certainly still valid; there may be no greater possible spur to a company than the knowledge that future loan funds may depend on improving present performance. Banks are also able to help in the event of company take-overs, with mergers or even in industrial re-structuring. In the book edited by Peter Readman, it is commented that 'The Bavarian banks are at this moment involved in restructuring the brewing industry in Southern Germany';[22] this kind of activity is perhaps better done by the banks, with aims of improving profitability, producing cost-cutting and increasing output, rather than by government, which may have primarily social aims in view. If civil servants fail in restructuring an industry, the public pays through increased taxes; but bankers have a marked aversion to losing money, and hence may be better at re-organising industry than government can become.

The role of West Germany's central bank, the Bundesbank, is relatively passive with regard to the financing of industry, but the bank does discount eligible commercial paper within the limits of the official 're-discount quotas', which are prescribed, (on the basis of the liable funds of banks) by the Bundesbank. The Bundesbank also provides advances against securities for up to three months (Lombard loans) which are intended to tide banks over any temporary liquidity shortages. Of course, the Bundesbank, as the central bank of West Germany, also acts as a lender of last resort to the banking system and sells (or repurchases) Federal Government Treasury bills in the market. It is interesting however to note that the total loans raised by general government (including short-term loans) in West Germany during 1970–73 have been between one-fifth and one-sixth of the loans advanced to the corporate enterprises sector.[23]

Corporate and quasi-corporate enterprises receive the greater part of loans and advances forwarded. If we take out the financial intermediaries of credit and insurance institutions, corporate and quasi-corporate enterprises received about two-thirds of the funds advanced to final users.

Table 4.22 shows the relative importance of the sources of capital funds for non-financial enterprises. Medium- and long-term loans from the banking system are the most sizeable flow of these funds. Some of

TABLE 4.22   Funds borrowed by non-financial enterprises in West Germany, 1970–74

as % of GDP	1970	1971	1972	1973	1974
Bills and short-term bonds	−0.03	−0.08	−0.07	0.13	0.07
Long-term Bonds	0.21	0.49	0.40	0.13	0.19
Shares and other equity	0.48	0.62	0.36	0.32	0.31
Short-term loans	3.96	3.19	2.75	2.48	2.54
Medium- and long-term loans	6.91	7.92	8.88	8.22	5.36

Source: Calculated from Tables 4.19, and A20–A23 in the statistical appendix.

these loans are in the form of schuldscheindarlehen', or loans against borrowers' notes. Short-term loans, on a contractual basis between banks and enterprises, are the second largest source of external funds. Long-term bonds and bills and short-term bonds are relatively small sources of capital. Shares and other equity, between 1970 and 1974, provided between a third to two-thirds of 1 % of GDP as new funds for enterprises.

The total issues of shares and bonds in West Germany for the period 1970–74 expressed as percentages of GDP, is shown in Table 4.23. Shares and other equity during that period varied from two-thirds to one percent of GDP, and non-financial enterprises received over half of this. Bond issues varied more, (from 1.99 to 3.63 % of GDP raised during the same period,) but non-financial enterprises received very little of this.

TABLE 4.23   The financial market in West Germany: new issues of shares and bonds, 1970–74

Year	New issues	DM m.	% of GDP
1970	Shares and other equity	6803	0.99
	Bonds	13637	1.99
1971	Shares and other equity	8012	1.05
	Bonds	19597	2.57
1972	Shares and other equity	7387	0.89
	Bonds	30333	3.63
1973	Shares and other equity	6179	0.67
	Bonds	25563	2.75
1974	Shares and other equity	7163	0.72
	Bonds	29377	2.94

Sources: Copied and calculated from Table 4.19 and appendices A20–A23.

In the light of that financial market, the most important financial intermediaries in West Germany, if we consider the situation from the viewpoint of providing funds for non-financial enterprises, are the credit institutions.

Table 4.24 summarises in outline the total flow of major medium- and long-term funds in West Germany. These average about 10 % of GDP, and about 60 % of this would not be available for lending if the private banks did not mediate to convert short-term resources to longer-term. The principal beneficiaries of this system are the non-financial corporate and quasi-corporate enterprises who receive these funds.

TABLE 4.24   Summary of West German saving-to-investment transformation, 1970–74

in DM m.	1970	1971	1972	1973	1974
Medium- and long-term funds forwarded	65197	80112	93011	94358	85801
Medium- and long-term funds as % of GDP	9.49	10.51	11.14	10.17	8.58
Short-term funds transformed to medium and long-term financing by the credit institutions	38773	47747	51807	45168	56977
Savings transformed as % of GDP	5.64	6.26	6.13	4.87	5.70
Medium- and long-term funds advanced to corporate and quasi-corporate non-financial enterprises	47445	60426	74131	76270	53626
Funds for non-financial enterprises as % of GDP	6.91	7.92	8.88	8.22	5.36

Source: Tables 4.19 and A20–A23 in the statistical appendix.

In conclusion it could perhaps be noted that observers from the City of London do not always express approval of the financial climate of West Germany. The integration of the financial-industrial system in West Germany may jar upon the susceptibilities of English-speaking bankers who are used to a clear separation between banker and businessman. The book edited by Peter Readman, for example, talks of the 'stranglehold' of the banks on the financial system, stating that there is 'cause for concern' and concluding:

It is difficult to see what effective action could be taken (by government) and even more difficult to see how a liberal financial climate could ever be established in Germany. [24]

This *anschauung* invites a potentially devastating reply. It is the economic failure of nations, not success on the West German scale, which needs effective action, and those developed countries which possess integrated financial-industrial systems are not notable for their low growth rates.

4.5 TRANSFORMATION OF SAVING TO INVESTMENT IN THE UNITED KINGDOM

The Department of Trade and Industry in 1970 listed 126 companies which were treated in that year as banking or discount companies in the UK for the purposes of the Protection of Depositors Act, 1963.[25] The list comprises six clearing banks (Barclays Bank Ltd., Coutts & Co., Lloyds Bank Ltd., Midland Bank Ltd., National Westminster Bank Ltd., and Williams & Glyn's Bank Ltd.); four Scottish banks (now reduced to two, for three of those listed — the Bank of Scotland, the British Linen Bank and The Royal Bank of Scotland — are now merged into the Bank of Scotland, while the Clydesdale Bank is the other independent Scottish bank); five other small deposit banks, 17 accepting houses (such as Baring Brothers Ltd. and Hambros Bank Ltd.); 13 discount houses, 65 foreign banks attracted by the capital markets in London (8 Australasian banks, 21 British Overseas and Commonwealth banks, 9 American banks and 27 foreign banks); 15 other banks and a discount broker.

The number of these banks is constantly changing, for foreign banks are still setting up in London, while there is still some scope for further integration of the UK banking system. The four major clearing banks — Barclays, Lloyds, the Midland, and the National Westminster — dominate the scene, however, and a reduction in their number seems unlikely, for a proposed merger of Barclays, Lloyds and Martins Banks was turned down by the Monopolies Commission in 1968. The clearing banks also have foreign and other offshoots which contribute to a great integration of banking in the UK.[26]

In addition to the banks, there is a large number of building societies which now possess assets rivalling the total funds of the London clearing banks. This is principally a post-war phenomenon, although the trend goes back a long way. In 1950 the gross deposits of London clearing banks were £6014m., while the building societies' shares and deposits totalled £1167m. (or 19.4 % of clearing bank deposits)[27]. By 1960, London clearing banks had gross deposits of £7236m., some 20.3 %

larger than ten years' previously; building societies' shares and deposits were up to £2950m., or 152.8 % more than their assets in 1950. (This was about 40.8 % of clearing bank deposits in 1960.) By 1969, clearing bank deposits were £10610m. — in contrast to building society shares and deposits of £8,652m., or about 81.5 % of clearing bank deposits. Clearing banks have obviously lost potential deposits due to the competition for deposits with, and the growth of, the building societies, resulting in the ratio of net bank deposits to GDP steadily falling; it was 65.0 % in 1947 40.7 % in 1955, 33.4 % in 1960, 29.7 % in 1965 and 28.3 % in 1969. In every year from 1962 to 1972, personal deposits with building societies exceeded deposits with the banking sector, and in some years (e.g. 1969, 1971) the increases in building society deposits were over twice that of bank deposits.

In 1971, however, deposits advanced because the banks began 'to do business in new areas, previously left entirely to their subsidiaries; these include the issue and holding of sterling CDs, dealings in the sterling inter-bank market and an expansion of foreign currency business.'[28] (Incidentally, data for the London clearing banks beyond Dec.1972 cannot be quoted, for beyond that date, data has been collected for all banks in the UK.)

Building societies and other non-banks are a significant feature of the British financial system. However, the non-banking financial sector has been principally a source of funds for government, local authorities, private house purchases, and consumer credit. Although the National Savings Bank, Trustee Savings Banks, building societies, pension funds and life assurance societies receive a considerable amount of the saving of the country, they do not act as a source of funds for industry (except in the case of new capital issues). A look at the total flow of funds may help put the situation into perspective.

The Eurostat national accounts tables are once again available to show how saving is converted to lending for the EEC country of the UK. The transformation from initial lending to final borrowing sector in the UK in 1970 is shown in Table 4.25. The table gives, in a very summarised outline, the following information.[29]

(i) The major source of saving in the form of currency and transferable sight deposits is the household sector, which provides some 64 % of these savings (line F20, Part I). Most of these savings are borrowed by the credit institutions (or banks) which onward-loan these and other funds (line F20, Part II).

(ii) A major source of 'other deposits held' in 1970 was a flow of

Table 4.25   Transformation of saving to lending in the UK, 1970*

Code	S10	S80	S40	S50	S60	S90	Total
Part I—Assets acquired by each sector (sources)							
F20	301	942	90	140	136	−136	1473
F30	−261	1502	2122	82	−	3433	6878
F90	−	1735	−	−	−	−	1735
F40	−	−	1629	4	−	−43	1590
F50	84	−399	98	197	−	124	104
F60	283	−698	96	637	2	141	461
F10	−	−	−	−	111	171	282
F70	215	−7	4004	4	225	−1100	3341
F80	207	64	1752	103	1525	529	4180
Total	829	3139	9791	1167	1897	3119	19942
Part II—Liabilities incurred by each sector (borrowers)							
F20	−	−	1273	−	100	103	1473
F30	−	−	7297	−	−362	−2	6878
F90	−	−	−	1677	58	−	1735
F40	252	−	754	−	560	24	1590
F50	189	−	45	2	−170	38	104
F60	18	−	155	39	−	249	461
F10	−	−	−	−	171	111	282
F70	1124	89	53	−5	−803	2883	3341
F80	1372	1316	71	17	1068	336	4180
Total	2955	1405	9590	1730	622	3640	19942

Key

F20 Currency and transferable sight deposits
F30 Other deposits
F90 Insurance technical reserves
F40 Bills and short-term bonds
F50 Long-term bonds
F60 Shares and other equity
F10 SDRs
F70 Short-term loans
F80 Medium and long-term loans
* in £m.

S10 Non-financial corporate and quasi-corporate enterprises
S80 Households
S40 Credit institutions
S50 Insurance enterprises
S60 General government
S90 Rest of world

Source: *Eurostat National Accounts, 1976.*

foreign funds into the UK; that foreign funds flow amounted to about half of other deposits (line F30, Part I). All of these funds plus additional funds flowing from government, became a liability of the credit institutions, which added these funds to their asset-base for onward lending.

(iii) Households insurance funds (line F90, Part I) became partly the liability of government, and principally the liable funds of insurance enterprises, which loaned them in turn.

(iv) Bills and short-term bonds were issued by non-financial enterprises (15.84 % of total), credit institutions (47.42 %), general government (35.22 %) and overseas organisations (1.50 %) and hence principally acted as means for some credit institutions and government to raise finance (line F40, Part II). These were almost entirely purchased by credit organisations, which also bought bills and short-term bonds flowing in from abroad (line F40, Part I).

(v) Seventy percent of long-term bonds raised in 1970 were issued by non-financial enterprises, although credit institutions (at 16.42 %) and the rest of the world (13.87 %) raised significant amounts. Government repaid some £170m. of long-term bonds previously issued (line F50, Part II). Insurance companies, (purchasing 44.47 % of long-term bonds issued and transferred between sectors) and the rest of the world (buying 28 % of such long-term bonds) were the two major purchasers, but non-financial enterprises (at 18.96 % of issues and transfers) and credit institutions (at 22.12 %) also made significant purchases. The households sector sold long-term bonds previously purchased to the tune of £399m. (line F50, Part I).

(vi) Issues and purchasers of shares and other equity were:

	Issues		Purchasers	
	£m.	%	£m.	%
Non-financial enterprises	18	3.9	283	61.4
Households	–	–	–698	151.4
Credit institutions	155	33.6	96	20.8
Insurance enterprises	39	8.5	637	138.2
General government	–	–	2	0.4
Rest of world	249	54.0	141	30.6
Total	461	100.0	461	100.0

The year 1970 was not a good one for the UK's stock market. Issues of shares were principally for overseas organisations; credit institutions did raise over a third of total issues, but non-financial enterprises raised small amounts. Households divested themselves of shares and other equity to the value of one and a half times the value of shares issues, with insurance enterprises buying heavily in the market.

(vii) Special drawing rights were exchanged between the UK and the rest of the world (or the IMF) (lines F10, Parts I and II).

(viii) The rest of the world and non-financial enterprises were the major recipients of short-term loans, and the UK government acted as a source of short-term funds in 1970, repaying short-term loans already acquired (line F70, Part II). The credit institutions were by far the most important source of these loans (line F70, Part I).

(ix) Medium- and long-term loans were advanced from and received by all sectors; however advances mainly came from credit institutions (41.9 % of advances) and government (36.5 %) while the recipients of large amounts were non-financial enterprises (32.8 % of receipts), households (31.5 %) and government (25.6 %) (from lines F80, Parts 1 and II).

This kind of summary of the activities of one year describes the nature and volume of financial transactions but is too detailed to permit easy comparative analysis. Data similar to Table 4.25 for the years 1971–74 is in appendices A24–A27.

A closer look at the activities of credit institutions seems desirable. Table 4.26 abstracts from these above-quoted tables the apparent time structure of the resources of UK credit institutions which are unusual in that over 95 % of their sources of funds seem to be short-term. British banks do not issue sizeable flotations of long-term bonds with the express purpose of acquiring funds for long-term onward lending, probably because, due to the functional separation of banking and commerce in the UK, the banks do not see their role as providers of long-term capital. If British banks do not accept that role, then the arguments for issuing long-term bank bonds — involving the spreading of risk through the banking system, the provision of relatively secure investments for unit trusts, pension funds and insurance companies, the useful conversion of new money on the capital market to productive investment, and the ability of the banker to act as a financial intermediary between the saver and the final user of funds — all these arguments may be seen as irrelevant. Whatever the reason, the apparent time structure of the resources available to credit institutions in the UK means that the conversion of short-term savings to longer-term loans is being done almost in the absence of long-term credit resources.

Despite the low level of long-term resources, British credit institutions do transform some short-term resources to longer-term loans. Almost 20 % of loans in 1970, nearly half of the loans in 1972, and on average about 11 % of loans in 1972–74 were medium- and long-term. At first sight, it looks as if the banks have taken very great risks in 1971. But as

TABLE 4.26 Credit institutions in the UK: transformation of borrowing to lending, 1970–74

in £m.	1970	1971	1972	1973	1974
Nature of borrowing					
1 Short-term resources					
(a) Currency and transferable sight deposits	1273	1667	3661	6352	3189
(b) Other deposits	7297	6229	14458	25142	14317
(c) Bills and short-term bonds	754	1502	3781	2286	−1170
(d) Short-term loans	53	514	1016	816	−190
(e) Total short-term	9377	9912	22916	34596	16146
2 Medium- and long-term resources					
(a) Long-term bonds	45	90	71	69	97
(b) Shares and other equity	155	266	663	258	68
(c) Medium- and long-term loans	71	74	144	78	442
(d) Total medium- and long-term	271	430	878	405	607
3 Total borrowing	9648	10342	23794	35001	16753
(a) % short-term	97.19	95.84	96.31	98.84	96.38
(b) % medium- and long-term	2.81	4.16	3.69	1.16	3.62
Nature of lending					
1 Short-term lending					
(a) Currency and transferable sight deposit	90	51	767	1153	212
(b) Other deposits	2122	1197	4920	10126	2743
(c) Bills and short-term bonds	1629	1159	1953	1118	486
(d) Short-term loans	4004	3352	13738	20444	11845
(e) Total short-term	7845	5759	21378	32841	15286
2 Medium- and long-term resources					
(a) Long-term bonds	98	2543	−592	190	−111
(b) Shares and other equity	96	352	681	38	−416
(c) Medium- and long-term loans	1752	2426	2856	2755	2594
(d) Total medium- and long-term	1946	5321	2945	2983	2067
3 Total lending	9791	11080	24323	35824	17353
(a) % short-term	80.12	51.98	87.89	91.67	88.09
(b) % medium- and long-term	19.88	48.02	12.11	8.33	11.91

Source: Tables 4.25 and appendices A24–A27.
Note: Line 1(b) includes time deposits and time savings of £1105m. (1970); £1441m. (1971); £2474m. (1972); £6323m. (1973) and £3006m. (1974).

reference to appendix A24 will show, in 1971 the UK government issued £3599m. of long-term bonds — 88.6 % of long-term bonds issued in that year — and this factor alone, if credit institutions purchased long-term bonds in proportion to amounts issued, explains about 20 % of funds apparently riskily converted from short- to long-term. When similar government advances of medium- and long-term loans are taken into account, the percentage of medium- and long-term lending by credit institutions falls a further five percent. Nonetheless, 1971 still stands out as a year when UK credit institutions advanced about 23 % of loans to non-government, and hence riskier, users.

A summary of the activities of UK credit institutions with reference to the medium- and long-term loans advanced is in Table 4.27. The 'natural level' of medium- and long-term loans would be only 0.5 % to 1.4 % of GDP, if banks did not transform the time-span of the resources. Because

TABLE 4.27   Credit institutions in the UK, 1970–74

in £m.	1970	1971	1972	1973	1974
1 Medium- and long-term resources borrowed	271	430	878	405	607
2 Medium- and long-term resources loaned	1946	5321	2945	2983	2067
3 Resources converted from short- to medium- or long-term	1675	4891	2067	2578	1460
4 Gross Domestic Product	50707	56636	62769	71759	81617
As % of GDP					
5 Medium- and long-term resources loaned	3.84	9.40	4.69	4.16	2.53
6 Resources converted from short- to medium- or long-term	3.30	8.64	3.29	3.59	1.79
7 'Natural level' medium- and long-term resources	0.53	0.76	1.40	0.56	0.74

Source: Table 4.25 and appendices A24–27.
Note: If term deposits and time savings were defined as a medium- or long-term resource, then line 6 would be diminished, and line 7 increased, by the following percentages of GDP from 1970 to 1974 respectively: 2.18 %; 2.54 %; 3.94 %; 8.81 %; and 3.68 %. However, we do not consider these adjustments to be appropriate, due to continuing large gap in timescale between most time savings and deposits (from 7-day notice deposit accounts to one-year or two-year term savings) and the requirements of medium-term (say 3 to 7 years) and long-term (over 7-year) loans.

some risks are taken, about 2.5% to 4.0% of GDP is available for medium- and long-term loans from the credit institutions.

The full extent of financial support for the non-financial corporate enterprises sector during the period 1970–74 is shown in Table 4.28. Bills and short-term bonds have provided a relatively small source of finance — from one-quarter to half of one percent of GDP — and new issues of shares and other equity have varied from an almost insignificant source of finance to over half of one percent of GDP. During the 1970–74 period, therefore, the UK stock market did not provide non-financial corporate enterprises with much capital. Long-term bonds varied even more as a flow of funds, than the stock market; at best, non-financial corporate enterprises received 0.63% of GDP in 1972, and at worst in 1974, more long-term bonds were repaid than issued. Medium- and long-term loans provided from 1.6% to 3.6% of GDP. This was the largest source of potentially productive investment capital for enterprises, if we ignore the short-term loans figures, which show a surprising increase in the 1972–74 period. Why did these short-term loans increase?

TABLE 4.28   Funds borrowed by non-financial corporate and quasi-corporate enterprises in the UK, 1970–74

% of GDP	1970	1971	1972	1973	1974
Bills and short-term bonds	0.50	0.26	0.29	0.39	0.54
Long-term bonds	0.37	0.51	0.63	0.21	−0.08
Shares and other equity	0.04	0.26	0.53	0.15	0.05
Short-term loans	2.22	1.39	4.76	8.49	5.52
Medium- and long-term loans	2.71	3.60	1.61	1.66	3.41

Source: Table 4.25 and appendices A24–A27.

The answer to this question is that the British government, led by Mr Heath in the autumn of 1972, tried to ensure the availability of funds for the expansion of productive industry. This was done through a Bank of England request, on 7 August, 1972, which asked banks to restrict lending for property and financial transactions and to give priority to financing industrial expansions. Unfortunately, shortly after this request was issued, Bank Rate started climbing from 6% to reach 9% before the end of the year, and special deposits totalling 3% of funds were called in from banks and finance houses. (The incidence of these special deposits was ½% Nov. 30; ½% Dec. 14; 1% Jan. 3; and 1% Jan.

17.) However, Bank Rate fell by stages to $7\frac{1}{2}\%$ in the first six months of 1973, and as it did, business confidence may have increased.

The call to advance funds to industry had some effect, for bank borrowing by industrial and commercial companies reached unprecedented levels in 1972 and 1973. Nearly £3000m. was borrowed in 1972 (the previous peak-year of 1970 was £1126m.) and over £4500m. in 1973. The sources of capital funds for companies are shown in Table 4.29 from which it is possible to chart the rise and fall of bank borrowing.

TABLE 4.29   Sources of capital funds for UK industrial and commercial companies, 1971–75*

Year	Total	Undis-tributed income	Capital trans-fers	Bank borrow-ing	Other loans and mort-gages	Ordi-nary shares	Deben-tures and pref-erence shares	Over-seas
1971	7153	4174	595	732	237	160	215	1040
1972	10593	5495	409	2988	158	326	290	927
1973	15959	8366	373	4504	794	107	51	1764
1974	16281	9104	364	4411	58	43	−56	2357
1975	13905	9339	442	659	463	966	56	1980

* in £ m.
Source: Economic Trends, Annual Supplement 1976, HMSO, Table 131.

In 1971 bank borrowing by industrial and commercial companies was about 10 % of the total sources of capital funds. During the years 1972, 1973 and 1974 this company borrowing represented over a quarter of their total capital sources. The peak level was during the fourth quarter of 1973, when bank borrowing by companies rose to over a third of their capital sources; however, special factors related to the October 1973 Arab-Israeli war may have contributed to that result.

Why could UK companies not use this financial support for investment? Company borrowing from UK banks is largely short-term; companies are required to repay the capital and interest within a few years at best, and most of the loans are of less than three years' duration. Capital funds in any year may appear to be coming out of bank borrowing, but they are actually being funded by company income over the next few years. Short-term loans therefore in most cases only provide investment capital if the company's cash flow could have provided the investment anyway; the advantages of short-term loans may be the enforcement of high company saving and the earlier provision of the capital item. Naturally there are some tax advantages in this bank borrowing for the companies concerned, despite the short period of the loan. These short-term bank loans have relatively high repayment rates, when annual repayment is considered as a percentage of the funds advanced, but this is a subject we will discuss in Chapter 5. The short-term nature of the loans has two main implications; first, the loans cannot be readily used for plant and machinery investment with a long repayment cycle or a low rate of return, due to the high repayment costs; and second, heavy borrowing in any single year will result in the need to roll-over loans in subsequent years, or alternatively the repayment of these loans will be a drain on future cash-flow.

TABLE 4.30   Contribution to capital funds source of UK industrial and commercial companies, 1971–75*

Year	Company capital funds as % of GDP	Undistributed income	Capital transfer	Bank borrowing	Other loans	Ordinary shares	Debentures and pref. shares	Overseas
1971	14.58	58.4	8.3	10.2	3.3	2.2	3.0	14.6
1972	19.27	51.9	3.9	28.2	1.5	3.1	2.7	8.7
1973	25.15	52.4	2.3	28.2	5.0	0.7	0.3	11.1
1974	22.15	55.9	2.2	27.1	0.4	0.3	−0.3	14.4
1975	14.93	67.2	3.2	4.7	3.3	6.9	0.4	14.3

* % of total funds.
Source: Calculated from Table 3.14 plus GDP data from *Economic Trends*, Annual Supplement 1976, HMSO.

When the uses to which these capital funds are put (Table 4.31) are related to the percentage sources of these funds (Table 4.30) it is possible to assess the purposes for which the extra funds were used. But perhaps the most striking aspect of the 1971–74 boom was the sheer speed of the increase of industrial and commercial capital funds as a percentage of GDP. In the period 1963–70, company capital funds as a percentage of GDP were never less than 11.5 % (lowest in 1967) and never more than 15.75 % (peak in 1964). By contrast, during 1972 and 1973, company capital funds increased their share of GDP by almost 5 % annually (Table 4.30, first column). Industrial and commercial companies found themselves awash with funds, which could not be used for fixed capital

TABLE 4.31   Uses of capital funds by UK industrial and commercial companies, 1971—75

Year	Total	Gross domestic fixed capital formation	Increase in value of stocks and work progress	Total liquid assets	Cash expenditure on acquiring subsidiaries and trade investments	Over-seas	Other items (residual)
(a) in £m.							
1971	7153	3470	759	1241	567	352	764
1972	10593	3796	943	2348	980	768	1758
1973	15959	4718	3526	2568	1557	2039	1551
1974	16281	5848	6089	56	839	1875	1574
1975	13905	7028	2382	2452	354	1808	−119
(b)% of total funds							
1971	100.0	48.5	10.6	17.3	7.9	4.9	10.8
1972	100.0	35.8	8.9	22.2	9.3	7.3	16.5
1973	100.0	29.6	22.1	16.1	9.8	12.8	9.6
1974	100.0	35.9	37.4	0.3	5.2	11.5	9.7
1975	100.0	50.5	17.1	17.6	2.5	13.0	−0.7

Sources: (a) from Table 133 of *Economic Trends*, Annual Supplement 1976; (b) calculated from (a).

formation due to their short-term nature. This obviously produced an investment challenge to the managers of industrial and commercial enterprises. Much of the extra funds improved company liquidity; the liquid assets of companies usually absorbed 5—10 % of new capital funds during the 1963—70 period; in 1971—73, liquid assets absorbed 16—22 % of these funds.

Several reasons could be suggested to explain this increase in company liquidity. It could have been that part of the money was earmarked for possible future fixed investment; economic and industrial uncertainties could have created a situation in which higher liquidity was desired; and possibly some managers borrowed money simply because it was available. In any case, fixed capital formation fell to an all-time low of less than 30 % of total capital funds in 1973, and the oil crisis in late 1973 and the following three-day week may have nipped many new investment proposals in the bud. A large involuntary investment of capital funds in stocks and work in progress was produced by the 1974 depression, when the contribution made by capital funds to liquidity was very low indeed (at 0.3 % of total capital funds). The borrowing boom was over, and had to be paid for in 1974 and 1975. Part of the debt was obviously rolled-over, together with the start of some new loans, in 1974, and bank borrowing in 1975 was less than 5% of capital funds, much below its 1963–70 average of 11.7% The wave of new issues in 1975 (up to £966m. from £43m. the previous year) may have been caused by the need for new long-term capital funds to reduce dependence on bank loans.

The attempt of the Heath government to increase industrial investment does, however, seem to offer several qualified lessons. There may be little point in increasing short-term bank borrowing to industrial and commercial companies, if that borrowing is intended to finance fixed investment. The highest level of company fixed investment during the 1971–75 years was in 1974, when 7.95% of GDP was invested; this is not much better than the 1965 peak year, when the comparable figure was 7.84%. Short-term loans from the banking system are likely to be used by industry for short-term uses. Short-term loans may produce some increases in trade investment and company integration (1972 and 1973 saw many company take-overs) and possibly some investments in stocks and work in progress, but very little else.

On the other hand, permanent increases in the profit level or the level of undistributed income as a percentage of GDP, would seem likely to lead in time to a higher level of new investment — provided political uncertainties did not create an environment in which today's profits would be at risk from tomorrow's governments. If the UK businessmen had access to cheap medium- and long-term investment finance, it seems likely they would invest it, as their counterparts do overseas. For the greatest lesson of the Heath boom is probably that unless the finance provided to UK industry is medium- and long-term, the fixed investments will not be forthcoming.

The new issue market in the UK does, however, provide some long-term capital for commercial and industrial companies, as does government and some financial institutions. The amounts of the long-term capital provided by investment and other government grants, loans and mortgages, ordinary and debenture plus preference shares, is set out in Table 4.32 for the period 1963–75 inclusive. Table 4.33 gives the same information as percentages of annual GDP. Investment and other government grants rose from insignificant levels in 1963 to 1966 to over 1.5% of GDP in 1969, and have since fallen to about 0.5% of GDP. Loans and mortgages provided, on average, about 0.5% of GDP. The total new issue market provided over 1% of GDP. In 1974—the year following the oil crisis—long-term capital sources would have virtually vanished had there been no investment grants, and if these grants had

Table 4.32   External long-term capital raised in UK by domestic industrial and commercial companies, 1963–75*

Year	Investment and other grants	Loans and mortgages	Ordinary shares issued	Debentures and preference share issues	Total
1963	13	124	123	212	472
1964	17	213	158	254	642
1965	20	266	63	345	694
1966	26	104	124	451	705
1967	236	35	65	350	686
1968	454	154	303	183	1094
1969	598	197	183	335	1313
1970	526	321	44	159	1050
1971	595	237	160	215	1207
1972	409	158	326	290	1183
1973	373	794	107	51	1325
1974	364	58	43	− 56	409
1975	442	463	966	56	1927

* £m., current prices
Source: *Economic Trends*, Annual Supplement 1976, Table 131.

been absent during the whole period, the capital provided to industrial and commercial companies would have been about 1.5 % of GDP.

For the purpose of rounding out the comparison of the UK on a similar basis to those of other countries, Table 4.34 gives the total net new issues of shares and other equity and long-term bonds in the UK. Shares and other equity issued by all companies (including financial companies) ranges from 0.21 % of GDP in 1974 to 2.76 % of GDP in 1971, averaging over 1.1 % of GDP. Long-term bonds varied from 0.56 % of GDP in 1970, when the UK government issued no new long-term bonds and repaid £170m. of them, to 7.17 % of GDP in 1971, when UK government issued long-term bonds valued at £3599m. (or 88.6 % of bonds issued, or 6.35 % of GDP).

Table 4.35 summarises the saving-to-investment transformation process in the UK. The total flow of medium- and long-term funds forwarded (which includes some inevitable double-counting of flows) was between 8 and 12 % of GDP. Savings transformed from short- to longer-term are about 3 % of GDP, except when the UK government issues large flows of bonds (as in 1971) when the absence of the defaulting risk may cause an abnormally high rate of transformation.

TABLE 4.33   Long-term external capital sources for industrial and commercial companies*

Year	Investment and other grants	Loans and mortgages	Ordinary shares issued	Debentures and preference shares	Total
1963	0.05	0.46	0.46	0.79	1.75
1964	0.06	0.73	0.54	0.87	2.19
1965	0.06	0.85	0.20	1.11	2.22
1966	0.08	0.31	0.37	1.36	2.13
1967	0.68	0.10	0.19	1.00	1.96
1968	1.21	0.41	0.81	0.49	2.92
1969	1.51	0.50	0.46	0.85	3.32
1970	1.21	0.74	0.10	0.37	2.41
1971	1.21	0.48	0.33	0.44	2.46
1972	0.74	0.29	0.59	0.53	2.15
1973	0.59	1.25	0.17	0.08	2.09
1974	0.50	0.08	0.06	−0.08	0.56
1975	0.47	0.50	1.04	0.06	2.07
Averages	0.64	0.52	0.41	0.61	2.17

*   % of GDP
Source: Calculated from Table 4.32.

TABLE 4.34   UK financial market: new issues of shares and bonds, 1970–74

Year	New issues	£m.	% of GDP
1970	Shares and other equity	461	0.91
	Long-term bonds	284	0.56
1971	Shares and other equity	598	1.06
	Long-term bonds	4060	7.17
1972	Shares and other equity	1732	2.76
	Long-term bonds	583	0.93
1973	Shares and other equity	500	0.70
	Long-term bonds	2070	2.88
1974	Shares and other equity	174	0.21
	Long-term bonds	902	1.11

The funds advanced to non-financial corporate enterprises—the bottom line in Table 4.35—have ranged from 1.6 to 3.6% of GDP. As this figure includes some nationalised industries, the amounts received by private sector industry were less than this.

TABLE 4.35 Summary of saving-to-investment transformation in UK, 1970–74

in £m.	1970	1971	1972	1973	1974
Medium and long-term funds forwarded	4180	5567	5302	6438	9616
Medium- and long-term funds as % of GDP	8.24	9.83	8.45	8.97	11.78
Short-term saving transformed to medium- and long-term financing by the credit institutions	1675	4891	2067	2578	1460
Saving transformed as % of GDP	3.30	8.64	3.29	3.59	1.79
Medium- and long-term funds advanced to corporate and quasi-corporate non-financial enterprises	1372	2038	1012	1188	2781
Funds for non-financial enterprises as % of GDP	2.71	3.60	1.60	1.66	3.41

Source: Table 4.25 and appendices A24–A27.

One method of analysing the sources of saving and the capital uses in the UK is to examine the net acquisition of financial assets (or liabilities) for each economic sector. If we deduct capital uses (or gross domestic capital formation plus increase in value of stocks and work in progress) from capital sources (defined as saving plus capital transfers) then the sectors which generate financial assets can be contrasted with the sectors which have financial deficits. Table 4.36 quotes this information for the period 1963–75 in the UK. Because of the way this table is calculated, if debt is used to finance capital investment or working capital, then there will be negative values for that economic sector, i.e. that sector will have increases in its financial liabilities; while if capital resources are higher than gross capital uses, then an increase in financial assets will result for that sector. As in France, Japan and West Germany, Table 4.36 shows that the personal sector is the major source of saving, although foreign investment in the UK also provides a source of funds. The savings which have been transferred between economic sectors over the 13 year period have been less than 5% of GDP. This low percentage is partially explained by the fact that these tables show net funds transferred between economic sectors; for example the lending of building societies and hire purchase companies (which are largely funds loaned by the

TABLE 4.36   Net acquisition of financial assets by economic sector in UK, 1963–75

Year	Public sector	Financial companies	Industrial and commercial companies	Personal sector	Overseas sector	Residual error	Funds loaned as % of GDP
1963	−833	9	421	492	−131	42	3.58
1964	−1003	−23	−127	592	355	206	3.94
1965	−851	−22	−123	970	26	−	3.19
1966	−968	−74	−141	1148	−101	136	3.88
1967	−1645	−97	169	933	298	342	4.99
1968	−1138	−224	228	648	272	214	3.64
1969	335	−468	−77	785	−460	−115	2.55
1970	708	−392	−759	1267	−733	−91	4.33
1971	−311	−285	499	800	−1084	381	3.42
1972	−1718	−229	1136	1346	−154	−381	3.82
1973	−2923	−523	469	2490	795	−308	5.43
1974	−5293	−700	−2500	5198	3422	−127	11.55
1975	−8280	−921	332	6276	1673	920	9.88
						Average	4.94
Total (£m.)	−23920	−3949	−473	22945	4178	1219 ±28342	
% of total	84.4	13.9	1.7	81.0	14.7	4.3	−

* Defined as equal to saving plus capital transfer less gross domestic capital formation less increase in value of stocks and work in progress: in £m.
Source: Economic Trends Annual Supplement 1976, HMSO, Table 118.

personal sector to the personal sector through financial intermediaries) are netted out of this table. Similarly loans made between organisations within each economic sector do not appear; Table 4.36 refers only to inter-sectoral lending.

Over the 1963–75 period, the public sector has consumed almost 85 % of the financial assets shown in this table. The efficiency of the transformation process, between savings offered to productive investment in industrial and commercial companies, was less than 2 %. Indeed if 1974 were not in the series, industrial and commercial companies would have acted as a source of funds for public and financial investment. Furthermore, since the amount of net investment benefit to industrial and commercial companies was less than half the cumulative residual error in the 1963–75 period, the only certain statement one can make is that the financial support given to UK industrial and commercial companies from debt capital was so insignificant that it is not clearly distinguishable from zero. It could hardly be said, on this evidence, that British industry is not standing on its own two feet, owing nothing (in terms of fixed capital funds) to anyone but its shareholders.

The UK financial system, looked at from the viewpoint of capital debts, seems to be primarily a means by which the UK government can raise the money required for the public sector. Yet it is in the public sector that capital finance may contribute least to long-term employment and output. The separation of the financial system from the industrial system in Anglo-Saxon economies may bear the major responsibility for this state of affairs; but before discussing this, it is necessary to look at the largest economy in the world, that of the USA.

4.6 TRANSFORMATION OF SAVING TO INVESTMENT IN THE USA

The American banking system can be thought of as a four-tier structure. First, there are about 9000 independent local banks, each operating within a single state of the USA and subject to state supervision. All of these relatively small banks have their deposits insured by the Federal Deposit Insurance Corporation, and for the majority of these banks, that is their only link with the Federal system. Second, there are about 4000 national banks, who are by that very fact members of the Federal Reserve System; and some large state and city banks are also members of that system by virtue of their size.

The Federal Reserve (or 'the Fed' as virtually everyone calls it) is the central bank of the USA. The Federal Reserve System was developed in response to the wave of bank failures in 1907; after considerable opposition, the Federal Reserve Act was passed in 1913. This set up the third tier of the US banking system — the 12 Federal Districts of the USA, which had one Federal Reserve Bank each — and these in turn are controlled by the fourth tier, the Federal Reserve System, located in Washington. The advantages of independent local banking have since been preserved as well as the creation of the necessary national banking structure in the USA under the watchful eye of the Fed.

The purposes of the Federal Reserve System are to assist small banks in the banking community to avoid failures (through the Federal Deposit Insurance Corporation) and to regulate the money and credit supply and the cost of credit in the USA. The fact of the Fed's existence made possible Roosevelt's 'New Deal' of the mid-1930s, for the Fed also acts as government bonds broker, providing a source of finance for the US government, as need be. Local state banks (who are not members of the Fed) have about 15 % of total deposits in the USA. These banks are often located in rural communities, and they frequently have a surplus of funds which they lend to a national or large state bank which is a member of the Fed. Any commercial bank, due to its membership of the Fed can either contribute to, or borrow from, the Federal funds market, which is the major mechanism of inter-bank lending and which is also the market in which the Fed, on behalf of the US government, raises or repays loans.

The transformation of saving to lending in the USA is complicated by the high degree of financial intermediation between saver and borrower. At local level, all bank branches collect liquid deposits and time savings and lend part of these to local customers, while canalising funds not required locally to their city branches or other banks for onward lending. City branches of banks, in the industrial centres of the country, are naturally the largest lenders to industry, with the result that there is a sizeable flow of funds within the banking system (though often not within the same bank) from rural and farming areas to the cities. The complexity of the intermediate lending procedures is such that the saving-to-lending transfer system is perhaps best understood in terms of the final users of funds and the original source of these funds.

Table 4.37 shows the total funds raised in credit markets in the USA between 1970 and 1973. The range of the breakdown of the total funds is sufficient to permit some fairly detailed analysis of the uses of saving in the USA.

During the 1970–73 period, for example, the US government raised funds as shown in Table 4.38. The central government's demand for funds in the USA has therefore represented a sizeable, but not a major, function of the credit markets. By far the greatest proportion of the funds raised by the US government has been in the form of the Public Debt Securities.

The state and local governments of the USA also raised funds in the credit markets from 1970 to 1973.

If the demands for funds of central, state and local government are added, the percentage of credit market funds absorbed by all government averages about 21 % in the 1970–73 period, from 11.8 % in 1973 to 29.4 % in 1971.

The funds raised by corporate equities on the stock market and by the issue of corporate and foreign bonds are shown in Table 4.40, both in

TABLE 4.37 Funds raised in credit markets by non-financial sectors in the USA, 1970–73

in $bn.	1970	1971	1972	1973
Total funds raised	98.2	147.4	169.4	187.4
US Government	12.8	25.5	17.3	9.7
(a) Public debt securities	12.9	26.0	13.9	7.7
(b) Agency issues and mortgages	−0.1	−.5	3.4	2.0
All other non-financial sectors	85.4	121.9	152.1	177.7
(a) Corporate equities	5.8	11.5	10.5	7.2
(b) Debt capital instruments	79.7	110.4	141.6	170.4
Analysis of debt capital: totals	57.6	84.2	94.9	97.1
(a) State and local government securities	11.2	17.6	14.4	13.7
(b) Corporate and foreign bonds	20.6	19.7	13.2	10.2
(c) Mortgages	25.7	46.9	67.3	73.2
composed of:				
Home	12.8	26.1	39.6	43.3
Other residential	5.8	8.8	10.3	8.4
Commercial	5.3	10.0	14.8	17.0
Farm	1.8	2.0	2.6	4.4
(d) Other private credit: totals	22.1	26.3	46.7	73.4
composed of:				
Bank loans	6.4	9.3	21.8	38.6
Consumer credit	6.0	11.2	19.2	22.9
Open market paper	3.8	−0.9	−1.6	1.8
Other	5.9	6.6	7.3	10.0
Debt capital by borrowing sector				
(a) Foreign	2.7	4.6	4.3	7.5
(b) State and local governments	11.3	17.8	14.2	12.3
(c) Households	23.4	39.8	63.1	72.8
(d) Non-financial business	48.0	59.6	70.5	85.1
of which				
Farm	3.2	4.1	4.9	8.6
Non-farm non-corporate	5.3	8.7	10.4	9.3
Corporate	39.5	46.8	55.3	67.2

Source: *Economic Report of the President*, Washington, 1975, Table C–54.

TABLE 4.38 US government funds raised in credit markets, 1970–73

in $bn.	1970	1971	1972	1973
Funds raised	12.8	25.5	17.3	9.7
As % of GDP	1.30	2.40	1.48	0.74
As % of total funds raised in credit markets	13.0	17.3	10.2	5.2

Source: Tables 4.37, 4.42.

TABLE 4.39   US state and local govt. funds raised in credit markets, 1970–73

in $bn.	1970	1971	1972	1973
Funds raised	11.3	17.8	14.2	12.3
As % of GDP	1.15	1.68	1.22	0.94
As % of total funds raised in credit markets	11.5	12.1	8.4	6.6

Source: Tables 4.37 and 4.42.

TABLE 4.40   New issues of shares and bonds for non-financial sectors in the USA, 1970—73

$bn.	1970	1971	1972	1973
Corporate equities	5.8	11.5	10.5	7.2
Corporate and foreign bonds	20.6	19.7	13.2	10.2
% of GDP				
Corporate equities	0.59	1.08	0.90	0.55
Corporate and foreign bonds	2.10	1.86	1.13	0.78

Source: Tables 4.37 and 4.42.

terms of billions of dollars and as percentages of GDP. Non-financial sectors of the economy received on average about 0.78% of GDP from the stock market, while on average almost twice this percentage of GDP was raised through corporate and foreign bonds. Because of the exclusion of financial sectors from this table, caution must be exercised in making any direct comparison between Table 4.40 and the total amounts raised by share and bond markets elsewhere calculated.

As Table 4.37 indicates, and as could be expected, private residential mortgages make up the greater proportion of all mortgages, although commercial mortgages constitute about one-fifth of the total. Consumer credit and bank loans to private customers account for most of the residue of other private credit.

The percentages of all capital funds are calculated for the period 1970–73 in Table 4.41. Corporate business has received, on average, about 35% of credit market funds during the 1970–73 period; about 3% more than households. US farms, and foreign capital raised in US credit markets, each take a few percent of the total funds advanced.

The finance of the total flow of funds advanced had a number of different sources, as Table 4.42 indicates. By far the largest single source of funds was private domestic deposits, which accounted for over 60%

TABLE 4.41 Distribution of total funds raised in USA credit markets, 1970–73

in % of total funds	1970	1971	1972	1973
US government	13.0	17.3	10.2	5.2
State and local government	11.5	12.1	8.4	6.6
Households	23.8	27.0	37.2	38.8
Farms	3.3	2.8	2.9	4.6
Non-farm non-corporate	5.4	5.9	6.1	5.0
Corporate business	40.2	31.8	32.6	35.9
Foreign	2.7	3.1	2.5	4.0

Source: Calculated from Table 4.37.

TABLE 4.42 Finance of funds advanced in USA credit markets to non-financial sectors, 1970–73

in $bn.	1970	1971	1972	1973
Total funds advanced to non-financial sectors	98.2	147.4	169.4	187.4
Financed directly or indirectly by:				
Private domestic non-financial sectors	63.3	83.1	105.8	124.3
(a) Deposits	66.6	93.7	101.9	88.8
of which: demand deposits and currency	10.5	12.7	16.7	12.6
Time and savings accounts	56.1	81.0	85.2	76.3
(b) Credit market instruments: net	−3.4	−10.6	3.8	35.5
US Government securities	−9.0	−14.0	1.6	18.8
Private credit market instruments	6.5	10.7	12.1	20.5
Corporate equities	−1.7	−5.3	−5.4	−8.4
Less: security debt	−0.9	2.1	4.5	−4.4
Other sources				
(a) Foreign funds	2.4	23.9	15.8	10.1
− At banks	−8.5	−3.2	5.2	6.5
− Direct	10.9	27.2	10.6	3.6
(b) Change in US govt. cash balance	2.8	3.2	−0.3	−1.7
(c) US government loans	2.8	3.2	2.6	3.0
(d) Private insurance and pension reserves	21.8	24.8	27.1	29.5
(e) Other	5.1	9.1	18.4	22.1
Gross Domestic Product	981.2	1061.1	1168.3	1302.1
Total funds advanced as % of GDP	10.01	13.89	14.50	14.39

Source: *Economic Report of the President*, Washington, 1975, Table C–54.

of credit market funds, except during 1973, when credit market instruments became a sizeable source of funds. Insurance and pension funds provided between one-fifth and one-sixth of total credit market funds.

Because the largest single source of funds for US credit markets is private domestic deposits, the saving of individuals (defined for this purpose as the saving of households, personal trust funds, non-profit making institutions, farms and other non-corporate business) is of interest. The assets in which individuals hold their savings determines, to some extent, the risk in the transformation process from short-term resources to longer-term loans.

The asset bases of the savings of individuals is listed in Table 4.42. As occurs elsewhere, the net savings of the personal sector is less high than its gross saving, for the gross savings of individuals are loaned through credit institutions usually as mortgages, bank loans and consumer credit to other individuals. The American source of this data includes saving for, and investment in, consumer durables, while other systems of national accounting (the British one, for instance) may assume that consumer durables are consumed at the time of purchase. So long as the approach is consistent, the assumption made about whether consumer durables are an act of investment or consumption does not matter because if consumer durables are defined as a net investment then the increase in gross financial assets must be set commensurately higher to give the same net increase in financial assets.

From Table 4.43, it would seem that Americans keep about 10% of their additional annual financial savings in currency and demand deposits. Most of their savings (about 50–60%) are kept in savings accounts. Corporate and foreign bonds have been purchased out of private saving during the 1970–73 period, although the level of purchase has varied considerably. Individuals have (on average) sold corporate equities in each of these years, and government securities were sold in 1970 and 1971 but purchased in 1972 and 1973. A fair proportion of individual savings has been in the form of insurance and pension reserves. Mortgages, consumer credit and bank loans for a number of unspecified purposes have been higher than the increase in net investment in housing, consumer durable assets and other assets, with the result that the total net funds available for lending to other economic sectors has been less than the increase in financial assets. Nonetheless, net savings by individuals has been by far the largest source of funds for credit markets; in this respect the USA is similar to many other countries.

Table 4.44 summarises the sources of funds for non-farm, non-financial corporate business for the period 1963–73. It would appear

TABLE 4.43   Saving by individuals in the USA[1], 1970–73

in $bn.	1970	1971	1972	1973
Increase in financial assets	80.6	99.7	124.4	138.2
Made up from:				
Currency and demand deposits	11.3	11.1	12.1	13.1
Savings accounts	44.4	70.3	75.4	67.7
Government securities[2]	−10.4	−14.5	1.6	24.7
Corporate and foreign bonds	10.7	9.3	5.2	1.1
Corporate equities[3]	−1.7	−5.3	−5.4	−8.2
Insurance and pension reserves[4]	24.3	27.7	30.3	31.6
Other assets	2.0	1.1	5.2	8.2
Net investment in:				
Non-farm homes	10.6	17.6	24.3	27.2
Consumer durables	10.6	16.5	24.4	27.1
Non-corporate business assets	6.6	11.0	10.6	15.4
Less increase in debt due to:				
Mortgage debt on non-farm homes	12.5	24.2	38.4	44.2
Consumer credit	6.0	11.2	19.2	22.9
Other debt[5]	13.7	21.9	28.2	20.5
Total	76.2	87.4	97.9	120.2

Notes:
(1) Savings by households, personal trust funds, non-profit institutions, farms and other non-corporate business
(2) Consists of US savings bonds, other US Treasury securities, US Govt. agency securities and sponsored agency securities and state and local obligations
(3) Includes investment in company shares
(4) Private and government life insurance and pension reserves
(5) Security credit, policy loans, non-corporate business mortgage debt, and other debt
Source: *Economic Report of the President*, Washington, 1975, Table C–21.

from this evidence that there has been a fairly steady fall in the percentage of funds coming from internal sources—almost 70% of funds were internally generated in 1964; the proportion is down to below half in 1973. Or, to put it another way, between 1963 and 1973 total funds were up by a factor of about 2.71; internal sources of funds less than doubled; external sources rose to about 4.34 times their 1963 value. Among these external funds, the growth of long-term credit market sources has been most consistent; short-term credit market and other funds have varied considerably in value.

Table 4.45 shows these funds sources as percentages of GDP. The total funds available to non-farm, non-financial corporate business has varied around 12.20% of GDP by only about 1.3% or so. American

TABLE 4.44   Sources of funds for non-farm non-financial corporate business in the USA, 1963–73

in $bn.	Total funds	Internal funds[1]	Total	External credit market Long-term[2]	Short-term[3]	Other
1963	65.0	43.9	21.1	8.2	3.9	9.0
1964	72.4	50.5	21.9	8.8	5.6	7.4
1965	91.3	56.6	34.8	9.2	11.2	14.4
1966	97.3	61.2	36.1	15.7	9.6	10.9
1967	94.0	61.5	32.5	21.6	8.0	3.0
1968	113.6	61.7	51.9	18.4	13.2	20.4
1969	118.1	60.7	57.4	20.0	18.9	18.5
1970	103.7	59.4	44.2	30.7	8.8	4.8
1971	120.4	68.0	52.5	41.8	5.0	5.7
1972	148.0	78.7	69.3	39.3	16.0	14.0
1973	176.2	84.6	91.6	34.5	32.7	24.5

Notes:
1 Undistributed profits (after inventory adjustment) and capital consumption allowances.
2 Stocks, bonds and mortgages
3 Bank loans, commercial paper, finance company loans, bankers' acceptances, and US Government loans
Source: *Economic Report of the President*, Washington, 1975, Table C–78.

TABLE 4.45   Sources of funds as % of GDP for non-farm non-financial corporate business in the USA, 1963–73

Year	Total	Internal	Total	External credit market Long-term	Short-term	Other
1963	10.93	7.38	3.55	1.38	0.66	1.51
1964	11.40	7.95	3.45	1.39	0.88	1.17
1965	13.29	8.24	5.06	1.34	1.63	2.10
1966	12.93	8.14	4.80	2.09	1.28	1.45
1967	11.82	7.73	4.09	2.72	1.01	0.38
1968	13.10	7.11	5.98	2.12	1.52	2.35
1969	12.64	6.50	6.14	2.14	2.02	1.98
1970	10.57	6.05	4.50	3.13	0.90	0.49
1971	11.35	6.41	4.95	3.94	0.47	0.54
1972	12.67	6.74	5.93	3.36	1.37	1.20
1973	13.53	6.50	7.03	2.65	2.51	1.88

Source: Tables 4.44 and 4.42 (for GDP).

commerce and industry (which is largely what the non-farm, non-financial corporate business represents) received from about 3.5 to 7.0 % of GDP from external sources. Only 1.3 to 4.0 % of GDP was supplied on a long-term basis, however, although there does seem to have been an increasing trend in the supply of long-term credit during the 1960s and early 1970s. Although corporate business in the USA does receive 30—40 % of the funds raised in credit markets, there may therefore be some legitimate doubt about whether the length of the credit is suitable for engendering long-term investment in plant and machinery.

One author has gone so far as to predict that the USA will be surpassed, first in income per head and then by total output, by the economy of Japan. It is the relatively low growth of the US economy, and the relatively low investment level in productive industry in the USA, which makes such prediction credible.[30] Another author, writing in 1963, put it like this:

> If we deflate western rates of growth in the way we are accustomed to do for under-developed countries,[31] the United States figure for the decade up to 1962 comes out at about 1 per cent — a figure insignificantly different from what we believe — on a very rough statistical basis — the rate of poor India to have been for the corresponding period.[32]

Fortunately, since 1963 the USA economy has performed much better. Yet it could perhaps do better still with a more adequate saving-to-investment transformation system.

4.7 RELATIONSHIPS BETWEEN FINANCIAL AND INDUSTRIAL STRUCTURES

There is a great range of different relationships between government, the financial institutions and the industrial structures in each of the five countries. Once again, limits of space permit only a short summary of the general position on this question in each country.

The role of the French government, in assisting economic growth in France, is basically twofold: first, there is an indicative planning procedure which, in the form of the National Plan, sets production goals for various industrial sectors of the economy, and explictly defines France's social and economic desiderata; and second, government financial agencies act to ensure the provision of investment credit to enable the objectives of the Plan to be fulfilled. The relationship between the production plans of a company and the objectives of the National Plan may therefore frequently be more important than the business connection between banker and industrialist, for the former broadly determines the prospects of a company receiving investment credit, while the latter may sometimes only be a social connection. In general, France's national planning system ensures that investment finance is available for large companies (which seem quite capable of defining some of their aims to co-incide with those of the Plan) for the expansion of nationalised industries, and for the growth of some family firms. However, due to the very variable standard of company reports in France, it is difficult to generalise about the average relationship between banker and businessman. The average levels of long-term debt in quoted companies' finance (at about 40% of the capital structure) argues for a fair degree of integration of the financial-industrial structure, yet there may have been a tendency for a high proportion of funds to be advanced to the largest organisations.

The probable position in France is that there is a high degree of involvement between major industrial producers and large banks, with some helpful contacts between family firms and bankers at local level, but there is a relative lack of information on the balance of emphasis in this area. French companies, as one book has commented, are loath to disclose some of their financial and other activities, even to potential investors.[33] One consequence of this is that the network of relationships between bankers and businessmen is not generally exposed to public view; only the aggregate flows of finance are readily available.

In Japan, the situation is radically different. Government's role is to act as midwife to the priority objective of rapid economic growth, and virtually all other national objectives are subordinated to that end. The financial-industrial structure is highly integrated—so much so, that major Japanese business groupings (the keiretsu or 'linked group') often have a large bank and other financial institutions which are part of the grouping. The companies in the Mitsubishi keiretsu, for example, have strong links with the Mitsubishi Bank, the Mitsubishi Trust and Banking Corporations, the Nikko Securities Company, and the Meiji Mutual Life Insurance Company.[34] Mitsubishi companies are active in warehousing, heavy industry, electrical products, atomic power, chemical machinery and chemicals, oil, steel manufacturing, chemical engineering, mining, and in the production of plastics, glass, cement, beer, and many other lines of business. It is not surprising that Mitsubishi is acknowledged to be a 'Sogoshosha' or general trading company.

Similarly, the Sumitomo keiretsu counts, as its financial members, the Sumitomo Bank, the Sumitomo Trust and Banking Company, the Sumitomo Marine and Fire Insurance Company, and the Sumitomo Life Insurance Company.[35] The Sumitomo keiretsu is also active across a broad bank of industrial activities. These linked company groupings are 'kinyu keiretsu', or financially-linked companies grouped around a large bank, to acquire the advantages of preferential credit through exchanges of shares and greater access to bank finance. There are many other examples of these kinyu keiretsu, such as the Mitsui Bank Keiretsu or the Dai Ichi Bank keiretsu, or the Fuji Bank keiretsu. Another form of linked group is the sangyo keiretsu — industrially-linked companies who cluster around a large company, and who may buy and sell products within the group.

All in all, it is difficult to avoid the conclusion that the financial-industrial structure in Japan is highly integrated. Bankers sit on the boards of industrial companies, and the power of banks is considerable. By law, no bank may hold over 10 % of the shares of any company, yet there is little to prevent companies in the kinyu keiretsu group from acquiring shares in other linked companies. In practice, loans advanced are more relevant than shares purchased, and it is not unknown for individual companies in a kinyu keiretsu to receive over 50 % of their loan funds from their linked financial companies.

A recent NEDO report pointed out that the three largest Japanese general trading companies have an aggregate turnover larger than the Japanese national budget, and that the average ratio of own capital to total capital employed is 3.4 %[36]. Without the great integration of the financial-industrial structure in Japan, neither of these results would seem likely.

West German banks are relatively well-integrated with the industrial structure. Banks may perform the role of industrial restructuring, and the power of banks in business is considerable because the banks are not only the major providers of industrial loan capital but also wield the voting powers of most equity shareholding. (West German shareholders usually allow banks to use shareholders votes as the banks see fit; shareholders are consulted on company issues, as they must be by law, but often are willing to surrender their voting rights to the commercial competence of the banks.) The government of West Germany distances itself from much of the industrial scene, except in the case of nationalised (or part-nationalised) industries. Although debt-equity ratios are high in West Germany, the banks have a great deal of information on the companies to which they advance funds; the presence and involvement of bank nominees on companies' boards may serve as a guarantee that investment funds are being well-utilised and that the company pays considerable attention to its financial position. The relative integration of banking and business in West Germany has helped create a confidence-creating financial-industrial system, through the greater commitment of financial institutions to providing funds for industrial growth.

The two Anglo-Saxon countries—the UK and the USA—are quite different. The financial structure and the industrial structure are quite distinct in both these countries, with only relatively minor exceptions. Banks provide an external financial service to the industrial companies; they do not generally offer investment credit (except for relatively short-term periods) and are not so involved with industry, through linked and acknowledged groupings, as described in Japan and West Germany.

The UK government does not involve itself in assisting industry, beyond providing systems of export credit guarantees and some preferential finance of investment in development areas. However, the British government has been impelled from time to time to mount rescue attempts (e.g. Rolls-Royce, British Leyland etc.) when the absence of internal financial discipline, and the lack of suitable systems for providing long-term investment capital in the UK, causes the financial collapse of major companies. UK banks do not generally acknowledge the need to be more integrated with industry; the rationale for this attitude is that if companies want investment capital, then they should go to the stock market.

The US financial and industrial systems are wholly distinct, although because banks are organised largely by state or region, there are more links between major city banks and the industrial community of their area than is the case in the UK. The range of possible kinds of financial transactions in the USA seems larger than anywhere else, for American ingenuity has given rise to a highly developed and flexible securities market and loan methods.[37] The American government does not act directly to affect US private investment levels, but exercises a policy of benign neglect, permitting free market forces to decide the availability and cost of new investment capital.

If the five countries had to be ranked in descending order of integration of banking with business, then the order would be (i) Japan (highly integrated) (ii) West Germany (well integrated) (iii) France (fairly integrated) (iv) the USA (close links in some cases) and (v) the UK (relatively unintegrated, with clear separation between banks and business). One indication of this level of integration is the relative ease with which businessmen become bankers, or indeed bankers are businessmen, where there is close financial-industrial integration, and vice versa. In the UK and the USA banks provide a service to their customers; in Japan and West Germany, the role of the banking system is predominantly to assist industry.

The reason for this difference in emphasis lies in the recent historical past. The end of World War II signalled the start of the industrial rebuilding of Japan and West Germany and (to a lesser extent) France. To help provide funds for industry, links were forged (or strengthened, where they had existed pre-war) between banks and businesses. Some economists during the post-war period commented that the war-damaged economies were growing faster than the UK and the USA because they were growing from a low consumption level; the implication was that Japanese or West German growth rates would fall as these economies approached Anglo-Saxon levels. Yet it seems to us that once links are established between the financial and industrial sectors, there is no particular reason why the level of investment funds should be reduced because real private consumption has reached a particular level. Present or past levels of consumption in the UK or the USA may constitute no economic barrier. One way of examining the priorities of the financial systems of different countries is to calculate the net funds borrowed by households as a percentage of total household savings. This is done in Table 4.46 where it can be seen that in Japan and West Germany, only a few percent of gross household savings are loaned back to households, while the lending of household saving to households is a

TABLE 4.46   Net borrowing of households as a percentage of their gross financial saving, 1970–73

Country	1970	1971	1972	1973
France	51.5	49.2	65.5	63.2
Japan	6.5	6.5	10.7	NA
West Germany	6.1	9.4	10.9	5.3
UK	44.7	57.5	80.9	54.3
USA	40.0	57.4	68.9	63.4

Source: Table 6.5.

major activity of the financial systems of France, the UK and the USA. The excess savings of households, which can be a major source of uncommitted finance, are considerably reduced in volume by the

French, British and American financial systems which loan funds to households for housing and consumer credit on a large scale. Household savings are therefore rather more converted to consumption and housing capital rather than to industrial investment in these three countries. If present consumption and an increase in the demand for housing are preferred to increasing industrial capacity, then the French, American and British financial approach is to be preferred, and if vice-versa, then the Japanese and West German financial systems show more merit. This subject will be raised again with a different emphasis in Section 6.2.

It is difficult to assess the precise degree to which financial investment (or the speculative purchase of pre-existing commercial paper) is occuring in these five nations. However, investment trusts in the UK and mutual funds in the USA tend to be purely financial investors; they do not generally provide new capital for enterprises, but collect saving to purchase pre-existing bonds, stocks and shares, providing no new investment capital to enterprises in that process, except when new issues are purchased. Investment trusts and mutual funds are therefore channels which largely transfer saving to an increase in commercial paper demands (and some consumption from the sellers of shares) in the secondary market. Most pension funds in the UK are in a similar position.

The net effect of these different national financial systems is to provide a flow of medium- and long-term finance for enterprises. These total funds are quoted, as percentages of GDP, in Table 4.47. The funds include new share issues by enterprises, new long-term bonds, plus medium- and long-term loans, for the three European countries in this

TABLE 4.47   Medium- and long-term external funds provided to non-financial corporate and quasi-corporate enterprises, 1970–73

% of GDP	1970	1971	1972	1973
France	4.51	4.79	4.92	5.00
Japan	7.99	9.65	8.33	8.46
West Germany	7.60	9.04	9.64	8.67
UK	3.09	4.35	2.75	1.77
USA	3.98	4.99	4.86	4.01

Source: Table 5.12.

table. Japanese funds are almost certainly understated, for Table 4.47 assumes only equipment funds are medium- and long-term; in practice, most short-term Japanese industrial loans are revolving credits, never repaid. It is nevertheless quite clear that in Japan and West Germany, there are relatively large flows of medium- and long-term finance for enterprises, while external funds are most scarce in the UK. The absence of integration of the financial and industrial sectors may be partially responsible for this result.

5 The Costs and Profits of Capital

5.1 THE THEORY OF CAPITAL GEARING

Within the Anglo-Saxon economies, there is a theory and practice of capital gearing which rationalises the reality and sometimes ensures, through banking prudence, that the percentage of debt in the capital structure of most companies does not exceed about 30 % of total capital employed. Both the theory and the practice of capital gearing are subjects which deserve to be dealt with in some detail.

It is as well to begin with a definition. The balance sheet definition of capital gearing (or leverage, as it is sometimes called) is the ratio between long-term debt and the total long-term capital employed. There is another way of looking at gearing, by defining it in relation to profit and loss account and to the proportion of company earnings taken by fixed interest stock. However, both definitions tend to equate to a similar situation and our concern here is with capital gearing. The gear ratio is the ratio of loan capital to equity capital. Hence in a company with total capital assets of £1m., if there are long-term loans of £200,000, the gearing is 20 % and the gear ratio is 0.25.

Gearing has two principal affects. First, it is aimed at producing a lower average cost of capital, and second, it alters the expectations of return to the shareholders. The mechanics of debt costs a good deal less than an equity flotation. The costs of the flotation of new issue capital depends to a great extent on the standing of the issuing company, but a new issue of about £1m. can cost about £250,000, while the costs of flotation are proportionately more for lower amounts. Loan capital, on the other hand, can be acquired from the banks at virtually zero initial cost. Once equity has been raised, the issuing company needs to pay steadily, if gently, rising dividends to maintain the share price and to support propitious market conditions for a future new issue, should one be required. In Britain average returns to the industrial shareholder have averaged 3–6 % in recent years:[1] with corporation tax at 52.5 %, this has

155

meant that the average costs of previously-issued equity capital could have ranged between 6 and 12 % of share prices to company profits before tax, but this issue is relatively complex (See Section 5.2). However, the recent depressed performance of the British stock market has given rise to the reverse yield gap — returns on fixed-interest stocks have exceeded equity yields, as they tend to do during a depression; new issues at present would have a very poor chance of successful flotation unless future dividend yields on these particular shares were at least 12 %, or unless they offered a good prospect of capital gains. The real costs of new equity capital would probably be about 20–25 % to company cash flow before tax, under current UK stock market conditions. It is difficult to see how a lower rate — of say 18 % to the company, yielding 9 % or so to the investor — would entice any but the most optimistic large investor, who could get a higher return from some banks, building societies or local authority bonds at no significant risk.

On the other hand, the cost of debt in the UK at present would be about bank rate plus 2 %, for a large company in good standing. It is therefore quite clear that even under the relatively high inflation circumstances of the last few years in the UK, debt costs much less than equity. The question for the investing company is the relative mix of debt and equity which should be used to minimise the average cost of company capital.

The theory on this point is fairly clear. Debt should not, theoretically, exceed about one-third of the total capital structure of a company, because since the interest on loans is guaranteed to be paid in good years or bad, it is argued that a higher proportion of debt would mean that in bad years, shareholders would find that most of the company's earnings were being swallowed by interest payments. Although very high debt seems to carry the risk of making the dividend payments (and hence the share price) more unstable, a judicious amount of debt gears upward the returns due to the shareholder. The presence of some debt, which carries less risk because it is secured and which receives a low fixed-interest payment before tax, produces a higher rate of return to the shareholder than a company financed by equity alone. Hence if a company is wholly financed by equity, the dividends would be lower, and therefore the cost of equity higher. On the other hand, if a large company attempted to finance itself largely by loans it could run into certain difficulties. As the proportion of loans to equity increased, the security of the loans would run out and hence bankers might well be unwilling to advance further loans except at higher rates of interest to reflect the larger risks. This situation is summarised in Figure 5.1. This shows the supposed costs of

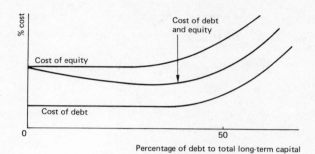

FIGURE 5.1   Conventional explanation of the theory of Anglo-Saxon capital

equity capital and debt capital, as well as the combined weighted average cost-curve of capital which results from these theoretical arguments.[2] The minimum point on the graph, at which the cost of capital is minimised, is the position at which the finance of the company is supposedly 'optimal'.

There is a number of difficulties with the theory of gearing, as summarised above. First, the theory is largely a rationalisation of average capital structures in Anglo-Saxon economies, and does not refer (except by implication) to the rest of the world or to individual firms. The Japanese economy in 1975 had an average debt-equity ratio of 85 % for industrial and commercial firms, and if high debt levels in quoted companies resulted in a very risky stock market, the Tokyo stock exchange should surely have collapsed by now. The fact that the Tokyo exchange has signally failed to collapse must cause some difficulties for the theory, unless the theory accepts having its area of validity restricted to the economies of the Anglo-Saxon world. Yet even in Anglo-Saxon economies, the proportion of debt in a company is not limited by the theoretical considerations set out above, but ranges considerably for reasons not directly obvious.

For example, a recent study of gearing in UK quoted companies found that the range of gearing was relatively wide and that there was no clear relationship between the type of industry and the amount of gearing which was permissible. For the 2870 quoted companies examined on 17 August 1973, the gearing percentages were found to be as shown in Table 5.1.

As Table 5.1 illustrates, the conventional theory about the company's capital structure has very little (if any) basis in observed statistical fact. It

TABLE 5.1   UK gearing percentages of quoted companies

At August, 1973	Gearing percentage ranges						
	0–9%	10–19%	20–29%	30–39%	40–49%	50–74%	75–100%
Number of companies	457	490	518	579	427	374	25
% of 2870 companies	15.9	17.1	18.0	20.2	14.9	13.0	0.9

Source: Robin B. Fox, Leverage in UK Companies, 1967–73—An Empirical Investigation, *Management Decision*, 1977, Vol. 1

is the more surprising, therefore, that the traditional view of gearing often tends to be defended, albeit in a modified form with a flatter saucer-shaped cost-curve of capital rather than the U-shaped cost-curve shown in older texts. In the absence of the theory, there would be no reason to believe that the average cost of company capital increases for high levels of debt, which does not have a probable rise in cost as the mix of debt in company capital increases. This would lead us to the conclusion that debt finance, being cheaper than equity, would confer the advantage of increasing the productive strength of a company. As Kahn has remarked vis-à-vis Japan, it makes no difference to the productivity of a machine whether it is funded by debt or equity.[3] The rate of investment may be the principal determinant of economic and company growth, and the mixed capital structure of the sources of finance of that investment may not matter very much, so long as that capital structure is low-cost. Furthermore, attempts have been made to examine the theory in the light of statistical data, most notably by Modigliani and Miller,[4] who have reported the discovery of a relatively flat cost of capital. However, Modigliani and Miller's results are not necessarily a refutation of traditional theory, for reasons can be advanced consistent with both.[5]

The traditional theory of gearing also tends to be an analysis of the theoretical position of loans in the long-term capital structure without considering the cash flow demands of short-term loans which are, in many cases, a greater risk to earnings than long-term fixed-interest debentures. Consider, for example, the data in Table 5.2. This table indicates considerable under-gearing in UK companies in the 1960s; indeed, until 1965, the bank advances to UK industrial and commercial companies are a large proportion of company liabilities and are generally short-term and although the stock of such advances has continuously risen, the loans are continually being repaid and renewed. The cost of repayment of short-term loans, because they include the repayment of capital, may be low if assessed at their interest-cost, but the

TABLE 5.2   Financial valuation of UK industrial and commercial companies, 1960–75

End-year in £m.	Market value of companies' liabilities				Total	Debt ratio	Companies' liquid assets
	Ordinary shares	Preference shares	Debentures	Bank advances			
1960	20120	1725	1654	1965	25464	14.21	3320
1961	18951	1618	1696	2170	24435	15.82	3314
1962	23995	1829	2440	2470	30734	16.00	3320
1963	30524	1848	2920	3042	38334	15.55	3699
1964	29304	1814	2924	3781	37823	17.73	3696
1965	31481	1797	3138	4240	40626	18.16	3675
1966	25975	1638	4558	4409	36580	24.51	3577
1967	34923	1562	4968	4692	46165	20.92	4050
1968	46243	1292	4948	5071	57554	17.41	4311
1969	40383	996	4671	5737	51787	20.10	4112
1970	33275	742	5223	6747	45987	26.03	4257
1971	47340	911	6334	7329	61914	22.07	5283
1972	56330	774	6112	10319	73535	22.34	7458
1973	50274	615	5290	15120	71299	28.63	9795
1974	21800	499	3788	18834	44921	50.36	9685
1975*	47100	600	4500	19800	72000	33.75	12000

*Provisional

Note: The debt ratio is the percentage of bank advances plus debentures to total assets.

Source: J. S. Flemming, L. D. D. Price and S. A. Byers, 'The cost of capital finance and investment', *Bank of England Quarterly Bulletin*, Vol. 16, No. 2, June 1976.

effect on cash flow can be very large. The traditional theory of gearing does not take into account the first requirement of company survival — that liquidity, with all its short-term problems, is paramount over profitability. An illiquid firm may go bankrupt immediately, and is at the mercy of its creditors and its bankers; an unprofitable firm, if it avoids illiquidity, may have the time to turn its financial situation around. Even a zero interest rate would not encourage fixed investment if the capital had to be repaid within days, weeks, or months. Hire purchase for consumers results in more consumer purchase of durable goods; long-term investment credit equally results in more fixed investment. The reason in both cases is the same; the borrower (whether an individual or a company) can afford the easy payments. Yet there is in nearly all writing about the costs of investment capital, an emphasis on the interest cost and a neglect of the cash flow cost. The interest rate is of course not irrelevant, but the repayment rate is crucial.

This may be a partial explanation for the reported disregard of the cost of capital in taking investment decisions. Robin B. Fox, for example, inquired into the attitudes toward leverage in 20 substantial quoted companies, and found that the cost of capital was seen as relevant in only five, out of the 17 companies who admitted to using discounted cash flow techniques to evaluate investment projects.[6] Six of his companies had apparently little or no understanding of the term 'optimal financing'.

In summary, therefore, the major difficulty with the theory of capital gearing is that it is largely a theoretical explanation of UK, USA and Anglo-Saxon practice; the lack of any statistical evidence for the theory must result in some doubt as to whether other equally logical theories could explain the observed range of debt-equity ratios in the nations of the west as a whole. Table 5.3 gives debt-equity ratios for industrial and commercial companies in 1970 for those five nations which are our chosen field of interest. The academic question might well be how we explain such a wide range of different national traditions in debt-equity ratios, and this could partially be done by reference to the differing national institutions for funding industrial investment, as outlined in the previous chapter.

Yet perhaps the more pragmatic question might be — if other countries had restricted themselves to the same debt-equity ratios as the UK, how much smaller would the asset bases of major quoted

TABLE 5.3   Debt-equity capital structures, 1970

1 *Country*	*2* *% Debt*	*3* *% Equity*	*4* *With a 22:78 Debt-Equity ratio, the size of all quoted companies in the economy would have been*
Japan[2]	85	15	about 19.2% of their size
West Germany[1]	57	43	about 55.1% of their size
France[1]	39	61	about 78.2% of their size
USA[3]	31	69	about 88.5% of their size
UK[1]	22	78	as occurred

Source of the debt-equity percentages:
[1] Peter Readman *et al.*, *The European Money Puzzle*, Michael Joseph, 1973, p. 138
[2] Bank of Japan figures
[3] Securities and Exchange Commission, NYSE
Note: The sizes quoted in column 4 refer to 1970.

companies in their economies be? The answer for four countries is shown in the fourth column of Table 5.3. Would the Japanese miracle have happend, if their major companies were 80 % smaller? What kind of world would we be living in, if all these countries in Table 5.3 had restricted themselves to the conventional wisdom that debt should never exceed about one-third of a company's capital structure? Of one thing we can be sure; it would not be similar to the actual world. Other countries would have major companies and economies which would be considerably smaller if they shared Britain's conventional wisdom about how to finance industrial investment.

Two important caveats must be added to the calculations in column 4 of Table 5.3. First, the imputed size of quoted companies in the West German economy is over-stated, because in that country certain debt-equity ratios are required by law, and this can result in West German banks converting loans into equity capital for the benefit of those wearing legal spectacles. Banks in West Germany not only advance loans for industrial investment; they also own about half of the equity of West German industry. A more valid estimate of the extent to which West German industry was originally funded might be about 80 % debt and 20 % equity. This would imply that if West German industry and commerce were limited to the British figure of 22 % debt finance the asset-based size of quoted companies in the West German economy might have been about one-quarter of their actual size in 1970.

Second, the French debt-equity ratios do not necessarily reflect the original source of the funds as the British figures do, for in France about 80 % of the medium- and long-term capital flows in the economy are controlled by government institutions, which canalise funds to business-men as capital loans, provided these businessmen can persuade the authorities that their company needs these funds to fulfil the obligations of the National Plan. The different debt-equity ratios shown in Table 5.3 probably reflect different levels of risk in funding capital investment in these economies partly due to the different degrees of integration of the financial-industrial systems in these nations (as outlined in Chapter 4) and partially resulting from the differing degrees of financial and fiscal support given by governments to their industrial sector.

However, the evidence, taken as a whole, seems to indicate that the conventional theory of capital gearing has no relevance to economically successful countries (such as Japan or West Germany). Indeed, the evidence perhaps indicates that Modigliani and Miller's suggestion that the minimum cost of capital may be at the point of 100 % debt could conceivably be correct.

5.2 THE APPARENT COSTS OF HISTORIC CAPITAL IN SECONDARY STOCK MARKETS

The weighted average costs of capital in each of the five nations can in principle be calculated if the average interest costs of debt and the average dividends paid on historic capital issues can be assessed. In practice, it is virtually impossible to do this. First, there is a deceptive similarity between the notions of debt-bonds in many countries, but further examination reveals that these loan categories, while conceptually similar, can be very different in practice. For example, much of the long-term company debt in United Kingdom consists of debenture fixed-interest stock, redeemable at some specified future date, and secured upon the property assets of the company in question; in Japan, apparently similar loans may be found to consist of unsecured loan stock, roll-over loans or investment credit bonds, perhaps with no specified capital redemption date, but with a specified date upon which the interest rate may be altered or the loan re-negotiated. Loan stock bonds in France and West Germany can also be quite different in terms or structure from their UK counterparts, depending upon the source and type of the loan. In some respects this difference in the nature of the comparison needs to be remembered, for in comparing the costs of capital between nations it is not simply the results of different debt-equity ratios which are being compared, but the capital cost outcomes of different socio-political-economic systems.

Second, there is no method by which to calculate the relationship between share values as they are, and the initial capital issued. Yet how can the true long-term costs of capital be assessed in the absence of this data? Some sources add an arbitrary few percent to existing share yields, to show the long-run cost of satisfying shareholders' expectations of a rising stock market, but the foundation of this procedure seems doubtful, and whether 2 % or 10 % is the correct figure to add depends upon the view taken of future share yields, future inflation rates and future interest rates. And is it possible to assume, in an international context in which shareholders only provided some 15 % of the capital for the expansion of Japanese industry, that these shareholders are in some sense entitled to the profits (whether re-invested or paid as dividends)?

National stock markets are also not independent. It is difficult to know whether and to what extent different stock markets throughout the world equalise equity yields, while discounting the expectation of future exchange rate alterations. The stock markets of the countries under consideration are obviously not one perfect world market, due to limitations imposed by national governments upon market forces which otherwise could cause either flights of capital or large inflows of hot money. For example, profits made in Japan cannot at present be repatriated to any foreign investing institutions; capital inflows to the Japanese stock market therefore rest upon either the hope of a future policy of greater profits liberalisation or upon a desire to get into and to remain within the Japanese market. Additionally, governments exercise market pressures which protect their national interests, as they see them. For example, if foreign buyers were to acquire a majority interest in any strategically vital companies, governments would almost certainly act to avoid potential security risks. Quoted companies may include strategically sensitive industries such as those involved in nuclear fuel processing, armaments, aircraft, and computers or electronics; these are industries in which most national governments would not permit foreign control.

There are sometimes additional and peculiar difficulties which distort stock markets; for example, there is a law in Japan that no foreign company may control over 49% of the ordinary shares of a quoted company, since the very low equity participation (down to 5% of capital structure) could in many cases enable foreign investors to acquire vast assets at low cost through the purchasing of the shares of a quoted company. Despite all these and other factors which may seem to limit the operation of a stock market as one world market, it cannot reasonably be doubted that stock markets have interacted to some extent to flow funds towards those markets where dividend yields are higher. However, dividend yields are only part of the story; they are, in a sense, similar to interest rates for if one national currency is weak the dividend yield available in that nation would need to be proportionately higher to attract or retain international investment. As Keynes pointed out, a rise in national interest rates (perhaps brought about by economic weakness) produces capital losses on the stock market which raises yields by pricing-down capital values. These observations are more relevant to the UK than to other nations, for during the past few years relatively higher rates of UK inflation coupled with price and dividend controls and a downward floating pound have wiped millions off UK share values. North Sea oil, lower interest rates and lower inflation with a steady pound are now reversing that trend.

Share yields, as at December each year, are shown for the five nations in Table 5.4 for the period 1970–74. There are some differences between the derivations and coverage of these yields.

TABLE 5.4   Share yields in national stock markets

%; end of period	Dec. 1970	Dec. 1971	Dec. 1972	Dec. 1973	Dec. 1974
France	4.47	5.28	4.55	5.40	7.82
Japan	4.03	3.12	1.78	2.42	2.66
West Germany	4.39	3.98	3.08	3.72	4.36
UK	4.67	3.51	3.33	5.28	12.48
USA	3.46	3.10	2.70	3.70	5.43

Source: Interest Rates, 1960–74, OECD.

Note: Profits and distributed income tax rates for these five countries for 1970 to 1972 were (in percentages):

Country	1970	1971	1972
France	50.00	50.00	50.00
Japan	26.00	26.00	26.00
West Germany	15.00	15.00	15.00
UK	40.625	40.00	40.00
USA	28.50	26.00	26.00

Source: NEDO, *Finance for investment*, March 1975, appendix A2.3.

The share yields for France are weighted average rates based upon a spread of 295 securities. For each security, the ratio between the last net dividend payment and the market price on the last Friday of each month share calculated; these individual share yields are averaged for each economic sector, and combined in the proportions of the capital values of these economic sectors. The yield quoted is the gross rate before tax.

Japanese share yields are based upon the simple arithmetical average yield of all shares quoted in the First Section of the Official List of the Tokyo stock exchange. (In 1974 this included 925 issues.) The calculated rate of yield quoted in Table 5.4 is the average rate of yield recorded on all business days in the month. Yield includes stock dividends.

The West German share yield quoted in Table 5.4 is the ratio of total dividends last declared dividend by the aggregate market value of all quoted shares at the end of the period. Withholding and income taxes are not taken into account.

The UK share yield is calculated from the prices of 500 industrial shares (excluding financial and property companies). Dividend yields are calculated as totals of last year's dividends (up to those recently declared) expressed as percentages of the total market valuations of the shares included. Market valuations are taken as daily arithmetical averages of middle market prices at close of business on each working day. Up to December 1972 in Table 5.4, earnings were taken as gross profit less corporation tax, gross preference dividends and all other charges. For 1973 and 1974 earnings are also net of unrelieved advance corporation tax.

The US share yields quoted in Table 5.4 are based upon 500 common stocks (425 industrial, 25 railroad, 50 public utility) selected by Standard and Poor and representing about 90 % of the total market value of all common stocks quoted on the New York stock exchange. The monthly yield is calculated by averaging weekly yields, which are calculated each Wednesday as the ratio of the total of latest-paid dividends to total market value for the 500 common stocks.

Under the circumstances ruling previous to the oil price rise following October 1973, dividend yields on the secondary market in most nations were relatively stable. In all of the five nations, dividend yields were usually some 3–5 %. The varying national levels of corporation tax increased these rates to between 3 and 12 %, which would seem to give some indication of the cash flow cost of previous issues of equity capital. However, this figure must be treated with caution, for the yields of shares are in most cases not related to their original price. Yields have been increased by marking down poorly-performing shares, and the marking up of good performers; high interest rates in recent years have caused a considerable mark-down of share prices virtually everywhere but Japan, where an appreciating currency makes low interest rates and low share yields feasible. The most that can be said is that, prior to 1973, the after-tax costs of equity to companies do not seem to have varied widely between nations (although a difference of a few percent could certainly make a large difference to international investment trusts). If the revaluations and devaluations of currencies in recent years were used to alter Table 5.4 to give real rates of return denominated in dollars, then the UK would show negative returns, USA returns (as the benchmark) would remain unchanged, Japanese and West German share yields would go much higher, and French rates would rise. However, such a table would show secondary market returns to international investors, not the cost of capital to national companies. Altered share yields in Table 5.4 after 1973 do not generally reflect a high cost of capital to companies, but a change of market prices. Costs of issued historic capital are still usually about 3–6 % after tax to the borrowing company. (New issue capital has naturally higher rates.) More precise estimates can apparently be made by taking tax rates (see note to Table 5.4) into account, but in view of the reservations expressed above, these estimates would be very approximate and hardly worthwhile.

The sizes of these secondary stock markets are very different. The

New York stock exchange is by far the largest, and the value of all quoted equities is about five times larger than the total value of UK domestic equities. (Due to large fluctuations in share values in the UK and the USA, there is no point in quoting a more precise multiplier.)

The value of all domestic equities on the UK stock market in 1971 was about the same size as the British GDP that year. (The price index of 500 industrial ordinary shares, comparing 1971 with 1975, was nearly 20% lower while GDP had increased by nearly 90%, so the comparison is now much less favourable.) During 1971, the French and West German stock markets had total domestic equity values of less than 20% of GDP. Japan has a stock market with total domestic equities of less than 10% of its GDP. All of these relative sizes must be treated with great caution, for when share yields are shown to have changed in Table 5.4, it is generally the total market capitalisation which has altered, not the level of dividends paid.

5.3 THE SCALE OF NEW INVESTMENT CAPITAL

When a company is about to place substantial amounts of new investment capital, there are three major sources from which the new long-term capital funds can come. First, and most cheaply, the company can invest its retained profits plus depreciation funds at no future cost to company cash flow. Second, it could attempt to raise the money by making a case to its local bank, and trying to acquire additional loan stock. The future cash flow costs of doing this would be dependent upon the rate of interest and the term of the loan. Third, if it was a quoted company, it could float some stock on the market, and the cheapest way of doing this would be by a rights issue.

There are of course other sources of funds which a quoted company could choose to tap. It could issue new stock, or preference shares — although these might disadvantage existing stockholders; or it could try to generate higher internal cash flows for investment by limiting credit to purchasers and seeking credit from suppliers. The majority of investment, however, is covered by the three main sources of finance listed above.

Within the five nations, there are great differences between the profits declared by companies and their underlying financial strength. British and American companies, dependent upon stock market quotations if they intend to fund investment from equity sources in future, declare relatively high profits and pay substantial profit or corporation taxes.

French, Japanese and West German companies, on the other hand, depending more heavily on debt finance, declare lower profits, while using debt finance to generate large amounts of depreciation allowances so as to write down profits into depreciation and hence avoid corporation or profit taxes. Table 5.5 clearly shows this tendency for the 50 largest (by criterion of total sales) companies in the five nations.

TABLE 5.5 Profits as a percentage of sales (1971) for the 50 largest national companies

Country	%
France	2.1
Japan	2.3
West Germany	1.4
UK	7.6
USA	5.3

Note: The 50 largest companies did not always have details of their profits and sales quoted in the source. In some cases, therefore, the percentages quoted above relate to the largest 50 national companies for which details were available.
Source: Calculated from *The Times 1000*, 1972/3.

In recent years UK companies have become quite alive to the possibility of utilising capital debt finance for the purpose of creating additional depreciation, reducing declared profits, and hence lowering the incidence of taxation. The British Treasury have also become more aware of this kind of financial manipulation, but despite proposed legislation upon the subject, it is obviously technically improper (as well as unfair to British businessmen) to forbid by law the kind of tax avoidance which is general practice overseas. It is very difficult for anyone to say whether a recent capital loan is required for a new wave of capital expenditure, and legislation (no matter how well worded and well intentioned) upon this topic carries the risk of being likely to reduce capital investment. The only sure method whereby the UK Treasury could produce an unbiased statement of total company profits would be by reducing the rate of corporation tax to the percentage cost of borrowing, when there would be no advantage in raising debt to reduce the profit level, for it would be literally unprofitable to do so. With corporation tax at 52.5 %, however, any company which is finding itself in a better profits position than dividend payments warranted, and which did not suddenly find a need for additional loan-provided investment capital, would be failing in its duties to its shareholders, itself and the nation. There is no law which prohibits arranging company affairs so as to minimise taxation, nor should there be.

Far from acting to ensure the maximum payment of company taxes on profits by law, some governments actively assist the writing down of profits into depreciation. Perhaps the most extreme example of this kind of activity is in Japan, where special depreciation, or depreciation allowances in excess of 100% of cost, are allowed on a range of investments.

The following list shows the range of special depreciation allowances which are eligible in Japan.[7]

+ 200% of cost	— on newly acquired business building, during the first five years of use
+ 100% of cost	— on facilities for the storage of crude petroleum, during the first five years of use
+ 50% of cost	— on machinery introduced to carry out the small- and medium-sized 'Industry Improvement Programe'
+ 33⅓% of cost	— on machinery required for the commercialisation of new technological ideas
	— on machinery in 'under-developed areas' and coal-mining districts
	— on designated capital investment of small and medium-sized enterprises
	— on improved machinery, during its first year of use (certain machinery qualifies only for 10% or 25% special depreciation during its first year of use).

It is difficult to know how widely these exemptions apply to Japanese industry, but if similar allowances were widely available in the UK, it must seriously be doubted if during the last ten years, UK industry would have paid virtually any taxes on profits, except for those taxes required by the need to generate some profits for the sake of paying dividends. Certainly the above list of special depreciation allowances in Japan would lead us to expect that despite the low declared profits of Japanese companies, depreciation plus retained profits might well be a high percentage of GDP. As we will see, this is indeed the case.

Depreciation allowances are an important part of national investment policies, for if depreciation is allowed at a high rate, an investment multiplier is created. If strict depreciation practices are followed, and depreciation allowances are permitted only to equal the historic cost of capital consumed, then the net capital stock (ignoring technical improvements, although in practice one cannot) would not increase.[8] If, on the other hand; depreciation allowances permitted plant and machinery which lasted ten years to have its capital recovered in four, then by the end of the fourth year (if the original investment was profitable) internal financing would permit the purchase of a second machine; by the end of the eighth year, internal financing could provide the capital for a third machine; and so on. If the recovery of current replacement costs of existing capital is permissible, then additional claims for depreciation allowances can arise due to inflation alone. These are not theoretical effects for depreciation claims in all developed nations are higher than capital consumption. 'Business saving', in the accompanying tables is equal to retained profits plus the excess by which depreciation claims exceed capital consumption.

The cheapest source of new capital is the internally generated funds of companies, which can be invested at no future cost to cash flow. There are two major sources of these internally generated funds. First, there are business savings — profits after taxation plus capital savings, principally due to the excess permissible claims of depreciation above capital consumption, but including other sources of saving, e.g. perhaps due to an increase in suppliers' credit, if any. These business savings are quoted in Table 5.6 for four of the five nations. (The national accounts of Japan do not break down internally-generated capital into business savings and depreciation, nor is the missing information available in OECD sources. This particular comparison will have to be made without Japanese data.) The second major source of internal company funds is capital consumption, but before we turn to examine that source, some comment on Table 5.6 seems required.

Corporate and quasi-corporate saving in France has tended to increase during the 1960s, from 3–4 % of GDP to about 3½–6 %. Saving from this source in West Germany is relatively high, between 4–5 % of GDP and shows no clear tendency to decrease, although the relatively high levels of 1960 and 1961 stand out. In the United Kingdom, however, a definite pattern of declining corporate saving seems to have typified the 1960s. If we look a little closer at the breakdown between public and private sector saving of corporate enterprises, then (as Table 5.7 shows) we can see that the decline in saving is principally in the

TABLE 5.6   Saving of corporate and quasi-corporate enterprises, 1960–71

Year	France Frs bn.	% of GDP	West Germany* DM bn.	% of GDP	UK £m.	% of GDP	USA $m.	% of GDP
1960	10.84	3.65	22.44	7.42	1634	7.22	13435	2.68
1961	10.93	3.39	20.05	6.01	1119	4.95	13423	2.60
1962	10.58	2.94	17.40	4.82	945	3.74	16298	2.93
1963	11.64	2.90	15.79	4.10	1510	5.61	16155	2.75
1964	15.24	3.43	19.61	4.65	1722	5.89	20120	3.20
1965	14.29	2.96	20.84	4.50	1734	5.55	24936	3.66
1966	19.08	3.68	20.43	4.15	1179	3.56	27362	3.67
1967	19.14	3.43	17.61	3.54	1269	3.63	24124	3.06
1968	26.86	4.39	28.17	5.21	1135	3.03	20891	2.43
1969	42.29	6.03	20.30	3.35	611	1.55	15388	1.66
1970	40.15	5.13	30.39	4.42	63	0.15	10980	1.13
1971	41.88	4.80	21.35	2.80	385	0.78	15797	1.51

* Figures include non-corporate enterprises.
Source: *National Accounts of OECD Countries, 1960–71*, OECD.

TABLE 5.7   Analysis of corporate saving in the
UK, 1960–71

£m.	Private	Public
1960	1759	− 125
1961	1352	− 153
1962	1101	− 156
1963	1534	− 24
1964	1771	− 49
1965	1788	− 54
1966	1315	− 136
1967	1427	− 158
1968	1259	− 124
1969	796	− 185
1970	502	− 439
1971	977	− 592

Source: As Table 5.6.

private sector, which in 1970 saved less than a third of the financial value of savings in 1960. Once inflation is taken into account, the real purchasing power of the 1970 private sector company saving was about one-fifth of the equivalent figure in 1960. UK public corporate enterprises ran at a deficit during the entire period. In the USA corporate saving seems to have peaked in the mid-60s and fallen since then. It is interesting to note that in the period 1960–65 corporate saving, which in the UK is largely derived from profits, was generally higher on average (as a percentage of GDP) in the UK than in our other three reference nations. However, in the late 60s, corporate savings as a percentage of GDP was lower in Britain and the USA than in France, Japan or West Germany.

The major source of internal company finance is depreciation. This is different from capital consumption, as capital consumption in economic terminology refers to capital withdrawals. Table 5.8 lists the capital funds arising from capital consumption in France, West Germany, the UK and the USA. Capital consumption as a source of funds has been relatively high in West Germany ($9\frac{1}{4}$–$10\frac{1}{2}$% of GDP), lower in France (between 7% and 8% of GDP) lower still in the UK. ($5\frac{1}{2}$–7% of GDP) and lowest in the USA (5–$5\frac{3}{4}$%). The relatively high West German percentage may be due to the inclusion of the capital consumption of non-corporate enterprises.

TABLE 5.8   Capital consumption as a source of finance in corporate and quasi-corporate enterprises, 1960–71

Year	France		West Germany*		UK		USA	
	Frs bn.	% of GDP	DM bn.	% of GDP	£m.	% of GDP	$m.	% of GDP
1960	20.88	7.03	24.42	8.07	1227	5.42	24908	4.97
1961	22.90	7.10	27.80	8.34	1383	5.71	26240	5.07
1962	25.36	7.06	31.79	8.81	1493	5.90	30067	5.40
1963	28.45	7.08	35.60	9.25	1586	5.89	31750	5.41
1964	31.40	7.06	39.03	9.25	1711	5.85	33860	5.39
1965	34.41	7.12	43.79	9.47	1865	5.97	36406	5.35
1966	37.62	7.26	47.92	9.74	2037	6.15	39515	5.30
1967	41.35	7.41	50.94	10.25	2166	6.20	42960	5.44
1968	44.81	7.32	54.22	10.03	2366	6.32	46847	5.45
1969	50.96	7.27	60.43	9.98	2572	6.51	51930	5.61
1970	59.01	7.54	70.50	10.26	2897	6.66	55153	5.67
1971	66.64	7.64	80.06	10.50	3300	6.72	60267	5.75

* Figures include non-corporate enterprises.
Source: National Accounts of OECD Countries, 1960–71, OECD.

Table 5.9 gives the percentage of internal funds which were generated by capital consumption during the period 1960–71. With the exception of France, there appears to have been an increasing dependence on

TABLE 5.9   Fixed capital consumption as a percentage of internal capital funds, 1960—71

Year	France	West Germany	UK	USA
1960	65.8	52.1	42.9	65.0
1961	67.7	58.1	53.6	66.2
1962	70.6	64.6	61.2	64.9
1963	71.0	69.3	51.2	66.3
1964	67.3	67.1	49.8	62.7
1965	70.7	67.8	51.8	59.4
1966	66.4	70.1	69.1	59.1
1967	68.4	74.3	67.6	64.0
1968	62.5	65.8	67.6	69.2
1969	54.7	74.9	80.8	77.1
1970	59.5	69.9	97.9	83.4
1971	61.4	79.0	89.6	79.2

Source: Derived from Tables 5.8 and 5.10.

funds generated from this source rather than business saving. The collapse of corporate profits in the UK, and their relative reduction in the USA and West Germany seems to explain this. It appears that reducing profits may have been a general feature of a number of western nations, rather than confined to the UK (although the rate of erosion of corporate savings in the UK, which caused dependence on capital consumption to rise to nearly 100% of internal funds in 1970, is unparalleled elsewhere). The reducing rate of profits which has produced the results quoted in Tables 5.6, 5.7, and 5.8 has been noted elsewhere[9]; it may, in our opinion, be due to the profits being 'competed down' by the availability of excess capacity and low cost investment in Japan, West Germany and (to a lesser extent) in France.

Total internal financing of gross capital accumulation in corporate and quasi-corporate companies is summarised in Table 5.10. Total internal financing as a percentage of GDP increased during the 1960s in France, Japan and West Germany, sharply reduced in the UK, and stayed at about the same level relative to GDP in the USA. The lower absolute level of internal financing in the USA obviously partially explains the lower investment rates there. However, before the full significance of investment financing to growth can be appreciated, it is necessary to examine the external capital funds available to industry in the five nations.

Table 5.11 puts into perspective the total external capital funds provided to non-financial corporate and quasi-corporate enterprises

TABLE 5.10 Total internal financing of gross capital accumulation in corporate and quasi-corporate enterprises, 1960–71

Year	France		Japan		West Germany		UK		USA	
	Frs bn.	% of GDP	10^8 Yen	% of GDP	DM bn.	% of GDP	£m.	% of GDP	$m.	% of GDP
1960	31.72	10.68	NA	NA	46.86	15.48	2861	12.63	38343	7.65
1961	33.83	10.49	26479	13.82	47.85	14.35	2582	10.65	39663	7.67
1962	35.94	10.00	28773	13.54	49.19	13.63	2438	9.64	46365	8.32
1963	40.09	9.97	31986	13.03	51.39	13.36	3096	11.50	47905	8.16
1964	46.64	10.49	39746	13.70	58.19	13.78	3433	11.73	53980	8.59
1965	48.70	10.07	40753	12.71	64.63	13.97	3599	11.53	61342	9.01
1966	56.70	10.95	51189	13.86	68.35	13.89	3816	11.53	66877	8.97
1967	60.49	10.84	65857	15.08	68.55	13.80	3435	9.84	67084	8.50
1968	71.67	11.70	82377	15.92	82.39	15.24	3501	9.35	67738	7.88
1969	93.25	13.30	98040	16.38	80.73	13.33	3183	8.06	67318	7.27
1970	99.16	12.66	119573	16.87	100.89	14.69	2960	6.81	66133	6.80
1971	108.52	12.45	124324	15.66	101.41	13.30	3685	7.51	76064	7.25

Notes:
1 West German figures include non-corporate enterprises.
2 Japanese figures are the capital funds provided internally each year by industrial and commercial enterprises.
Source: For all except Japan: National Accounts of OECD countries, 1960–71.
For Japan: Monthly Statistics of Japan, Bank of Tokyo, Oct. 1971.

TABLE 5.11 Total external capital funds provided to non-financial corporate and quasi-corporate enterprises, 1970–74

Year	France		Japan		West Germany		UK		USA	
	Frs bn.	% GDP	10^8 Yen	% GDP	DM m.	% GDP	£m.	% GDP	$m.	% GDP
1970	68.442	8.74	126259	17.82	79204	11.53	2955	5.79	49434	5.08
1971	68.477	7.86	173208	21.82	92687	12.12	3412	5.99	61175	5.83
1972	83.312	8.52	200562	22.13	104107	12.47	4904	7.77	77707	6.75
1973	101.210	9.13	217694	19.61	102229	11.02	7817	9.55	94835	7.37
1974	–	–	166607	12.58	84671	8.76	7706	7.46	97750	7.05

Sources:
For European Nations: Eurostat, 1970–74
For Japan: Monthly Statistics of Japan, Bank of Tokyo
For USA: Economic Report of the President, Washington, 1975

from 1970 to 1974 in the five nations. These range from 6–10 % of GDP in the UK to 12–22 % in Japan. However, the pertinent question about this capital finance may be whether it can be used, without high business risk, for longer-term investment in fixed assets. The proportion of the finance which is available as medium- and long-term funds is therefore of some interest, and is quoted in Table 5.12. Britain and the USA do not seem to offer their companies access to sizeable medium- and long-term external finance as West Germany and Japan do. Medium- and long-term capital funds for enterprises are less than half the level (as a percentage of GDP) in Britain and the USA, than they are in West Germany and Japan. Britain in particular seems to be caught in a curious kind of capital trap when the banks advance funds to industry (as they did in 1973, at government's indirect request via the Bank of England). The time structure of the available capital alters — companies, being able to get short-term capital, may not seek long-term capital — and hence less capital is available (as a proportion of the total) as long-term finance. Table 5.13 illustrates this effect, which does not seem to have applied elsewhere during the 1970–74 period.

TABLE 5.12   Medium- and long-term capital funds provided to non-financial corporate and quasi-corporate enterprises, 1970–74

Year	France		Japan		West Germany		UK		USA	
	Frs bn.	*% GDP*	*10⁸ Yen*	*% GDP*	*DM m.*	*% GDP*	*£m.*	*% GDP*	*$m.*	*% GDP*
1970	35.343	4.51	56614	7.99	52206	7.60	1579	3.09	38733	3.98
1971	41.778	4.79	76610	9.65	68954	9.04	2475	4.35	52386	4.99
1972	48.082	4.92	75496	8.33	80485	9.64	1738	2.75	55958	4.86
1973	55.465	5.00	93923	8.46	80451	8.67	1449	1.77	51625	4.01
1974	–	–	51302	3.87	58610	6.06	2759	2.67	50610	3.65

Note: It has been assumed that equipment funds for non-financial corporate enterprises in Japan are de facto medium- and long-term funds.
Source: As previous table.

TABLE 5.13   Medium- and long-term funds as a percentage of total capital funds, 1970–74

Year	France	Japan	West Germany	UK	USA
1970	51.64	44.84	65.91	53.43	78.35
1971	61.01	44.23	73.39	72.54	85.59
1972	57.70	37.64	77.31	35.44	72.01
1973	54.80	43.14	78.70	18.54	54.43
1974	–	30.79	69.22	35.80	51.77

Source: Table 5.12 as % of Table 5.11.

Finally, we can calculate from previous tables the total medium- and long-term capital funds made available for fixed investment by corporate and quasi-corporate enterprises in these five nations. This is done in Table 5.14. It seems clear that fixed capital funds are most adequate in Japan (where economic growth has been rapid) plentiful in West Germany (where growth has been high) fairly high in France, and lowest in the economic growth laggards of the UK and the USA. However, the relative equivalence of capital funds in the UK and the USA as a proportion of GDP is misleading, for (as we have shown elsewhere) much of the corporate and quasi-corporate investment finance in the UK goes into nationalised enterprises, which have no public counterparts (in industries such as steel, telephones, railroads and airlines) in the USA.

TABLE 5.14 Total medium- and long-term finance made available (sum of internal and external funds) as % of GDP

Year	France	Japan	West Germany	UK	USA
1970	17.17	24.86	22.29	9.9	10.81
1971	17.24	25.31	22.34	11.86	10.90

Sources: Sum of Tables 5.10 and 5.12.

5.4 THE COSTS OF NEW INVESTMENT CAPITAL

Before we can calculate the costs of new external capital supplied to industry, it is necessary to examine the interest rates charged by various sources of loans to industry in the five nations. There are so many possible interest rates, and banking conditions vary so widely between the five nations, that any short examination of this subject runs the risk of being misleading. Nonetheless, an annotated table of interest rates is capable of giving a broad picture of external capital costs in the five nations, as listed in Table 5.15. This table is a guide to the interest rates which may be charged in specific cases, but does not approach a definitive survey of all cases.

Companies wishing to acquire funds for development in France have several major options. First, they could seek a short-term loan (and short-term in France is defined as between 3 and 7 years) from a bank. Line 1(a) of Table 5.15 shows to minimum and maximum interest

TABLE 5.15   Interest rates charged on loans to industry, 1970–74

as at end December	1970	1971	1972	1973	1974
France					
(a) Medium-term loans (3–7 yrs)					
Minimum rate	8.10	7.60	7.65	10.95	13.00
Maximum rate	11.60	11.10	11.15	14.45	16.50
(b) Equipment loans by the Crédit National	9.25	9.25	8.50	10.00	12.00
(c) Issue yield of private company bonds	8.84	8.78	8.19	9.66	12.05
(d) Hire-purchase of equipment					
Minimum	11.20	10.20	9.70	13.00	15.00
Maximum	15.20	14.20	14.50	17.40	19.50
Japan					
(a) Short-term business bank loans	6.25	5.50	4.50	7.25	9.25
(b) Long-term business bank loans					
(i) Non-regulated rates	8.346	8.287	7.766	8.210	9.105
(ii) Regulated rates	7.305	6.882	5.916	7.701	9.582
(iii) Most preferential rate	8.500	8.200	7.700	8.600	9.900
(c) Issue yield of industrial bonds AA	8.046	7.730	6.984	8.181	9.696
West Germany					
(a) Day-to-day loans	7.47	5.77	6.69	11.89	8.35
(b) 3-month loans	8.12	6.63	8.60	13.20	8.60
(c) Loans against securities	7.50	5.00	6.50	9.00	8.00
(d) Issue yield of industrial bonds	8.70	7.90	8.00	NA	NA
United Kingdom					
(a) Short-term loans					
Minimum rates	8.00	5.50	8.50	14.00	13.00
High rates	13.00	9.50	12.50	18.00	17.00
(b) Actuarial mortgage rates	8.98	8.44	8.98	11.71	11.71
(c) Secondary market yield of 20-year industrial bonds	10.82	9.19	10.37	13.51	19.36
United States					
(a) Short-term loans to business	8.07	6.18	6.33	10.08	11.64
(b) Long-term bank loans to business	8.31	6.44	6.67	10.68	12.16
(c) Secondary yield of corporate bonds	8.35	7.75	7.47	8.05	9.56

Sources: Interest Rates, 1960–74, OECD; *Economic Trends, March 1975*, and the 1976 Supplement, HMSO.

charges on such loans. The lower rate would be charged if the credit could be re-discounted at the Banque de France or the other credit institutions (i.e. if the proposed investment could be seen as necessary to the French National Plan). Credits which could not be so mobilised would have a higher interest rate. Secondly, the company could seek a longer-term loan, exceeding 7 years in duration, by approaching the Crédit National, which is a major specialist source of longer-term business investment funds. In 1973 the Crédit National advanced long-term loans totalling Frs 3.8bn., while by 1975 this total had grown to about Frs 7.6bn. This para-public banking institution therefore issues loan funds at the rate of about a third to half of one percent of GDP per annum. The Crédit National can advance up to 20-year loans, but most loans are actually between 7 and 15 years; interest rates charged are at line 1(b) of Table 5.15. Although the amount of any single loan is unlimited, loans above Frs 2.5m. are made only with the approval of the Commissariat du Plan, and loans below Frs 50,000 are exceptional. Other banking institutions such as the big three nationalised banks (the Banque Nationale de Paris, the Crédit Lyonnais and the Société Générale) and the Crédit Industriel et Commercial are capable of extending long-term loans from their own long-term deposits. The interest rates charged on such loans would depend largely upon the standing of the borrower, but on average these loans would not cost much more than the Crédit National rates.

Thirdly, the company could issue shares or bonds on the stock market; line 1(c) of Table 5.15 refers to the issue yield of bonds — the cost to issuing companies would be about 3 % more than this in the first year of issue, and about $\frac{1}{2}$ % higher annually thereafter. An indication of the dividend cost of new share issues can be acquired by looking at the share yields in Table 5.4; to these yields must be added the costs of flotation, which can be considerable for small issues. Finally, a French company could consider the hire purchase of equipment over a few years (generally up to 3 years) although the interest charges for doing this are relatively high.

Businessmen in Japan have an initial choice between cheap short-term bank loans (less than 1 year, but capable in most cases of being rolled-over at a new rate of interest at the end of the period) and longer-term, usually more expensive bank loans. There are three distinct rates for these longer-term loans; first, there are the low regulated rates which are provided by government institutions for long-term investments which are for the promotion and development of key industries; second, there is the 'most preferential interest rates for long-term loans' which is applied to basic industries such as shipping and electric power companies; and third, there is a free market rate for long-term industrial loans; this is quoted at line 2(b) (i) in Table 5.15 and is the average interest rate on long-term loans granted. The most typical interest rate is the most preferential interest rate which is the basic rate for long-term bank loans. Japanese companies can also issue shares or bonds to raise long-term capital. Japan has a system which categorises bond issues into four classes (AA, A, BB, and B) according to company size as defined by capital assets, net worth, dividends paid etc. Corporate bonds in the same bond classes have uniform issue terms. For companies which are the thirty Japanese giants with the best credit ratings the issue yield of corporate AA bonds was as shown in line 2(c) of Table 5.15. For the corporate bonds issued by about 150 class BB and thirty class A companies with excellent credit ratings, the costs of capital via bond issues is about 1 % higher, as line 2(d) of Table 5.15 indicates. Prior to mid-1972, industrial bonds were redeemable 7 years after issue, but this maturity period was extended to 10 years for most bonds after July 1972.

In West Germany, nearly all long-term borrowing by enterprises is based upon interest terms freely negotiated between banks and their customers. (Maximum rates were quoted prior to 31 March, 1967, but official ceilings have been abandoned since then.) Evidence about interest rates charged is collected in retrospect. Interest rates for day-to-day loans, 3-month loans and advances against securities (or Lombard loans) for up to 3 months are shown in lines 3(a), 3(b) and 3(c) respectively of Table 5.15; these rates are averages based on daily returns for December of the years quoted. Issue yields of industrial bonds are also quoted up to 1972, but since then industrial bonds have been replaced in West Germany by long-term loans against borrowers' notes (Shuldscheindarlehen). This replacement was largely brought about by a 2.5 % tax on new issues of industrial bonds, first raised in 1970. Industrial bonds used to cost about 3 % more than the issue yield for flotation, and about 3/8 % p.a. thereafter. It seems probable that industrial bonds were abandoned largely because long-term loans against borrower's notes became cheaper to the recipient company after the tax was introduced on new bond issues. This would imply that long-term bank loans are available to West German companies at the day-to-day loan rate plus less than 2 %.

In the UK, most short-term bank lending is at between 1 % to 5 % more than the base rates of the London clearing banks, and these minimum and high rates are quoted in line 4 (a) of Table 5.15. Company debentures in the UK, have tended to be issued at about the actuarial mortgage rates, which are quoted for comparison at line 4(b) of Table 5.15. The secondary market yield of 20-year industrial bonds gives an indication of the yield which a new issue might have to offer to ensure a successful flotation, although the costs of flotation (which vary considerably with the market's assessment of the risk) need to be added to this in the first year of issue. However, this secondary market yield is based upon 15 bonds, and may not reflect the expected new issue yield of industrial bonds. (Incidentally, issue yields of UK company bonds cannot be reliably calculated due to the smallness of the issues in recent years — and issue yields of all bonds is not a relevant statistic, for the majority of government stock is initially purchased by the Bank of England, and this distorts market yields.)

The cost of loans in the USA is set out in Table 5.15 lines 5(a), 5(b) and 5(c). Short-term loans to business (defined in the USA as less than a year) have the condition attached to them, in USA banking practice, that about 20 % of the loan must be kept in an interest-free account of the lending institution. There are no other charges, but the effect of this condition is to increase by a quarter the interest rates on the money actually made available; businesses ask for 25 % more money than they can use, and pay interest on the whole of the loan, while withdrawing only up to 80 % of the loan. The additional costs of raising short-term loans in the USA are effectively equal to a quarter of the interest rate. Long-term bank loans to business are available at only about $\frac{1}{2}$ % p.a. more than short-term loans. The secondary yield of corporate bonds is the market yield of the monthly unweighted average of 10 industrial, 10 public utility and 10 railroad bonds rated Aaa and Baa by Moody's Investors' Service. Yields are computed on adjusted daily closing prices. These rates can give only a very by-and-large idea of the bond yield necessary to ensure successful flotation; the gap between new issues of industrial bonds and seasoned long-term corporate bonds may be too large.

For the 1970–74 period, we can sum up the costs of medium- and long-term capital in the five nations. It must be emphasised that the following summaries are approximate, but nontheless relate to the best estimate which the authors can make upon the basis of the information available. Costs for other periods can be derived from quoted sources.

5.4.1 CAPITAL COSTS IN FRANCE

(a) Gross business internal funds, typically at about 10–11 % of GDP, can be invested by corporate and quasi-corporate enterprises at no future cost to cash flow.

(b) Medium- and long-term investment capital of about 4–5 % of GDP is available for investment by industrial and commercial companies. A fifth of this capital is share issues, costing about 8 % in the first year and 5 % p.a. thereafter; about a tenth is bonds, costing 12 % in the first year and 9 % annually afterwards; about a further quarter is long-term finance, costing say 10 % annually for loans averaging about 10 years; most of the rest is short-term loans averaging around 5 years and costing about 12 %, but 5 % of the total is a state grant costing nothing. The average repayment cost to cash flow of this capital is about 0.6 to 0.8 % of GDP in the first year falling by about 0.05 % of GDP in the second year, i.e. the effective repayment rate is about 15.5 % of funds advanced in the first year and 14.5 % of the initial loan in the second and subsequent years. A relatively low proportion of annual internal business funds is being geared up to pay for medium- and long-term capital.

(c) Short-term loans (less than 3 years) of about 3 % of GDP are also available for use by industrial or commercial companies. The average duration of these loans, which are made at about 10 % is less than a year; repayment costs in the first year therefore exceed the value of the loans made.

5.4.2 CAPITAL COSTS IN JAPAN

(a) Gross business saving, typically about 13–17 % of GDP, can be invested at no future cost to company cash flow.

(b) Long-term equipment loans totalling about 8–10 % of GDP are available from a number of sources. About 7 % of GDP is available from the banking system as roll-over equipment loans costing a little over 8 %. The rest is composed of stock and shares and industrial bonds costing about 3 % for new share issues (of 0.3 % of GDP) and about 9 % for new bond issues (of 0.7 % of GDP). Equipment loans of 8 % of GDP therefore cost an estimated 0.63 % of GDP to future company cash flows.

(c) Short-term roll-over loans of about 8 % of GDP are available for periods of up to a year at about 7 % p.a. These revolving credits need never be repaid; the annual cost of the additional money borrowed each year is about 0.56 % of GDP.

5.4.3 CAPITAL COSTS IN WEST GERMANY

(a) Gross business saving, typically at 14 % of GDP, can be invested by companies at no future cost to cash flow.

(b) Medium- and long-term bank loans were over 70 % of the new borrowings of corporate and quasi-corporate enterprises, or about 12.0 % of GDP. About two-thirds of these loans were longer-term and the remainder medium-term but the average period of these loan categories is difficult to determine. Perhaps longer-term loans may be about 10 years, while medium-term loans could mean about 5 years, but this can be only a guess. Assuming that guess, for the purpose of making a rough calculation of capital costs in 1973, when interest rates for long-term industrial loans were about 10 %, the repayment costs of medium- and long-term bank loan capital in 1973 may have been about 1.5 % of GDP. Bills, short-term bonds and shares amounted to about 0.5 % of GDP, and their cost, in total was less than 0.1 % of GDP.

(c) Short-term bank loans of about 4 % of GDP were available to West German business in 1973. Again, there is no evidence of the duration of these loans, but they were probably less than a year. They would therefore cost more, in first-year cash flow terms, than the loans made.

5.4.4 CAPITAL COSTS IN THE UK

(a) Internal funds show a declining trend; there is no typical figure. During the 1960s, between 12 and 7 % of GDP was represented by these funds, which can be invested at no future cash flow cost.

(b) External capital funds of about 2.5 % of GDP — at an interest rate of about 7.5 % p.a., or a future cash flow cost of less than 0.2 % of GDP — are available from the financial market and from government grants for industrial and commercial companies.

(c) Short-term loans of up to two years' duration, equal to about 2 % of GDP and at an interest rate of (say) 10 % are also available from banks. These would cost at best 1.14 % of GDP per annum, if they were all two-year loans.

5.4.5 CAPITAL COSTS IN THE USA

(a) Internal funds, typically about 7–9 %, can be invested at no future cost to company cash flow.

(b) External capital funds of about 2–4 % of GDP, costing about 8–

10 % p.a. or 0.3 % of GDP, are available as long-term credit from the financial market.

(c) Short-term loans of up to 7 years' duration, most of which are less than two- or three-year loans, are available at cost of about 10.0 %. If these are on average two-year loans of 2 % of GDP (from 1 % to 4 % is the range) then they will cost about 1.2 % of GDP p.a. to repay.

5.5 THE PROFITABILITY OF PLANT AND EQUIPMENT INVESTMENT

Let us begin by assuming that businessmen invest when it is profitable to do so. This is an assumption with which few economists would quarrel; but what do we mean by the term 'profitable'? We surely mean that the increased income produced by a new unit of investment will exceed the charges set against that investment.

A simplified example may help to make the point. Suppose the equipment-output ratio in an economy is 2. Then an equipment investment project of say £1m. will produce added value of £500,000, which must pay for all the increased inputs to produce that additional output. Among these inputs, the share of increased output taken by wages and salaries will be the largest; probably 60 % or so. This will leave only some £200,000 p.a. to pay for the costs associated with the capital investment, and the costs of all other inputs. If the cash flow costs of capital, or the repayment rate on borrowed capital, exceeds 20 % of the initial loan, then the investment project is non-viable in the sense that it is not self-funding. In this context, the repayment rate is more important than the interest rate charged, for a low interest rate on a short-term loan can choke off more investment projects than a higher interest rate over a longer period.

Table 5.16 shows the percentage repayment rate associated with debt for particular periods of years and for various levels of interest. The crucial point which we would like to emphasise is that the repayment rate determines whether a project is self-funding or a liability to company liquidity. At a particular interest rate, the longer the term of a loan, the lower the repayment rate and hence the more investment projects which become viable. If only short-term loans are available, then only investment projects with very high rates of return are viable. If loan funds are available for two years at 14 %, then investment projects need to earn over 60 % return on capital to fund their own cash flow repayments. In these circumstances, only the most productive invest-

TABLE 5.16   Percentage repayment rate associated with debt

Number of years of payment	Interest rate %							
	6	8	10	12	14	16	18	20
1	106.0	108.0	110.0	112.0	114.0	116.0	118.0	120.0
2	54.56	56.09	57.60	59.17	60.72	62.31	63.86	65.44
3	37.41	38.80	40.21	41.63	43.07	44.52	46.00	47.48
4	28.86	30.19	31.55	32.93	34.32	35.74	37.17	38.62
5	23.74	25.04	26.38	27.74	29.13	30.54	31.98	33.43
6	20.34	21.63	22.96	24.32	25.71	27.14	28.59	30.07
7	17.91	19.21	20.54	21.91	23.32	24.76	26.23	27.74
8	16.10	17.40	18.74	20.13	21.56	23.02	24.52	26.06
9	14.70	16.01	17.36	18.77	20.22	21.71	23.24	24.81
10	13.59	14.90	16.27	17.70	19.17	20.69	22.25	23.85
11	12.68	14.01	15.40	16.84	18.34	19.88	21.48	23.11
12	11.93	13.27	14.68	16.14	17.67	19.24	20.86	22.53
13	11.30	12.65	14.08	15.57	17.12	18.72	20.37	22.06
14	10.76	12.13	13.57	15.09	16.66	18.29	19.97	21.69

ments are viable. On the other hand, if capital loans are available for 10 years at 14 %, the repayment rate falls by two-thirds, and much more investment is stimulated. If the interest rate and the period of a loan are known, then Table 5.16 shows the rate of return an investment project has to earn to be at least self-financing.

A high level of investment in a country is often said to be due to business confidence. Is there a better definition of business confidence than an improving, or non-deteriorating, liquidity position? Self-financing investment projects, or investment projects which generate cash flow, at worst do not damage and at best improve liquidity.

Table 5.16 also demonstrates that a lengthening in the term of the loan usually reduces the repayment rates more significantly than a change in interest rate. If term loans lasting 3 years at 12 % were lengthened to 4 years, this reduces the repayment rate by about 9 % p.a. during the first 3 years (down from a repayment rate of 41.63 % for 3 years to 32.93 % for 4 years) and this new repayment rate is lower than a 3-year loan at a zero interest rate. The annual repayments of a 6-year loan at 16 % are less than the annual repayments of a 3-year loan, at 2 %. Long-term loans make it easier for corporate investors to pay, much in the same way as consumer credit makes it easier for consumers to purchase large items. With corporation tax at 52.5 %, this is equal to an effective interest rate subsidy for capital loans to profitable companies, for interest payments are a charge against pre-tax profits.

This table can be used to illustrate precisely how it would be possible for British companies to use long-term bank loans to minimise taxes on profits. Suppose a British firm expected its gross profits to be about £1m. for the next 10 years. Corporation tax would take £5.25m. of this, and only £4.75m. would flow, over ten years, into profits after tax. Yet suppose a 10-year capital loan of £5m. at 14 % could be negotiated. The repayment would cost 19.17 % of the total loan annually—or £958,500; this would produce a taxable profit of £41,500 as opposed to £1m. a year, thus reducing tax liability by over £0.5m. p.a. The whole of the annual repayment rate is eligible for deduction from pre-tax profits, for the interest on a capital loan is an allowable charge and the capital repayments are equivalent to depreciation allowances. In this example, a stream of future earnings totalling £4.75m. over ten years can be converted into a present sum of £5m., in addition to future income after profits tax of £197,125 over 10 years. In fact, profits are seldom so predictable, but depreciation can sometimes be adjusted to meet the need to cancel out abnormally high profits while losses can be carried forward to profitable years. This kind of financial operation protects profits and is allowable overseas; it would be highly profitable in Britain, and help act as an investment spur, if long-term industrial bank loans became available.

We can generalise the example given in the previous paragraph to calculate the cash flow cost, to profitable companies, of debt. If a company is profitable and these profits are high enough to cover the interest and capital repayments associated with debt, and so long as interest payments are an allowable charge against pre-tax profits while capital repayments are equivalent to the incidence of depreciation, then the annual cost of capital to profitable companies is as shown in Table 5.17.

Caution must be exercised in interpreting the figures in this table, for it is unlikely that the Inland Revenue would permit a capital investment to be depreciated over one, two, or three years, except in special circumstances. Nonetheless, the table shows the cost to profits, in cash terms, of these short-term capital loans. If a loan of £100,000 is made for 1 year at 16 %, then the fact that the capital and interest is all repaid in the first year does not affect the fact that no matter how depreciation is spread over subsequent years the total cost of this loan is £55,100 to post-tax profits, so long as the rate of corporation tax remains at 52.5 %. The after-profits repayment cost of a ten-year loan at 16 % is less than

TABLE 5.17 Percentage repayment rate associated with debt for profitable companies

Number of years of repayment	Interest rate %							
	6	8	10	12	14	16	18	20
1	50.35	51.30	52.25	53.20	54.15	55.10	56.05	57.00
2	25.92	26.64	27.36	28.11	28.84	29.60	30.33	31.08
3	17.77	18.43	19.10	19.77	20.45	21.15	21.85	22.55
4	13.71	14.34	14.99	15.64	16.30	16.98	17.66	18.34
5	11.28	11.89	12.53	13.18	13.84	14.51	15.19	15.88
6	9.66	10.27	10.91	11.55	12.21	12.89	13.58	14.28
7	8.51	9.12	9.76	10.41	11.08	11.76	12.46	13.18
8	7.65	8.27	8.90	9.56	10.24	10.93	11.65	12.38
9	6.98	7.60	8.25	8.92	9.60	10.31	11.04	11.78
10	6.46	7.08	7.73	8.41	9.11	9.83	10.57	11.33
11	6.02	6.65	7.32	8.00	8.71	9.44	10.20	10.98
12	5.67	6.30	6.97	7.67	8.39	9.14	9.91	10.70
13	5.37	6.01	6.69	7.40	8.13	8.89	9.68	10.48
14	5.11	5.76	6.45	7.17	7.91	8.69	9.49	10.30

Notes:
1 The above table shows the annual cost of debt to profitable companies, i.e. the cost to post-tax profits of debt. See text for examples.
2 The table is equal to Table 5.16 multiplied by the after-tax profits proportion $(1-t)$ where corporation tax (or t) is equal to 52.5%.

the original value of the loan, due to corporation tax. Inflation is sure to make the real repayments equal a smaller fraction of the real value of the original loan. Corporation tax therefore acts as an unwitting subsidy to capital investment, and this may not have been widely appreciated in the UK due to the lack of long-term bank loans for capital investment.

In these circumstances we find it difficult to understand why various groups have, from time to time, advocated subsidies to the interest rate for industrial investment in the UK. The difficulty is with the term of the loans available, which affects repayment cash flows dramatically, and not with the interest rate, which has much less effect. Nonetheless, various groups and individuals have advocated an interest rate subsidy to manufacturing investment, as though that was where the problem lay. The 1972 Industry Group, for example, have used some of our previous work (acknowledging this privately in a letter to one of the authors) to argue the need for lower interest rates on capital investment; indeed their submission to the Committee to Review the Functioning of Financial

Institutions (otherwise called the 'The Wilson Committee') makes this point quite strongly. In addition to missing the basic point, there are many inherent difficulties with these proposals. What, for example, would prevent the lender factoring the loan at a higher and more usual rate of interest? Would there not be a tendency for reduced-interest rate loans to finance unprofitable investments, thereby achieving more investment but a lower profitability? We find it difficult to imagine a more powerful subsidy than the rate of corporation tax, which warns the lender that if his intended investment is profitable, then the real cost of loan capital may well be negative, while unprofitable investments will be comparatively expensive.

However, let us examine the profitability of a hypothetical British industrial company in which the capital-output ratios, stock ratios and manpower requirements are equal to the average values of UK manufacturing industry as a whole. It has been calculated in Section 3.4 that the capital-output ratio for UK manufacturing industry may have been about 1.25 in 1970. This sounds relatively good; but let us calculate the profits in which this may result.

Suppose £125,000 is invested in new net investment. Then, with a capital-output ratio of 1.25, this should produce output of £100,000 p.a. Now the stocks required to service this level of output would be, including work-in-progress, fuel, raw materials and finished goods, perhaps about 40 % of the annual output. In other words, an investment of £165,000 is required in the first year—£125,000 for fixed plant and £40,000 for stocks—to produce output of £100,000 p.a. The work force would probably claim, if this was an average industrial company in 1970, some 73 % of the value of the output, or £73,000. This would leave £27,000 return on an investment of £165,000—or about 16.4 % return on capital. If the machinery lasted less than the six years taken to recover the capital, the investment would not be worthwhile. If the repayment cost of capital is above 16 % p.a., then any new investments in UK industry, if these are likely to earn only the average rate of existing investments, are not an asset to cash flow. The question could be asked; is an investment in UK industry which gives 16 % return on investment while the capital is being depreciated, and 8 % thereafter (with corporation tax at 52.5 %) really worthwhile? Would not the entrepreneur be better off by putting his money in a building society? It would certainly carry less risk over a short-term period, although in today's inflationary world an investment in real assets is sooner or later worth more than paper investments. Taxation and the large share of output taken by salaries and wages have combined to make much of

British industry only marginally profitable. If companies are not permitted to earn returns on investment which exceed the repayment rates of new capital investment, then there is no incentive to invest. This seems so obvious a principle that it should hardly need to be stated, yet no attention seems to have been paid to creating an environment in the UK which would satisfy this principle. Ideally, companies should be permitted to make tax-free annual returns on capital investment equal to at least the interest rate on government bonds; otherwise, there is no reward for risk. The earned income of companies should always exceed the unearned income available from government bonds; otherwise an invitation to shut down is being offered to the owners of industry. But this kind of concept is probably too far removed from current taxation orthodoxy to be acceptable.

The previous calculation of the rate of return in British industry began with the assumption that new investments would earn the same rate of return, and have the same capital-output ratio, as existing industrial investments. This would not be the case. Modern plant and machinery generally requires less men to work with it, and has a lower capital-output ratio, than existing fixed capital assets. This arises partly due to the improved state of technology—the embodied technological progress of new plant and machinery, which results in a lower capital cost for higher output levels—and is also partially explained by the improved labour-replacing or labour-assisting aspects of new machinery. Both of these effects improve potential returns to corporate investors, for the lowered capital-output ratio means less capital input for the same output, and the lower manpower requirement results in less output being consumed by wages and salaries. In the source used to derive Table 5.18, Japan's Economic Planning Agency have assessed the amounts of new fixed capital required to generate output of ¥100m. in 1963 and 1967. Included in the 1967 graph is a small labour-replacing investment component, but the form of presentation does not lend itself to detailed analysis. It does, however, let us see what the marginal capital-output ratios may be for a range of industries.

Table 5.18 is probably greatly affected by the economies of scale. Very large-scale investments have been made in most industries in Japan, and a lower size of operation would probably have higher capital-output ratios. Despite this reservation, the calculation of profitability on new investments with these kind of capital-output ratios is remarkable.

About £0.8m. net investment in fixed assets in industry could lead to output of £1.0m., if Japanese capital investment results could be transplanted to the UK. The amount this would tie up in stock

TABLE 5.18 Net capital-output ratios in Japanese industry, 1963 and 1967

Industry	Capital-output ratios	
	1963	1967
Manufacturing	0.82	0.80
Food	0.75	0.77
Textiles	0.81	0.75
Paper and pulp	1.34	1.22
Chemicals	1.05	0.93
Ceramics, stone and clay products	0.96	0.95
Iron and steel	1.98	1.62
Non-ferrous metals and products	1.30	1.46
General machinery	0.70	0.67
Electrical machinery	0.60	0.45
Transportation machinery	0.70	0.80

Note: This table is derived by reading numbers off a graph, and hence could be inaccurate from this source in any one figure by up to ± 0.03.
Source: *Economic Survey of Japan, 1969–70*, Economic Planning Agency, Japanese Government; Chart 15, p. 17.
Note: Table 5.18 shows the net capital-output ratio, after deducting elimination and depreciation, required to produce an additional unit of output in each Japanese industry. The original table actually shows the net capital required to produce ¥100m.; i.e. ¥82m. of net capital assets were required in 1963 in manufacturing industry to produce ¥100m., and so on.

investment would again be about 40 % at most — say, £0.4m.

If the new plant and machinery required about 60 % of the value of output to be spent on wages and salaries and other costs, then an annual profit of £0.4m. could be had from a total investment in fixed assets and stocks of £1.2m., or 33 % return on investment. If the repayment costs of capital were significantly less than this, investment would boom. In Japan, with large-scale investment funds available at less than 10 %, it would be surprising if investment in manufacturing industry were low, against that potential profit level.

The procedure used to calculate cash flow profitability in the previous examples, is set out below.

(i) Divide the new net fixed capital investment by the capital-output ratio, to calculate the annual output of the investment.
(ii) Multiply the output by the stock ratio, to calculate the required investment in raw materials, work-in-progress and stocks.
(iii) Add the stock level to the net fixed capital investment; this is equal to total investment capital tied up.

(iv) Deduct from gross annual output the costs of labour and other costs to calculate the net surplus.

(v) Divide the net surplus by total capital investment to calculate the rate of return on investment. If this exceeds the repayment cost of capital, then the investment is profitable. If it does not, then the investment is a liability to cash flow.

By following the above steps, it is possible to show that cash flow profitability =

$$\frac{1.0 - L}{C + S} - r$$

Where L = the ratio of labour and other non-capital inputs to output

C = the capital-output ratio

S = the ratio of stock to annual output

and r = the repayment rate of capital investment.

This formula highlights a number of useful generalisations. Prime among these may be the observation that a low capital-output ratio is no guide in the profitability of investment; profitability also depends on the deductions from the value of output. Generally, those industries with low capital-output ratios have high labour costs and vice-versa. Examples may help to make this point more clearly.

In the garment industry, fixed capital investment per worker is generally low. (This may not be the case in ten years' time when large plants, with pattern cutting and stitching machines become the rule, but it is the case today.) The fixed assets for most production workers consists of sewing machines and a building in which to work. The capital involved in setting-up small garment workshops is low, and manpower costs absorb most of the value of the output. Competition is relatively intense, because there is little capital at risk (much of the capital is either in purchasing or leasing part of a building) and the technology is so simple in principle that almost anyone could go into this business. But despite a low capital-output ratio, the manpower-intensive nature of the business and keen competition keeps profits low.

The petrochemical industry is at the other end of the scale. Investments per worker are very high indeed. The value of the immense platforms in the North Sea for example, is gigantic by comparison with the total salaries of the workers upon these rigs. Some petrochemical processing plants seem quite deserted; although they are always staffed, the staff is not in evidence. Low capital-output ratios in the petrochemical industry, however, do not imply low profits. Even if the capital-output ratios are lower than in manufacturing industry, the amount which is deducted from the sales revenue by the costs of labour and other costs is small compared with the value of the product. The technology is costly and complex, and requires huge investments. Established firms in the industry have an immense advantage against the newcomer, who would have neither supplies nor an appropriate distribution network nor points of sale. Competition therefore tends to become oligipolous.

All economic outputs, short of total automation (and even then, there are engineers) are the joint product of capital and labour. Most of British industry lies between the extreme manpower-intensity of the garment industry and the extreme capital-intensity of the petrochemical industry. It is technically possible, through an analysis of the manpower costs of each UK industry, to arrive at approximate estimates of the profitability of investment in individual manufacturing industries, but such a task is beyond the scope of this book.

The purpose of this section has been threefold; first, to show the rate of return a capital investment project has to earn in order to fund at least its own repayments; second, to show that the repayment cost of capital to profitable companies would be low if long-term investment credit were widely available in the UK (this is certainly not the case at present, as this chapter shows) and third, to indicate a method of assessing cash flow profitability, commenting on this method.

The circumstances which would encourage a high rate of fixed capital formation do not seem to have been created in the United Kingdom. This may not be due to a lack of profitability, on new investments, but may lie in the lack of long-term industrial investment credits.

The differences in observed investment roles in various countries may be partially explained by the assumption that investment occurs up to the point where the repayment rate for the investment equals the return on the investment. Hence in the UK, growing companies run up against liquidity problems due to the expensive repayment rates associated with short-term loans, while in Japan fewer liquidity problems arise due to the availability of long-term investment credits. Yet the problem is not purely economic or financial; part of the difference lies in the historical industrial traditions.

5.6 TWO DIFFERENT INDUSTRIAL TRADITIONS

It seems from the evidence that within the community of developed western nations there are two types of capital structure, each resulting from the historical background of the nation within which it is found.

The Anglo-Saxon capital structure seems to rest upon low debt and high equity-ratios, where most new company investment is financed from the internal sources of depreciation and retained profits, with the stock market acting as a relatively small source of new investment funds. The alternative western capitalist tradition, as operated in Japan and West Germany, has a high debt and low equity capital structure, where a major source of the new long-term company investment is bank loans (which provide new investment capital of between $9-20\%$ of the GDP) where depreciation of assets previously acquired through debt is a large source of internal investment funds, and where the stock market also provides a relatively small source of new investment funds. France seems to occupy an intermediate position between the two types of capital structure. It can hardly be doubted that the sources of industrial investment capital (as a percentage of the GDP) are more adequate in Japan, West Germany and France than they are in the USA or the UK. It is also difficult to deny the observation that those nations with high debt ratios in the capital structure of their companies have been most successful in the economic growth league tables.

The theory of optimal financing, which is sometimes used to justify the observed low debt levels in Anglo-Saxon countries, is academic in the sense that it is an interesting, unproven theory. High debt levels in the capital structures of some countries seem to have been associated with the advantage of relatively rapid economic expansion.

There are perhaps two sets of reasons why debt usage by industrial and commercial companies leads to more rapid economic growth. The first set of reasons is to do with the practical operations of industry while the second set relates to economic theory and functioning of the banking system.

As Abegglan has commented[10] in the context of Japanese industry, the high usage of debt to fund a company's operations may seem to carry higher financial risk, but, on balance the apparent disadvantage of heavy and regular interest payments may be more than cancelled out by the reduced business risk. The improvement in the level of output and the productivity of the company due to the introduction of capital machinery may more than meet the interest payments, hence improving company liquidity and providing increased growth. The introduction of machinery tends to result in higher productivity through the improved technology associated with younger machinery. High investment also leads to a great magnitude of industrial change, to the building of larger plants and optimum-size factories, hence providing increased productivity through the economies of scale.

These pragmatic reasons fail to explain why funding industry via the banking system is so much more efficient than using a stock market for the same purpose. There are several inter-related causative factors. The most powerful factor is theoretical and economic, but has extensive social and industrial ramifications. Put at its most deceptively simple, it is that the use of the banking system to finance industrial investment results in all the mechanisms of credit creation acting in favour of the investors in the community.

Consider a banker advancing a loan to an industrialist. As soon as the banker credits the industrialist's account with the loan, the sum total of the money in bank accounts increases by the amount of the loan. This increases the ability of the banker to lend to another industrialist. Nor is this observation cancelled out by the payment of the amount loaned by the industrialist to some other party; so long as the payment remains within the banking system, the general observation—that the banking system as a whole increases its ability to lend every time it places a loan—stays true. Loans create credit, which in turn creates more loans—hence if the banking system is used to advance loans to industry, a limited amount of personal savings can lead, under appropriate conditions, to a large amount of investment. Indeed, the velocity effect of loans in creating credit is so marked in Japan that one economist[11] has suggested that Japan's investment-saving equilibrium equation could be usefully considered as:

$$Is + Id = S + D$$

Where
Is = Savings-backed investment
Id = Debt-induced investment
S = Savings
D = Debt

The same author[12] has pointed out that 'operational possibility of the Shimomura model' can be approximated by a 'credit-creating Japanese economy' in which the long-term industrial investment credit supplied by the trading banks is 10 % of the GNP in excess of any savings made in the economy. However, the implications of that observation are more appropriate to a book about economics than one about investment finance.

This credit-creation effect may lie at the root of the virtuous cycle of high investments leading to more rapidly increasing income, which in turn stimulates the higher savings which provide further investments. Industry as a whole becomes more adaptable, more adept at managing the changes associated with the perpetual introduction of new and improved machinery and more socially skilled at handling the inevitable human problems associated with industrial change. Furthermore, if the investment credit supplied to industry has a low repayment cost (in cash flow terms) then high investment is less likely to damage company liquidity and investments are more likely to be self-financing. The prime danger in company expansion—the over-trading route to bank-ruptcy—could therefore be avoided by rapidly-growing companies.

Another crucial difference between providing investment funds through the banking system, as opposed to a stock market, lies in the relative efficiencies of the transformation process from short-term savings into medium- and long-term investments. If investments are funded from debt, then the initial availability of investment funds is approximately 70 % of new bank savings (excluding that 30 % or so of funds which bankers have learnt prudently to keep in short-call cash and securities to avoid a run on the bank[13]). When industrial investors are given priority over personal customers, the efficiency with which national savings in bank loans are transformed into productive plant and machinery investments can be relatively high.

On the other hand, if a stock market is used as the accredited major source of long-term external funds, the only productive money canalised to the investing community is the amount of the new issue capital. Some financial investment in previously existing shares may occur, thereby inflating paper values and providing a large secondary market for shares and bonds, but this does not assist the would-be entrepreneur or corporate investor to instal more plant and equipment. At worst, the stock market may act as a money sponge, soaking up capital which could be productive into an increase in the value of paper assets, or to permit saving to finance consumption, if a seller of shares uses the sale as a source of income. Hence the efficiency of the transformation process from savings via the stock market into the provision of long-term investment funds may be rather low. Given the natural preference for security in savings, the result is likely to be a shortage of long-term investment credit, adequate medium-term loans for working capital, and the use of the banking system for the advancement of short-term loans. Savings flowing through a banking system into productive investment is the least inflationary expenditure that can be envisaged; it is that investment expenditure which will increase productive capacity soonest; and that expenditure is therefore greatly to be preferred to the stimulation of demand via a government deficit (which is the usual Keynesian use for savings in a depression situation). Investment credits expand supply and reduce unemployment by increasing productive capacity, just as a government deficit increases demand and reduces unemployment. An increase in the level of investment credit of a country, other things being equal, would increase that country's economic growth rate by increasing the rate of capital accumulation. And the increased economic capacity, in turn, would produce generally beneficial effects on welfare; on employment, inflation, and living standards. But this is the subject of the next chapter.

6 Welfare and Economic Growth

6.1 THE INTERNATIONAL COMPARISON OF REAL INCOMES

In Chapter 2, the income levels in five nations were quoted in dollars per head, as calculated by the United Nations, for 1960 and 1970 (Table 2.3). The rates used to convert GDP per head into common currency were the prevailing dollar exchange rates[1]. There is a number of reasons why these rates do not represent the real purchasing power of the disposable incomes of households in an economy. First, the exchange rates are (at best) the market rates necessary to balance the external monetary demand and supply of a currency. Exchange rates are therefore related to the equalisation of the total values of imports with exports. A country which consumes much of what it produces, and imports a great deal while exporting too little in value terms, could have a relatively high standard of living due to the high internal consumption levels, while possessing a low exchange rate due to the weakness of its trading position (e.g. the UK). Conversely, a country with a strong trading position, such as West Germany, may sometimes have an exchange rate which is higher than justified by comparative living standards vis-à-vis other nations.

Second, as mentioned in Chapter 2, official exchange rates for developing countries may not reflect market rates. Black markets in local currencies may no longer exist in Hong Kong, Japan or in the oil-rich states of the Middle East, but it is difficult to visit some of the developing countries of Asia or Africa without noticing the currency black market. The rates quoted by Swiss banks for the redemption of the unused non-convertible currencies of developing countries may be a better guide to market rates than the official exchange rate. However, this kind of factor does not affect the convertible currencies of the five nations which are our chosen area of comparison.

Third, exchange rates are sometimes subject to sudden devaluations or revaluations. The appreciating currencies of Japan and West Germany and the depreciating currency of the UK do not have a pro rata effect on living standards within these countries. The real purchasing power of household incomes based on all household purchases in the economy is generally more stable than the exchange rate, which affects only import and export prices.

Economists have been aware of the deficiencies of using exchange rates to convert national incomes into common currency for over two decades. It would be premature to say that the problem of international comparisons of real incomes has been wholly solved, but there has been some progress in developing a suitable methodology for calculating indices of real living standards, together with a supporting logical rationale.

One approach, used by Gilbert and Associates,[2] was to measure for a number of countries the quantity of national products in their components, partly by deflating expenditure on national income components by relative prices adjusted for quality comparisons, and partly by measuring quantities of national product directly, where this data was available. These different production profiles of the quantity of output for different countries can then be aggregated to comparable financial totals by using the prices of one country, if a one-to-each comparison of the real purchasing power of total income of that country with every other in turn is desired. Alternatively a system of weighted price levels (derived from national values and output) can be derived in order to arrive at some reasonable basis for making each-with-each comparisons. In order to place these levels of real national product at comparable prices on a common basis, the data must be deflated by the population numbers of each country to arrive at real national income per head.

Dr W. Beckerman reviewed the studies of the real purchasing power of national incomes up to 1966 and suggested a new and interesting method of estimating real incomes.[3] He proposed that the relative level of real per capita private consumption could be estimated fairly reliably by establishing the relationship (in the form of a multiple regression equation) between the total real per capita private consumption and some of its most correlated components. However, although this method seemed promising, the standard errors associated with the predictive equations were relatively large, and implied the possibility of a substantial error in the prediction of real per capita private consumption in any individual case. In one of the tables quoted, therefore, Beckerman quoted the extrapolated Gilbert and Associates figures for

European countries: Table 6.1 shows part of that table.

These results indicated that the official exchange rates were not a good indicator of real private consumption. An exchange rate comparison would lead one to presume that living standards in the UK were about half of USA levels, while the reality may be that UK private consumption in 1960 was about 60 % of USA levels. Exchange rates for 1960 could also lead to a serious under-estimate of real private consumption in Japan and West Germany and, to a lesser extent, in France.

TABLE 6.1 Predicted indices of real private consumption per head, 1960

Country	Index	Index at official exchange rates
France[2]	54.3	47.4
Japan[3]	28.7	12.6
West Germany[2]	56.1	41.2
UK[2]	61.7	49.9
USA[1]	100.0	100.0

Notes:
1 USA in 1960 = 100
2 Based on Milton Gilbert and Associates data extrapolated to 1960
3 From modified non-monetary indicator method
Source: Wilfred Beckerman, *op. cit.*, extract from Table 5, p. 36.

Table 6.1 also implies that Japan's exchange rate in 1960 may have been considerably undervalued. An undervaluation of Japan's currency may have led to a strong trading position due to the cheapness of exports, and may therefore have understated real living standards and the real relative size of Japan's economy, although in the long run pressures are likely to be generated, forcing the value of yen upwards. Similar arguments apply to West Germany, although the UK case may be more complex. Considerable undervaluation of the pound may not lead to a balance of trade surplus if there is inadequate industrial capacity to supply total domestic and foreign demand; the result may be more inflation with relatively lower growth, due to lack of capacity in the UK during the 1960s.

If it is assumed that real private consumption rises at the same rate as

GDP growth, we can extrapolate the indices of real private consumption in 1960 to 1970. This is done in Table 6.2. Real private consumption indices for 1960 were increased by the 1960 to 1970 GDP real growth rates, then deflated by USA growth from 1960 to 1970 to derive the index in Table 6.2 column 1. Reference to Appendixes A6, A8, A10, A13 and A15 will show that this procedure is fair for comparisons between France, West Germany and the USA in 1970, albeit 1970 Japanese and British real private consumption levels could be understated by 17 % and 5 % respectively.

TABLE 6.2   Calculated indices of real private consumption per head, 1970

Country	1 Calculated index of real private consumption	2 Index at official exchange rates (see note 1)
France	65.5	59.4
Japan	55.9	39.3
West Germany	61.8	54.5
UK	57.9	45.1
USA	100.0	100.0

Notes:
1 All indices in this table are comparisons against USA = 100.
2 Indices of per capita product at constant prices in 1960, used in the derivation of column 1 above: France, 63; Japan 39; West Germany 69; UK 81; and USA 76 (all compared with 1970 = 100).
Source: Data for index of per capita product of constant prices; Table 180, *UN Statistical Yearbook, 1974*. Index of real private consumption calculated as explained in text. Ultimate source of index of official exchange rates; Table 188 of *UN Statistical Yearbook, 1974*.

The major difference between these tables of real per capita consumption in 1960 and 1970 is that Japan, previously at about half the European standard of living, has attained European levels of real private consumption. The fastest-growing West European country in this group in the 1960s—France—has approached a living standard of some two-thirds of that of the USA. The three EEC nations quoted here are however within a fairly narrow band — from 57.9 to 65.6 — of the standard of living in the USA.

A comparison of 1960 with 1970 reveals the following.

(i) France gained ground against USA living standards, but the difference between the index of real living standards and the exchange rate remained approximately constant, with the exchange rate indicating a consumption level some 6 % of USA private consumption below the index of real private consumption.

(ii) Japan improved its real private consumption level tremendously, and its exchange rate became more realistic, although of the four nations compared with the USA, the difference between the real private consumption level and that implied by Japan's exchange rate was greatest.

(iii) West Germany's exchange rate is the only one which in 1970 implied a higher level of private consumption than actual.

(iv) UK living standards, due to low growth relative to those of the USA, lost ground by that touchstone, but the understatement of UK living standards using the exchange rates appears to have been reasonably constant, on the basis of this limited evidence. More recent evidence indicates that the market exchange rate between the pound, compared with consumer purchasing power parities, is such that in October 1975, relative prices in Bonn and Paris were 129 and 131 respectively (compared with a standard of 100 in London).[4] Incomes net of tax would therefore have to be about 30 % higher in Bonn or Paris to purchase a basket of goods equivalent to one brought in London. However, comparisons based upon prices in some EEC capitals are not necessarily a good guide to the consumer purchasing power in the whole economy, so too much should not be made of these statistics.

The low level of UK private consumption implied by the conversion of GDP in common currency using the exchange rate value of the pound sterling does not reflect the reality; British households, in terms of real private consumption and the associated welfare values, are better off than they seem. The UK, however, cannot exploit the price advantage of the lower exchange rate as Japan does, principally due to low productive capacity in the UK. The British therefore do not primarily have a living-standards problem; they have a trading problem, which in turn affects living standards. The trading problem can be solved only by higher industrial capacity; this requires more investment. In turn, higher rates

of investment require more surplus saving than seems to be available in
the UK at present.

6.2 FACTORS AFFECTING THE LEVEL OF HOUSEHOLD SAVING

The savings of households are the major source of uncommitted saving
in all the five nations. As such, this saving (if transformed in time-span
by a new banking system) may be the principal source of external new
investment capital for industry, as we have shown at some length in
Chapter 4. The factors which may determine the level of these personal
savings are therefore of interest, especially if the adjustment of these
factors could produce a higher level of saving.

The gross saving of households for the period 1965–70 is shown in
Table 6.3. Although this saving refers to households, the figures include,
in every case, the saving of small unincorporated business, and the
saving of private non-profit institutions serving households. It is
generally impractical to separate out, even on a theoretical basis, the
income arising from a business partnership from the income of the
partners. With small businesses, the separation of an individual's

TABLE 6.3   Gross saving by households, 1965–70

Saving by households	1965	1966	1967	1968	1969	1970
France Frs bn.	37.31	40.31	45.70	48.31	50.61	70.22
Japan ¥bn.	3792.7	4546.3	5803.6	6961.5	7959.6	–
West Germany DM bn.	35.76	35.04	35.31	41.09	47.74	53.58
UK £m.	2229	2444	2370	2561	3122	3289
USA $m.	28432	32527	44369	43887	42875	59661
As % of GDP						
France	7.81	7.77	8.18	7.92	7.25	8.97
Japan	10.27	12.31	13.29	13.45	13.30	–
West Germany	7.74	7.12	7.11	7.60	7.88	7.80
UK	6.28	6.47	5.94	5.94	6.77	6.49
USA	4.14	4.32	5.58	5.06	4.59	6.08

Sources: For France, West Germany, USA: *National Accounts of OECD
Countries 1960–71*, OECD, Table 10.
For Japan: *Economic Statistics Annual 1970*, Statistics Department, Bank of
Japan, Mar. 1971.
For the UK: *Economic Trends, Annual Supplement 1976*, Table 20. GDP data
from Appendix A 28.

income from that of the business he/she owns is also an impossible line to draw. Hence the inclusion of estimated non-corporate business saving with that of households. By 'gross personal saving' is meant the net increase in fixed resources (such as dwellings and non-corporate business assets) plus the gross increase in financial assets. American figures for gross household saving also include net investments in consumer durables, which other national accounts generally treat as a consumption item.

The highest rate of saving by households is in Japan, averaging about $12\frac{1}{2}\%$ of GDP for the 1965–69 period. French households, saving about 8% of GDP, rank second in this table but are well below comparable Japanese household saving. West German household savings seem remarkably stable, at between 7 and 8% of GDP. The households of the UK and USA saved least.

However, while these personal saving rates are interesting, they do not show either the funds supplied by households to the credit markets nor the funds taken by households from those markets. A table of the financial transactions of households is required for that purpose.

Table 6.4 shows the funds supplied to, and taken from, the aggregate financial institutions by the households of the five countries. The net surplus of the saving of households to the financial system is also calculated. Table 6.5 puts these flows of funds into perspective as percentages of GDP.

Japanese households stand out as relatively high savers, providing an average of 10.6% of GDP, during the 1970–72 period, to financial markets. These same households borrowed, on average, only 0.87% of GDP during the same period, with the result that almost 10% of GDP was provided by the surplus saving of households to Japanese financial markets. During the 1970–72 period, about 62% of these surplus savings were canalised to corporate businesses, 20% to foreign investment and the residual 18% went to the Japanese government, public corporations and local authorities.[5] The build-up of high levels of foreign investment is a recent phenomenon designed partially to offset Japan's embarrassingly large trade surplus; in 1968, for example, there was only ¥377bn. of foreign investment —equivalent to about 8% of surplus household saving in that year, much lower than the 20% of the 1970–72 period. Since Japanese foreign investment is done largely by the business sector, Japanese households are indirectly providing about 8% of GDP to industry and commerce. This system of priorities, of putting economic growth first, has had its consequences in terms of a poorer social infrastructure. Japan in 1970 may have had a real private

TABLE 6.4   Gross financial saving and net borrowing by households, 1970–73

	1970	1971	1972	1973
France—Frs m.				
(i) Gross household saving	52170	74509	92670	87174
(ii) Household borrowing	26601	36660	60779	55086
(iii) Net household saving	25569	37849	31891	32088
Japan— ¥bn.				
(i) Total personal saving	6147	8052	11858	–
(ii) Consumer borrowing	398	523	1272	–
(iii) Surplus of personal sector	5749	7529	10586	–
West Germany—DM m.				
(i) Total household saving	55147	63324	76061	73079
(ii) Household borrowing	3367	5844	8251	3889
(iii) Net household saving	51780	57480	67810	69190
UK— £m.				
(i) Total household saving	3139	4653	6246	8032
(ii) Household borrowing	1405	2677	5050	4363
(iii) Net household saving	1734	1976	1196	3669
USA — $bn.				
(i) Total household saving	80.6	99.7	124.4	138.2
(ii) Household borrowing	32.2	57.3	85.8	87.6
(iii) Net household saving	48.4	42.4	38.6	50.6

Sources: For France, West Germany, UK: *Eurostat National Accounts*, from portions reproduced at appendices A17–A27, plus tables 4.1, 4.19 and 4.25.
For Japan: *Monthly Economic Statistics*, Bank of Japan.
For USA: *Economic Report of the President*, Washington, 1975, Table C–21 (also partly reproduced in Table 4.43).

consumption level similar to that of the UK or West Germany, but the housing quality was apparently well below European levels, which Table 6.6 illustrates. As the Japanese Economic Planning Agency remarked on this table:

Japan's per capita stock of social overhead capital is only about half as compared with West Germany and Britain. Especially with respect to housing, Japan's level is only about 40 % with respect to the two countries.[6]

In West Germany, household savings are also relatively high, and as in Japan, they are not canalised back to household borrowings to any great extent. During the 1970–73 period, Table 6.5 shows that West German households received, as housing loans and consumer credit,

TABLE 6.5 Gross financial saving and net borrowing of
households as % of GDP, 1970–73

Country	1970	1971	1972	1973
France				
(i) Saving	6.66	8.54	9.45	7.68
(ii) Borrowing	3.40	4.20	6.19	4.85
(iii) Net Saving	3.26	4.34	3.25	2.83
Japan				
(i) Saving	8.67	10.14	13.08	—
(ii) Borrowing	0.56	0.66	1.40	—
(iii) Net saving	8.11	9.49	11.68	—
West Germany				
(i) Saving	8.03	8.30	9.11	7.87
(ii) Borrowing	0.49	0.77	0.99	0.42
(iii) Net saving	7.54	7.53	8.12	7.45
UK				
(i) Saving	6.19	8.22	9.95	11.19
(ii) Borrowing	2.77	4.73	8.05	6.08
(iii) Net saving	3.42	3.49	1.90	5.11
USA				
(i) Saving	8.21	9.40	10.65	10.61
(ii) Borrowing	3.28	5.40	7.34	6.73
(iii) Net Saving	4.93	4.00	3.30	3.89

Source: Table 6.4 converted to percentages of GDPs.

TABLE 6.6 International comparison of tentatively-calculated housing stock,
1968

$bn, 1968 prices	Japan	West Germany	UK	USA
Fixed assets	237	300	252	1886
Machinery & equipment	125	158	131	774
Social capital	111	141	120	1111
(of which, housing)	61	90	82	743
Per capita; in $100				
Social capital	11.1	24.3	21.8	55.3
Housing	6.1	15.5	15.0	36.9

Source: *Economic Survey of Japan, 1969/70*, Economic Planning Agency,
Japanese Government, Table 79, p. 73.

only about 0.67% of GDP — or about 8% of their savings of 8.33% of
GDP. Thus 7.67% of GDP was available as the surplus saving of
households, to be borrowed by other economic sectors.

Perhaps one basic difference which distinguishes Japan and West Germany from the other three nations is the smaller scale of consumer credit and housing mortgage banks (or building societies) in these two countries. Much of the saving in Japan is for house purchase; it is easier to acquire a mortgage in West Germany, but about one-third of the cost of the house must first be saved. An absence or restriction of credit for house purchase forces higher savings. This stands in contrast to the UK and the USA, where 90 % mortgages are available to individuals.

In France, as Table 6.5 indicates, household saving during 1970–73 was at about 8.0 % of GDP, but about 58 % of this was returned to the household sector as credit, largely for housing.

In the UK and the USA, household saving during the 1970–73 period as a percentage of GDP (at 8.88 % and 9.72 % of their respective GDPs) were on average higher than in France and West Germany. However, the percentages of household saving re-loaned to households through the financial system — at 60.8 % in the UK and 58.5 % in the USA during the 1970–73 period — meant that (as in France) there was relatively less surplus saving by households.

If the surplus saving of households is to be increased, three kinds of measures seem theoretically possible. First, incentives could increase the gross financial saving of households. Second, legal measures could be taken by governments to limit the extent to which households tap the financial system for credit. Third, some (if not most) actions by government could simultaneously increase saving by limiting credit to households. The discussion of this subject can be curtailed if the reasons for the very high personal saving ratio in Japan are discussed in contrast to the very low UK rate, for these two national extremes indicate the range of possible factors affecting a relatively high or low surplus of household saving.

It has elsewhere been argued that, in the UK, when hire purchase and consumer credit is restricted by government action, savings increase, and vice-versa.[7] The comparatively high level of personal savings in Japan — exceeding 20 % of disposable income in recent years — is obviously partially explained by the need for the Japanese to save prior to the purchase of a large consumer item, as consumer credit is virtually non-existent in Japan.[8] This suggests that the household savings can be increased by regulations concerning the availability of hire purchase debt to consumers. However, this could well be electorally unpopular.

A recent OECD report on Japan[9] has suggested that one of the contributing reasons for the high level of personal savings in Japan is the tendency of Japanese employers to award part of wages in the form of periodic overtime payments and six-monthly bonuses. Overtime and bonuses are also paid in the UK, but they are not generally paid in the same way as they are in Japan, which has a higher proportion of lump-sum payments for overtime and bonuses at the end of quarterly or six-monthly periods. These irregular cash earnings (which have reached 25 % of total pay in recent years) seem to be regarded by employees as a windfall and are much more likely to be saved than regular income. The graph in the OECD report shows what may be a reasonable correlation between changes in total bonus payments and personal savings.

The same report has also said that the principal reason for the high personal savings ratio in Japan is the inadequate Japanese social security system. That statement, however, seems in partial contradiction to the high security produced by Japanese life-time employment procedures; social security in Japan may be less, but company security is generally higher. Some Japanese saving is probably for old age, and it seems that UK benefits in that case are higher than those available in Japan. Obviously the highly developed UK social security system may be one reason why UK personal saving is lower than in Japan, yet since the level of UK benefits is now generally below those available in the majority of other EEC nations, this can provide only a partial explanation of why UK savings are low. On the other hand, in recent years in the UK household financial savings have increased sharply and this may be partially related to uncertainties about employment.

The personal saving ratio in both the UK and Japan has also increased in recent years because of the world-wide phenomenon of higher inflation. It seems to be now fairly firmly established that for many nations an increase in the rate of inflation results in a higher level of personal saving.

While it could not be argued that any UK government either could or should consciously accept a policy of increasing inflation, or reducing the level of social security in order to increase the personal saving ratio, it does seem that higher surplus household saving could be created in the UK by limiting consumer credit and adopting an incomes policy which at least partially involved six-monthly bonuses rather than percentage increases.

Another method of increasing both the saving level, and the stability of savings made, is through the banks' structuring of interest rates for time deposits. Table 6.7 shows the Japanese interest rate structure, which offers considerably higher rates for one-year term savings than for ordinary deposits. Still higher rates are available for long-term savings, through loan trusts. These term savings have considerable

TABLE 6.7   Interest rate structure in Japan

In annual percent-ages	Official discount rate	Prime rate (all banks)	Contract interest rate (all banks)	Deposit rates of all banks		Yields of loan trusts	
				ordinary	1-yr term	2-year	5-year
1971	4.75	5.50	7.593	2.25	5.75	6.45	7.27
1972	4.25	4.50	7.045	2.00	5.25	5.95	6.82
1973	9.00	7.25	7.186	2.50	6.25	7.70	8.52
1974	9.00	9.25	9.113	3.00	7.75	8.20	9.02
1975	6.50	6.75	9.099	2.50	6.75	7.20	8.32

Source: *Monthly statistics of Japan, December 1976*, Bureau of Statistics, Office of the Prime Minister.

advantages; they increase the stability of the deposits in the banking system by ensuring that a 'leading indicator' is available to banks about the minimum level of their time deposits over the next year — and this assists the transformation of saving to investment by reducing the risk of sudden withdrawals. Banking instability is reduced, as sudden changes in interest rates (between building societies and banks, for example) do not produce such large swings of saving from one institution to another. Term savings have little disadvantage to savers, because if the money is required in a hurry, a one-year bridging loan can be provided wich will discount the term saving into ready cash, all the while creating credit and an additional transaction for the bank. On the other hand, sudden withdrawals have a financial penalty, and hence this will be done only in emergencies; term savings encourage financial planning by households. Term savings and such an interest rate structure can also assist to provide a better basis to make saving more readily available for longer-term investment. Rapid economic growth obviously assists a high rate of saving, and this factor is probably relevant to household saving ratios everywhere.

Some of the financial assets of households are represented by investment trusts, pension funds and securities. Investment trusts are not a large feature of the Japanese financial scene. They are large-scale phenomena in the UK and the USA. The major function served by investment trusts (mutual funds in the USA) is financial investment. Investment trusts should ideally provide a source of some new funds for investment. Pension funds in the UK are in a largely similar position; part of the savings of both institutions should if possible be canalised to investment, partly through the purchase of guaranteed long-term bank bonds, to new productive capital formation. The primary financial activity of investment trusts and pension funds is to purchase pre-existing bonds and stocks on the secondary market, but this does not preclude them from buying new long-term bank bonds and other new issues.

The rise of the building societies in the UK has also utilised household saving for house building. No similar sizeable industrial credit banks exist in the UK, and these are a necessary innovation. The living standards of households and the employment of individuals depend upon a balanced use of the surplus saving of households.

6.3 INFLATION, ECONOMIC GROWTH AND LIVING STANDARDS

The economic sector which makes the greatest gains from high economic growth rates are households, which generally receive over 60 % of the national income and whose expenditure share of economic output varies, in the five countries, from about 50 % for early-70s in Japan to nearly 65 % in the USA of 1975. (See statistical appendices A6, A8, A10, A13 and A15 for annual percentages of national income taken up by consumer or household expenditures.) Living standards of households are therefore the prime reason and justification for governments wishing to increase their economic growth rates. However, attempts to increase economic growth through increasing the pressure of demand are likely to result in some inflation which will erode the living standards of part of the population. This brings us to the question: is there a trade-off between inflation and economic growth? Is there a tolerable level of inflation, or is inflation the unmitigated economic evil it is generally assumed to be by politicians?

Inflation has sometimes been talked about, in the political arena, as if it were one of the worst afflictions of the British economy. There is certainly some justification for this, for inflation re-distributes national income in predictable, but electorally unpopular, ways. Yet, in 1967 Micheal Stewart, writing about Keynes's effect on economic theory in general and British economic experience in particular, was able to observe that it was difficult to take seriously the suggestion that rising prices could be as great a domestic social and economic problem as mass unemployment.[10] (Internationally, as he went on to observe, things were different, as inflation could erode our ability to pay our way in the world—barring devaluation.) It is however an accurate observation that Japan, had, between 1950 and 1970, a much higher rate of inflation than Britain, and economic growth in Japan more than compensated for that higher inflation rate. This suggests that if it is desirable rapidly to increase living standards with full employment, some inflation may be unavoidable. There may be a trade-off between the rate of economic growth and the rate of inflation. Let us consider what the nature of that trade-off might be, by examining the gains and losses to a hypothetical statistically average individual in the economy.

The households of an economy have two types of assets. First, they possess fixed assets—a stock of housing, and other consumer capital such as furniture, cars, TV and radio sets, and so on; and second, they have certain monetary assets and liabilities—perhaps principally a flow of income, a stock of saving and debts largely given by the sum of hire-purchase liabilities and mortgages. The general effect of inflation is to increase the replacement price of existing household assets and to increase present incomes while decreasing the purchasing power of past savings and the burden of debt. So long as the real purchasing power of household incomes has risen, the inflationary rise in the price of existing household assets may not seem to matter. Yet if present income were to be infinitely preferred to the price of acquired assets and the value of past savings, this would set no limit to the rate of inflation. This is clearly illogical, as high inflation is a major cause of economic instability. It may be preferable to examine how inflation affects the total potential purchasing power of households, not only the income constituent of that purchasing power.

The potential purchasing power of households is equal to their savings plus their earnings. (By 'savings' is meant the net financial assets of households.) Inflation alters this potential savings-plus-earnings purchasing power, for the value of goods and services which savings can purchase is eroded if the inflation rate exceeds the average interest rate given on savings. It is possible to calculate how high the inflation rate may rise before the real gains in the purchasing power of earnings are cancelled out by the loss of purchasing power in savings.[11] Of course, this calculation will not refer to the position of any individual within the economy but only to the statistically average individual.

Inflation for its own sake is quite insupportable, but some inflation for the sake of promoting a rapid build-up of capital equipment in private industry and consequently better employment prospects in the UK, may be a necessary evil. It seems that a 2–3 % increase in capital machinery in private industry, if funded in the worst possible way, by printing money, could produce 2–3 % more inflation initially, and perhaps 2–3 % more inflation due to multiplier effects in the second year. This may be tolerable in exchange for a rise in real income of 1 to 1.5 %. Looked at in this light, some inflation may sometimes be the price for higher economic growth. That kind of inflation can be regarded literally as an investment — a temporary erosion of purchasing power in return for a higher real income in all future years. In the long run, the standard of living in a country is more important than its price level, relative to some earlier period. The exchange rate can, and will, find its own level, distort it how governments may, for intolerable pressures are generated in the form of vast flows of finance if the rate is artificially set too high or low. It is the level of real private consumption per capita which truly matters in the longer run.

The essential links between inflation and investment are the multiplier, which may be about 2 for the UK economy,[12] and the capital-output ratio. As savings are presently spent in the UK, with perhaps only a third of total saving canalised to productive investment, it is difficult to advocate, with a capital-output ratio of 7, that 14 % more inflation is worth 1 % more growth. The very low rate of return on investment in public corporations and the zero rate of return (in terms of marketable output) of public expenditure is currently reducing the overall capital-output ratio for the UK to a very low level. But if the situation changed so that private investment could be stimulated in the UK by the provision of long-term investment credit, and if as a result 2–3 % more inflation during two consecutive years produced 1–1½ % higher real consumption in all subsequent years, it seems possible that, under certain circumstances, this could be worthwhile.

Yet the situation described in the previous sentence represents the connection between inflation and growth in one set of its worst aspects, for inflation need not be a necessary concomitant of economic growth at all. If the public sector borrowing deficit were reduced, and if the funds thus freed were canalised to cheap, long-term investment credit for British industry, then total economic demand would be no higher in consequence while productive capacity could grow apace.

In this section, some of the effects of inflation, and its possible relationship to economic growth in some circumstances, have been briefly discussed; but the many causes and theories of inflation, whether cost-push, demand-pull, cost-plus, or due to the money supply or perhaps the bargaining power of trade unions, are too large a topic for this book.

6.4 INVESTMENT AND EMPLOYMENT

It is a well-understood paradox of economic affairs that policies which intend one result can have the opposite effect. Interference with some market forces can be done only at considerable risk. Hence, if prices are fixed too low, shortages follow, and rationing or black markets may result; if fixed too high, there are surpluses, which the state is obliged to purchase. It seems possible that the attempt of the British government to keep employment high during the post-war period has led to increasing unemployment levels in the UK. The reasons for this are relatively complex, and well-rooted in the official UK economic philosophy.

The British government tries for the most part to manipulate the UK economy through the management of demand. Other developed Western nations (excepting the USA) have arranged matters so that the private investment level can be stimulated when necessary, by increasing investment credits to the economy. There are a number of implications in this difference in economic philosophy. The discussion of this topic can be curtailed if we consider the contrast between the two extremes of British economic philosophy and that of Japan.

When the Japanese economy goes into a depression, the high continuing level of new plant and machinery investment results in unemployed people or spare resources being absorbed by the capital-goods sector of the economy; the result is that after virtually every cyclical economic boom, there is an inbuilt tendency for the rate of investment to increase and the productive basis of the economy becomes stronger.[13] In the UK, on the other hand, every depression tends to result in the deliberate creation by government of jobs in service industries, where productivity gains are usually harder to make due to the fixed high manpower inputs; hence the UK comes out of a depression with a larger services sector and with its growth poential impaired. The Japanese economy grows out of a depression through government-assisted investment booms, stimulating the expansion of industrial supply prior to the subsequent consumer demand, and this process leads to high growth with some inflation; the British economy comes out of a depression through government-assisted consumer booms, stimulating the expansion of consumer credit and higher demand, and this process leads to persistently higher inflation with some growth.

In Japan, economic booms tend to lead to real growth as high stock levels, high productive capacity and keen competition keeps prices down. In the UK economic booms rapidly run up against the productive ceiling of the economy, price inflation results, imports get sucked in, and the value of the pound may fall.

The Japanese diversion of savings to private productive investment results in a kind of investment race between firms, where a premium is put on competent and realistic management, co-operative unions, and the fast growth of the company, for the gains from new investment and rapid growth of output are very high. The British use of savings for short-term consumer and industrial finance and government expenditure results for the most part in a more service-oriented society, where output is more nearly fixed or very inelastic, and one man's loss is more obviously another's gain. The Japanese system is, in the longer run, a flexible wealth-creating system, while the British one tends to be more wealth-sharing.

In Japan, public and government savings really do finance investment, and as the economy grows, increases in saving leads to a virtuous cycle of increased investment, increased employment and higher growth. All the mechanisms of credit creation in Japanese banks act in favour of providing funds to the industrial investor. In the UK, the growth rate is dependent on the attitude of government to capital and to profits; price controls can reduce profit levels and therefore lower the ability of the economy to grow. Capital transfer tax, requiring to be paid out of taxed income, in many cases is likely to destroy within years the capital accumulations of generations; higher private savings are not canalised into growth, but into short-term consumer, business and government consumption, and to some extent, into paper assets on the stock market. Credit creation in the UK banking system acts in favour of short-term consumption. It is difficult to escape the conclusion that in the UK those price controls which are the cost of union co-operation in wage restraint, have led during the last few years to a vicious circle of UK decline, which the inadequacy of the saving-to-investment transformation process has not ameliorated.

Investment credit within a nation acts directly to increase capacity; consumer demand affects capacity only indirectly, and there is no guarantee that consumer demand will increase the nation's industrial capacity — it could equally well increase the imports from another nation. Indeed, in the UK this seems to be the usual result.

The Japanese investment-funding technique and economic philosophy — involving growing the economy through investment credit booms, financed if necessary through a deficit — seems much more effective than the British practice of trying to grow the economy through a recovery of consumer demand.

Both techniques create employment, but in Britain the employment is created almost directly and this has been the major aim of government policy; while in Japan the employment is created indirectly, through increasing productive investment which needs to be manned.

There are hopeful signs, however, that British governments will not continue to divert saving from the industrial sector, where it can provide output and jobs, to the creation of additional demand. Nevertheless there is a risk that savings will simply lie unutilised unless these funds are converted to cheap, long-term investment credit for final industrial users — and what is the point of the public sector reducing its borrowing requirement if industry is not to be given access to the funds freed? The use of saving to create additional employment, as Keynes suggested, is of course laudable. But is it not preferable to permit industry to create productive employment, rather than have government introduce work experience programmes, additional public works, and employment subsidies? To build pyramids in the UK would doubtless increase employment and demand, but there is not a large consumer market for pyramids. It seems to us that the UK government might be better advised to create the correct conditions for rapid economic industrial development rather than assist the development of non-productive employment.

It is an ironical reflection that the British government, by putting public welfare and high employment first, has swallowed up rising amounts of capital and created a slowly rising standard of living and rapidly rising unemployment; while the government of Japan has created a rapidly-rising standard of living and public welfare.

So much for the difference in economic philosophy; what difference is there in the consequences of public and private investment in the UK? Additional investment has three effects which are important for the economic welfare of a nation. First, investment acts as an immediate stimulant to the employment level. While new investment is taking place, more people are employed, but this is a two-edged sword; investment plans and out-turns are notoriously unstable; if investment creates employment while it is increasing, it results in unemployment when it is reduced. Short-term changes in the investment level produce short-term changes in employment. Second, investment sometimes increases the productive capacity of the nation, especially so if that investment is in output-assisting plant and machinery. This effect is generally held to be the major moral justification for investment, in that it increases the possible level of future consumption albeit at some cost to present consumption. Third, productive investment generally requires the employment of additional manpower, which is continuously employed in the long term to help produce the additional output. Various types of investment expenditure result in different combinations of these three effects.

Consider, for example, an investment in social overhead capital, such as a road-building project. The effect on employment would be immediate, and labour would be employed to construct the road, reducing the unemployment level. Demand would be stimulated by the additional wages of the newly-employed or, to be more precise, demand would rise by the aggregate difference between the total previous income of the unemployed from benefits, and their total new income. Additionally, demand for some earthmoving equipment would probably increase, benefitting the manufacturers of that equipment. A new road, however, produces no marketed output (if it were a toll bridge or a toll tunnel, at least some future income for the project, and future employment in the bridge or tunnel authority, might result) and certainly it is difficult to argue that future exports would be increased by any road project. Some involved abstract arguments, such as the way in which a good roads systems in particular and good communications in general assists economic growth, could be advanced; but the linkage between improved social overhead capital and higher marketed output is less than direct (especially in the UK, where standards of social overheads capital are capable of standing comparison with other economically developed nations). Where the benefits of investment are not measurable, this does not imply that they are absent; it does, however, indicate that those who would prefer these investments have a more difficult case to argue. What is the purpose of having a good roads system and adequate housing if the price of this may be continuing high unemployment? The exact mixture of these different social priorities obviously needs to be balanced by politicians.

Investments in productive industry (either by companies or by public corporations) do not simply employ manpower during their placement, but employ workers continuously afterwards. The wages of these workers are paid from the increased output. As we have shown in Chapter 3, there is much more output and employment generated by new net investments in private companies, rather than public corporations. The issue in this chapter is the long-run effect of Keynesian demand-management, using the investment policy of public corporations to stimulate new investment and employment, both in the short and long term.

Table 6.8 shows the net capital stock (at replacement cost), value of

TABLE 6.8   UK net capital stock, output and employment incomes in companies and public corporations, 1962–72

£ bn. Year	Net capital stock (at replacement cost)		Output		Employment income from	
	Companies	Public corporations	Companies	Public corporations	Companies	Public corporations
1962	20.7	10.1	14.489	2.646	10.385	1.868
1963	22.1	10.8	15.466	2.807	11.331	1.930
1964	23.9	11.8	16.803	2.983	12.314	2.023
1965	26.1	12.9	17.968	3.163	13.292	2.138
1966	27.9	14.1	18.852	3.303	14.330	2.215
1967	28.7	16.6	19.367	3.589	14.628	2.393
1968	31.3	18.2	20.641	4.035	15.570	2.630
1969	34.8	19.6	21.524	4.227	16.679	2.735
1970	39.6	22.0	23.304	4.336	18.583	2.941
1971	44.7	24.7	25.594	4.750	20.306	3.243
1972	50.1	27.2	28.342	5.358	22.404	3.694

Source: Tables 13 and 63 of *National Income and Expenditure, 1973*, HMSO.

TABLE 6.9   Relation of UK net capital to output and employment

Year	Net capital-output ratios		Rate of return on capital (%)		Employment return on net investments (%)	
	Companies	Public corporations	Companies	Public corporations	Companies	Public corporations
1962	1.43	3.82	70.0	26.2	50.2	18.5
1963	1.43	3.85	70.0	26.0	51.3	17.9
1964	1.42	3.96	70.3	25.3	51.5	17.1
1965	1.45	4.08	68.8	24.5	50.9	16.6
1966	1.48	4.27	67.6	24.4	51.4	15.7
1967	1.48	4.63	67.5	21.6	51.0	14.4
1968	1.52	4.51	65.9	22 2	49.7	14.4
1969	1.62	4.64	61.9	21.6	47.9	14.0
1970	1.27	5.07	78.7	19.7	46.9	13.4
1971	1.75	5.20	57.3	19.2	45.4	13.1
1972	1.77	5.08	56.6	19.7	44.7	13.6

Source: Calculated from Table 6.8.

output and employment incomes generated by companies and public corporations during the period 1962–72. Table 6.9 shows the capital-output ratios, income rate of return on capital (i.e. the increase of the capital-output ratios) and the employment incomes generated, as a proportion of net investment. The capital-output ratios are derived from Table 6.8 and are the ratio of net capital stock at replacement cost to net output at current prices; inflation is therefore cancelled out in both dividend and divisor, although it is not the same inflation which is cancelled out, for the net capital stock is inflated by the price-index of capital goods, while the output is inflated by the price-index of produced goods and services. The consequence is a valid (if complex) net capital-output ratio.

One of the virtually indisputable facts about the UK economy during this century is the increasing role of public-sector investment. In the period 1900–14, the public sector took some 16.22 % of gross domestic fixed capital formation. In the period between the wars (1920–38), the figure was 24–33 %, while in the post-war period some 40–50 % of gross fixed investments have been in the public sector. To some extent, this increasing role of public sector investments is due to post-war national-isations and to the larger role of the UK government in the post-Keynesian scheme of things; but the trend is nonetheless a cause for concern, for the governemnt use of investment money may provide a short-term palliative to unemployment while increasing the long-term unemployed. An example can help illustrate how this may occur.

Suppose the UK government decides to increase investment in public corporations as a means of reducing unemployment in the short term. A boom in the investments of public corporations will certainly produce some employment—but what will this do in the longer term? For every £250m. investment, there will be about £100m. of net investments. (See Table 3.19; only about 40 % of the gross investments of public corporations produces net investments.) These net investments will give rise to annual output valued at less than £20m., and to employment worth about £13m. (This is derived by looking at the rate of return on net capital, and the employment return on net capital, given in Table 6.9). The efficiency of the public sector in generating continuing wealth is about 8 % (£20m. return on £250m. invested) and in generating continuing employment, about 5.2 %.

Now if the original investment sum was generated by government borrowing, then the real rate of return is undoubtedly lower than the interest charge; only the borrowing power of government can afford that kind of investment. If the investment money was raised by taxation of company income or by reducing company profits, then there has been a diversion of capital from a productive position to a less productive one.

Companies require about £190m. to generate £100m. of net investments, which leads to about £60m. of increased output and about £45m. of additional employment. The efficiency of continuing wealth-generation (output to gross investments) seems about 32% and the employment generated, as a proportion of input investment, is about 24%.

Private sector companies are therefore about four times better at generating output and over four and a half times better at producing employment than public corporations. If we assume that new investment would not lead to the withdrawal of some existing plant and equipment, then the picture improves considerably. Companies would require about £100m. in investment to generate £60m. of output and £45m. of continuing employment, if new investments were as productive and labour-intensive as the existing ones; while public corporations, with that same £100m. of net investment, would generate £20m. of output and £13m. of continuing employment, on the basis of the same assumption. In terms of net investments, private sector companies are three times better at generating output and almost three and a half times better at providing employment than public sector corporations. Yet if Keynesian economics is used to justify the employment of the unemployed, through increasing public sector investments which add little to output, then a cycle of collapse can be engendered as more and more low-productivity, low-employment-providing investments cannot be financed indefinitely. Borrowed money has a natural limit of availability; investments have to be paid for; the generation of demand without the provision of reasonable increases in supply is not viable in the long run. The aim of investment is not merely a short-term increase in employment, but the long-run creation of wealth and jobs. An economic philosophy for the UK which aims at the longer term seems quite feasible.

7 A Possible Transformation Policy for Britain

7.1. THREE CHOICES FOR BRITAIN

We have already put forward the view in previous chapters and elsewhere [1] that a country's economic growth rate is crucially dependent upon the efficiency of the transformation process which transfers short-term savings in the banks and longer-term savings in financial institutions into long-term plant and machinery investments in the factories. Our conclusion was that UK manufacturing industry was, and is, suffering a relative disadvantage, especially compared with industry in West Germany or Japan, due to the paucity of long-term external investment finance in the UK and its availability elsewhere. This book lays out the evidence for that viewpoint in more detail than could possibly be covered in an article.

Elsewhere we have pointed out that Japanese industry pays less — in cash flow terms — for much more external finance than its British counterpart. [2] This underlines the nature of the relative disadvantage suffered by British industry. Our purpose in this book is not to criticise the British investment-financing mechanisms, but to indicate the complex inter-locking nature of the social, political and financial set-up in the UK which has produced, and is producing, a relatively low level of private investment.

Although this book is specifically aimed at those who may be interested in understanding British investment-funding problems, the major factor responsible for low British growth is part of the common Anglo-Saxon heritage. It is the funding of private sector investment largely from retained profits and equity, rather than from large flows of external debt and the depreciation provision this produces, which is a major factor in the low investment behaviour and relatively low growth of the Anglo-Saxon economies. [3] The social concomitant of that

217

different investment-funding tradition is the separation of banking from business in Anglo-Saxon economies. The implications of this, and the suggested solution to the problem, are therefore not for Britain alone, but for all Anglo-Saxon economies, and the solutions may possibly also have some relevance to the economies of the developing world. But as with any suggested solutions to complex economic problems there are difficulties. One of the difficulties, for example, may lie in economic understanding.

Many economists assume that the level of investment in an economy is determined by exogenous forces which cannot be greatly affected by the actions of government. Economic textbooks typically explain differing national investment levels in abstract terms such as the different national business propensities to invest, and variations in this level are ascribed to alterations in business confidence.

It seems to us that, on the evidence given by international comparisons, the actual position may be somewhat different. It is almost axiomatic that businessmen cannot invest if they do not have the finance to do so. Even if finance for investment is available, unless the terms and conditions of that finance are such that profits can be made without a liquidity crisis (that is unless the repayment rate for capital borrowing is less than the earnings of capital) then investment is less likely to occur. The average national propensity to invest may be largely determined by the extent to which businessmen can make cash flow profits by investing cheap, long-term capital. Consequently, the different degrees of the availability and the associated costs of long-term industrial finance in different nations may partially explain the different investment rates. Business confidence could be defined as the absence of threat to the liquidity position. The different levels of investment in national economies may be largely explained by the proposition that marginal investment projects occur up to the point at which they threaten cash flow. This seems so obvious a principle we are amazed no-one appears to have suggested it before.

The lack of large-scale, long-term credits for British investment — a function which is partially provided overseas by the banking system — must therefore inhibit investment considerably. The clearing banks of Britain have recently gone on the defensive, launching a series of advertisements explaining that it is not their fault that investment is low, for the money is there to be borrowed by British industry.[4] These defensive advertisements have been produced in response to a call from the National Executive Committee of the Labour Party to nationalise the four main clearing banks[5]. One of the arguments put forward to support this nationalisation is that British banks do not provide funds for industrial development, as happens overseas. The clearing banks' response to this argument is that the work horse of British industry will not drink the funds currently provided. But the lending of British banks to industry has been, and is, largely short-term. Agricultural loans are typically seed-time to harvest — less than six months — and if part of these loans were intended to fund capital investment (although they are not) the rate of return on capital would have to be over 200 % p.a. in order to clear payments on time. On one-year loans, industry would have to find capital investment projects repaying 100 % plus the interest charged to fund their investment from its own cash flow, and on two-year loans, only projects with a return of over 50 % could be considered. There can be precious few investment projects with these rates of return. It is therefore not surprising that the NRDC and the CBI are able to tell the Wilson Committee (the Committee to Review the Functioning of Financial Institutions) that 'there is no shortage of investment finance, only a shortage of viable investment propositions'. Investment finance is no different from many other economic factors; if it is cheap, then using a great deal of it becomes feasible; if it is dear, then there is a shortage of viable investment projects due to price rationing.

To use short-term funds to provide large-scale capital investment can be the road to bankruptcy, due to the inability to fund the repayment rates, as some firms have discovered. Some banks, of course, do advance business loans of up to seven years' duration, but it cannot be pretended (nor has it ever been maintained) that these loans form a significant share of British banking business. The best defence of the British clearing banks against the proposed nationalisation would be that they currently provide significant amounts of long-term loans to British industry; and this defence cannot be used in the banking advertisements, for it is not true at present. But non-provision of investment funds is however not the fault of the banking system; it is the consequence of an Anglo-Saxon economic history, in which the financial system and the industrial system have kept themselves quite distinct. Anglo-Saxon prejudices and rationalisations about the proper ratio of debt to equity would limit the forwarding of investment loans by the banks, even if the provision of long-term investment credit became the accepted practice of British banks. Not only institutions but attitudes need to change, but they do not need to change by much. Bankers who provide vast amounts of loan capital for West German or Japanese industry do not need to become part of the management of industry except at times of financial crisis when their expertise is sought. Bankers have every right to ensure that there will be a proper return on the money they advance, and this requires some investigation of the prospects of capital investments. The banker helps ensure financial viability; the manager does the rest.

At present, the UK rationale of investment funding is quite different. Long-term company capital is supposed to be provided by internal savings and the capital market; banks are there only to provide short-term finance and loans against securities. It seems that this rationale is one factor which helps produce low investment and growth in the UK.

There are three main choices for the future funding of British industrial investment. First, nothing or very little may change; second, there could be a higher state involvement in banking; and third, banks could provide long-term funds for industrial investment on the German or Japanese pattern. These three main choices lead to very different outcomes for the future of Britain.

If nothing happens to increase the level of British industrial investment, then Britain's industrial capacity and living standards will continue to decline relative to other developed nations. Unemployment, which has been cyclically increasing on underlying trend since the early 1950s, will probably rise to above 2 millions in the early 1980s. Social and class conflict would thereby be exacerbated. Some British capital, management and skills may move overseas, to where the rewards are higher. The strains on the British economy due to being within the EEC may become very great, and lack of British economic competitiveness could force a retreat from full economic union in the EEC, perhaps relegating the UK to an outer ring of second class EEC members. It is conceivable that Scotland could seek independence, thereby breaking up the United Kingdom, for while success has a hundred fathers, failure is an orphan, and the continuing economic failure of the UK would become increasingly difficult for a resource-rich region to tolerate. Many problems are soluble with money: relative poverty magnifies difficulties. The UK could become, if present trends persisted, an economically weak off-shore island, balkanised by internal disputes, facing a relatively rich European mainland.

In a book published in 1972, Glyn and Sutcliffe, two committed socialist authors, concentrating on the squeeze on profits in Britain in particular but making out a similar case for other developed economies of the world, stated their belief that the solution to the problem must be a revolutionary socialist one.[6] They remark that although economic miracles operated in post-war Western Europe and Japan, nothing miraculous happened in the USA or Britain, and that the secret of rapid economic growth and investment eluded these economies[7]. It seems to us, however, that dirges for the funeral of capitalism (if that is any longer an adequate word to describe the mixed economies of the developed West) may be somewhat premature. It would be equally possible to write a book about the very low share of wages and salaries in Japan[8], and conclude that all western economies may follow Japan's external investment funding procedures. Glyn and Sutcliffe seem quite blind to the possibility of investment credit economies in the future of the West, even as Marx was blind to the possibility of a real rise in the standard of living. Projections of short-term trends unaltered into the future may well provide erroneous predictions; it was ever thus.

If Britain were declining as a matter of democratic choice — if a majority of the people of Britain had indicated that they actively wished a continual, deliberate relative economic decline — then decline would indeed be inevitable. But it does not seem that the relative decline of Britain results from consent; it appears more likely that decline may be happening due to historical economic drift, which does not indicate the presence of an economic policy, but rather the absence of an adequate one.

The Left of the Labour Party, in proposing to nationalise the banks and perhaps the insurance companies, certainly seem to have a policy. The question is whether such a policy would be successful in reversing the UK decline. Politicians have no particular ability to re-invigorate any industry, as the affairs of nationalised industries illustrate. On the contrary, politicians seem to have a capability to 'waste the labours of the people under the pretence of caring for them', to use Jefferson's choice phrase. The major financial experience of politicians is with the national budget, dealing with billions of pounds. This does not necessarily produce an economic perspective which is helpful in considering the problems of the average industrial company. The vast over-investment in plant and machinery in nationalised industries, where returns are relatively low, perhaps testifies to the lack of an adequate economic oversight of nationalised industries, whether by politicians or civil servants. If bankers were instructed to advance funds to industry, rather than to place funds where they would be likely to earn their keep, then this may be a formula for the greatest wastage of money yet envisaged. Politicians and civil servants seem quite inadequate to monitor the credibility of the needs of industry.

Consider, for example, the nationalisation of British Leyland. The Ryder Plan called for £2,800m. to be invested. Since Leyland employs about 110,000 people, this amounts to an incredible £25,000 additional capital investment per head. Even allowing for differences in price levels, and for new-model investment, this vastly exceeds the levels of investment per man in Datsun in the Japanese car industry (quoted at the end of Chapter 4). If British Leyland used the money to bring their production levels up to Japanese standards (at about £12,000 equipment per man) then they would produce about six times more output — this would be more cars than the number produced by all of the French car industry in 1975. This raises the question of what British Leyland were going to do with all that money. We have no doubt that all that capital could, in fact, be used. It is possible to use any amount of money by increasing the social overhead capital involved in industry. Very few companies or individuals experience problems in consuming money; in creating additional wealth, considerable difficulties are often experienced. The essential point is that it seems unlikely that any banker, mindful of receiving a good return on his money, would have consented to such vast investment expenditure. It is to the credit of the NEB that they apparently regard the Ryder plan with a jaundiced eye.

The nationalisation of an industry usually involves changes in a number of the industry's characteristics. The industry is usually made a monopoly, and hence becomes less responsive to market forces from the customer and more responsive to political pressure from their Minister. Would this be desirable in the British banking system? Most important decisions in nationalised industries — levels of investment, pricing, future planning and manpower, for example — are submitted to a political veto. As the company can no longer go bankrupt, selling becomes less important than satisfying political pressures, and no matter how great the losses become, government will ultimately be obliged to underwrite them. In the long run, however, the managers of the industry may emphasise income and profitability, for they make the discovery that the less money they request from government, the fewer issues which need to be politically referred and hence the lower the political leverage which can be exercised.

They are not, however, alone in that discovery. Politicians wishing to manipulate the electorate may instruct nationalised industries to hold prices down in pre-election years, and thereby run these industries into a loss-making position where those industries are sometimes made subject to a more day-to-day control. It is not that the managers of nationalised industries or political leaders deliberately choose to run nationalised industries in this fashion. It is as if the pattern of social and political pressures produces an almost automatic momentum towards an uneasy power-sharing between politicans, civil servants, and managers. A number of studies, the most recent of which is the NEDO Report on

Nationalised Industries, have set out proposed remedies to the perceived defects in the management, control and accountability of nationalised industries, but it remains to be seen if the proposals of that report will be implemented. Is it desirable that the management of British banks should operate in the kind of managerial limbo normal in other nationalised industries?

The overall affect of nationalisation on attitudes within an industry is probably not beneficial. The work force may not be slow to realise that the managers and the Board of Directors are no longer in charge of the company, and appeals can be made directly to politicians on vote-catching electoral issues such as the employment policy of the company. Managers discover that many decisions are subject to considerable delay in implementation, as the wisdom of these decisions is politically monitored and some apparently settled matters are politically reversed. Where the results of the decisions of nationalised industries are not believed to be politically acceptable, inquiry after inquiry may be launched to study the industry. This can hardly improve morale within the industry. Customers no longer complain so directly about deficiencies of the industry at the point-of-sale; they write letters to the newspapers and to politicians instead.

Finally, politicians discover to their cost that the one important industrial variable — the productivity of the industry — is not within their control, although this may have been the rationale behind nationalisation. The only effective power politicians exercise over the industry may be the right to appoint its top managers. Yet the very act of nationalisation has made the task of these managers very different; managers learn that it is more important to avoid mistakes than successfully to take risks. The pressures of the market place upon the top management of a nationalised industry are less than the political pressures, for top management is answerable for performance to politicians, not to shareholders for commercial success or failure. This does not seem to be the desired behaviour of the banking system. In the long run, government itself can become a virtual prisoner of the monopoly, although this does not seem to be acknowledged in the UK. This possibility is widely recognised in the USA — for example, the American government some years ago awarded computer contracts to Honeywell rather than IBM because it was reasoned that if IBM became much larger, it would be virtually the sole supplier of some vital computer equipment. The Japanese government also seems to have a policy of never permitting any one supplier to dominate any major consumer or industrial market.

If banking in the UK were nationalised, and if the Minister, management, workers and customers of banking responded to national- isation according to their behaviour patterns in previous national- isations, then the outlook for the British economy might indeed become bleak. The nationalised banking system would probably be used not only to advance funds to industry, but also to increase the involvement of government in virtually all aspects of industrial production. It is doubtful if government would discriminate between funds advanced to industry arising from taxation, and funds advanced arising from the appropriation of private savings. It is one thing for the French government to tap over 80 % of capital flows in the economy to transform short-term saving into medium- and long-term investments via a largely public and para-public banking system using indicative planning to identify preferred investments; it is another thing entirely for the National Executive Committee of the Labour Party to propose the nationalisation of British clearing banks and insurance companies as a short cut to the nationalisation of the UK economy, via government appropriation of savings and direction of investment funds. Further- more, there is no developed western nation which is growing more rapidly than the UK due to the presence of a nationalised banking system in that nation. All the evidence points the other way.

Japan is growing very rapidly because of the investment-funding conditions which have been created enabling private industry with help from private banks, to produce the goods. West Germany has about 300 private banks, most of which are interwoven financially with industry. Para-public banks in France help create the conditions for the rapid deepening of investment capital, but there is no forcing of funds; private industry has to come forward with viable investment proposals. There are no nationalised banks providing a service to the public in the USA.

The proposed nationalisation of the clearing banks seems to fall into the category of cures which are worse than the disease. The British government is capable, through legislation and market pressures, of altering the policy othe banking system with regard to the provision of long-term loans for industry. British banks have always responded to direction, as bank lending during the Heath boom illustrates, and it seems to be a little excessive to try to correct some unsatisfactory aspects of bank lending by a monolithic nationalisation.

It seems that what may be required is a change in emphasis within the British banking system, rather than outright nationalisation. British banking should have the additional and major function of providing some long-term capital to UK industry. But the banks cannot make that necessary change alone; supportive legislation may be necessary. The third way — the voluntary transformation of the clearing banks system from within — seems to hold out the greatest prospects of a more successful, rapidly-growing UK. If this conclusion is accepted, then there is a large range of policies which may be capable in total of improving the UK's investment levels and economic performance.

7.2 WHAT NEEDS TO BE DONE

The analysis conducted in this book helps us to pinpoint where and how the UK system has failed to facilitate adequate productive industrial investment, but this analysis would fail its purpose if it did not also provide a practical prescription for curing the UK's low-growth low-investment behaviour. The example of Japan indicates how the United Kingdom could adapt its institutions to facilitate a higher rate of economic development, although the extent to which the following suggested growth-accelerating solutions are politically acceptable is a difficult judgment to make. We believe, however, that it is essential that UK industry should not be obliged to suffer indefinitely under a long-term competitive disadvantage in international markets, as they might do if there is a continuing inadequacy of cheap external long-term capital finance in the UK.

It is as well to begin by recognising the size of the problem. In recent years, British commercial and industrial companies have invested about 4 % of the UK's GDP in the economic engine of plant and machinery; the business sector in Japan now invests 15–20 % of the Japanese GDP in plant and machinery. In France, and West Germany, private sector investment in plant and machinery runs at about twice the UK rate. (See Tables A6, A8, A10, A13 and A15 in the statistical appendix.) If the United Kingdom is to grow at an adequate rate compared with its major partners in the EEC, private sector investment needs to be approximately doubled, while for a Japanese rate of economic expansion, the UK private sector investment level would need to be more than trebled. That perspective indicates the scale of the problem, and all recent British governments have been unanimous in holding the opinion that the level of private sector investments should be, at the very least, substantially increased. The method of increasing industrial investment seems simple in principle. The cost of external investment capital needs to be cheapened, and the scale of investment funds increased. This can perhaps best be done by increasing surplus savings, and improving the efficiency of the saving-to-investment transformation process. External funds, once available, will increase gross business saving via depreciation, while protecting some profits from taxation. But this simplicity of conception does not diminish the complexity of operating such policies.

The industrial and commercial companies of any nation can invest their internal funds — from depreciation and retained profits — very easily. One indirect aim of government policy should be to increase these gross business savings. These gross savings can be increased by introducing current cost accounting procedures and higher depreciation allowances (e.g. by allowing the current cost of the replacement of existing assets to be claimed as depreciation). The extent to which businesses can invest external funds depends upon two factors; first, the level of savings elsewhere in the economy, and second, the availability of these savings for investment. The level of non-business savings in the economy depends for the most part upon the personal savings ratio, or the proportion of disposable income which private individuals choose to save. One other possible source of savings is excess government income but for the most part this is not relevant as the British government is not noted for its ability to achieve a large taxation surplus. The large Public Sector Borrowing Requirement indicates the opposite is true, and before funds can flow to industry, the British government needs to reduce its requirement for the lion's share of available saving. In Britain, public investment has usually had precedence over private investment; if higher economic growth is desired, private investment should be given priority, at least for a period.

Yet even if the PSBR declined, there is still the problem of which channel should be used to flow investment funds towards industry. Much of the personal savings of the UK is in the banks; industry receives a good proportion of these savings, but presently only as short-term loans. A large amount of the UK's personal savings is in the form of institutional investment, in insurance and pension funds; the institutions which hold these savings generally invest in some combination of equities, debentures and central and local government bonds. It could be argued that the insurance companies and pension funds should be able, because of the longer-term nature of their source of savings, to provide new capital for industry, but with the exception of some purchase of new equity issues and the purchase of some loan stock to develop North Sea oil, this has not occurred. The institutional investors in the UK do not seem to have the necessary contacts to provide a large-scale source of new investment capital for British industry; pension funds and insurance companies are by their nature and structure, centralised and relatively conservative investors, and where they do provide new capital, this is generally done through an intermediary such as a merchant bank. Only the clearing banks in the UK, like their counterparts in West Germany and Japan, seem to have the necessary infrastructure to canalise saving to investment through a comprehensive understanding of industry's needs at the local level.

The four main clearing banks in the UK are therefore the only possible candidates for the task of canalising investment funds to industry. There is of course the possibility that the clearing banks might not wish this role; but why should they not accept it? No other party could do it as efficiently. It would give the banks in Britain the same role as their counterparts in Europe, and this role for the banks may in the long run be not only inevitable, but also desirable, to reverse the relative decline of the clearing banks.

The prime reason for the inability of British bankers to advance long-term loan funds to industry is the seemingly short-term nature of their source of savings. This could be partly solved by the introduction of time deposits, that is, one-, two- and five-year savings deposits which offer higher interest rates to the depositor and provide the basis for the advancement of long-term loans by the banker. As mentioned previously, these time savings need not inconvenience savers, as, if these time deposits are required in a hurry, they can be converted into cash by bridging loans. Also, nothing prevents UK clearing banks from doing as banks do abroad — selling long-term bank bonds on the market, so as to spread the risk of lending long by borrowing long from other financial institutions (e.g. insurance companies and pension funds) who may have long-term resources.

Another of the reasons sometimes used by British bankers to explain their policy of not advancing long-term investment funds to industry is that there is a shortage of savings for that purpose in the UK compared with other nations. The reasons for making personal savings are not illogical, and the relatively low level of surplus personal savings in the UK may be due to a number of related factors.

The absolute level of personal saving, and the extent to which savings are available for industrial investment, could be raised by increasing restrictions on consumer credit and hire purchase over a number of years. Consumers would need to save prior to purchasing large items; aggregate consumer demand could to be stimulated by allowing, in higher net wage increases, amounts slightly larger than the consumer credit which was being phased out. It seems likely that households might prefer higher incomes with higher savings and paying cash, rather than lower incomes and savings with more consumer credit, yet the level of overall consumer demand can be the same in either case. The run-down of hire purchase and consumer credit will obviously not only result in higher personal savings, but will also release funds which banks can apply to industrial investment. The policy seems to have obvious benefits to both consumer and industry, and appears to be a desirable option. However, to run down consumer credit could well be unpopular until the longer-term benefits were appreciated. Such a policy might not be electorally popular, and hence might therefore be politically impractical. If very high private capital formation is required, this policy nonetheless needs to be considered. The introduction of restrictions on consumer credit need not be drastic; it could take the relatively gentle form of fixing bank-supplied consumer credit at a particular monetary level, which inflation could erode.

Government could also assist a higher level of personal saving by formulating wage guidelines to encourage lump-sum bonuses as part of an incomes policy. For example, if the incomes policy for the 1979/80 wage round were a norm of $+6\%$ this could perhaps be paid in three separate parts; an increase in the basic pay rate of $+2\%$, and two six-monthly bonuses of $+2\%$ of annual income. This kind of policy, practised over a number of years, could eventually enable a high proportion of income to be paid in six-monthly bonuses and could lead to a very high level of saving indeed. Inflationary pressures would be minimised, as lump-sum payments would tend to be used, in the absence of consumer credit, either to save for a rainy day or to purchase a large consumer item. Bonuses, in the absence of consumer credit, tend to act as a partial replacement to consumer credit; lump-sum payments tend to be saved until enough bonuses have accrued to enable consumers to afford relatively expensive items. Hence an incomes policy, involving bonuses, balances the withdrawal of consumer credit by enabling high-cost goods to be purchased in similar volumes as previously. Higher personal savings by a majority of the population could perhaps lead in time to an improved personal awareness of self-provided financial security, as unforeseen financial demands would have less distressing effects.

In the last analysis, however, somebody needs to take the risk involved in transforming short-term bank savings into long-loaned investment credit. This could be done by the banks on their own initiative (as happens in West Germany), or by banks supported by government guarantees against failure (as happens in Japan) or by government public and para-public banking (as in France). It must be obvious to everyone that no British government could allow any of the four major clearing banks to fail, so the practical risks involved in the transformation process are small, as there is a de facto support in any case. From the point of view of the efficiency of the transformation process from savings to private investment, the French system is least efficient (as public investment is given priority), the German system is moderately efficient, as it converts available saving but does not produce very high investment levels, while the Japanese system is superbly efficient. The constructive voluntary co-operation of both banking and government in creating industrial investment credit seems to be the most efficient option.

There are some necessary measures which the UK government could introduce to effect an improvement in the efficiency of the transformation process from short-term savings to long-loaned investment credit. The apparently missing link in this transformation process in the UK is a kind of investment credit bond, and we have not been able to discover whether it is missing because it is illegal or because it is merely unconventional. Perhaps a definition is desirable; by investment credit bond we mean a long-term capital loan made by a banker to an industrialist, on the conditions that the money will be used for productive investment, that the capital will never be repaid, and that the sole obligation of the industrialist is the payment of periodic interest on the loan, while the interest rate can be altered by the bank to the then realistic rate at two- or three-yearly or longer intervals. Whether this kind of capital loan is illegal or novel is, in the end, irrelevant; the lack of supportive legislation and the absence of a common UK banking practice permitting investment credit bonds are almost certainly inhibiting the proper transformation of public savings to industrial investment in the UK. Banks in the UK are currently able to argue that their role does not lie in providing long-term industrial capital; the legislation of investment credit bonds, and a clear green light from the government to the banks that this is indeed one of their proper functions, could change that attitude. It certainly does not seem that investment credit bonds are about to be spontaneously invented by the cautious UK banking community, while there are legal doubts about the possible consequences of the provision of investment credit bonds. This kind of roll-over loan is the cheapest conceivable form of industrial investment capital. There are no initial charges in raising it; it is flexible in amount; it provides a sound financial basis for industrial expansion, without interference in industrial efficiency. The interest payments on investment credit bonds should be allowable, like other bank loans, against profits before tax—this will make investment credit bonds, so far as businesses are concerned, a cheap and efficient source of large scale capital. The cheapness of those investment credit bonds will make many more industrial investments highly profitable, and this should help ensure a much higher rate of investment in the UK.

It would be quite wrong, however, for a UK government to will the end of increased investments through legislation of investment credit bonds without willing the means. The Bank of England at present holds some 16.5 % of UK bank deposits, perhaps principally to avoid excessive credit creation in the banking system. As the Japanese have discovered, credit creation acting in favour of the investing sector of the economy is no defect. The Bank of England, on receiving suitable assurances from the UK banks that funds made available would be applied to long-term investment credits, and after setting cash limits (which either inflation or policy would erode) on consumer credit, could slowly lower the level of special deposits and the reserve ratio to nil.

The UK banking system is nothing if not versatile. With the restriction of consumer credit, the legislation of investment credit bonds, and the unblocking of reserve assets, it seems quite possible that British bankers would develop their main market and would become as the German, French and Japanese bankers are —they would increasingly become aggressive, shrewd and evaluative lenders of long-term capital to the industrial and commercial sector of the economy. With the strengthening of the existing links between British banks and industry, which would have adequate capital for the creation of additional capacity, the British economy would experience its first investment-led boom, growing out of the depression through the construction of additional industrial investments. Some of the unemployed would be usefully engaged in the capital goods industries; eventually consumer demand would increase and industry would be better placed to meet these additional demands than previously. British industrial investments, freed from their reliance on retained earnings would steadily rise as the efficiency of the transformation process improved. The capital goods sector would grow in strength, employing an increasing proportion of the unemployed, pushing unemployment down, laying the foundations for more rapid UK growth in the 1980s. The efficiency of the UK transformation process would only be about 16 % or so initially but it would rapidly rise as British banks adapted to their new role.

Ultimately, a high proportion of bank savings could be canalised into productive capital formation, and British banks would look for ways to augment their own loanable bonds through borrowing from savings banks and insurance companies. Additionally, the long-term trend of money away from clearing banks towards building societies should preferably be stemmed. In the interest of providing finance for industrial investment, the banking system should become capable of offering some long-term savings accounts with tax-free interest. This would provide some additional term savings which the clearing banks could apply to long-term industrial investment, and would enable the banks to compete for deposits with building societies on a more equal footing. Legislation to permit this activity by the banks should be considered by the UK government.

Furthermore, once the investment financing system was working well, there would be no difficulty for the Bank of England in stimulating the overall level of investments in the UK economy by placing Bank of England loans with the banks. This process is performed in Japan through the discounting of investment credit bonds at face value (or down to 95 % of face value) by the Bank of Japan; this procedure leaves the accounts of both the central banks and the local banks in balance, but it is a credit-creating and liquidity-increasing process which enables further cycles of investment to occur. The Bank of England must in any case stand behind those British banks which advance long-term funds to industry, for the transformation process can be risky, and only the widely known willingness of the Bank of England to discount invest-ment credit bonds in the event of a run on any particular bank, can make the transformation process possible. It is interesting to note that the Chancellor of the Exchequer referred, in his April 1976 budget speech, to the possibility that medium-term industrial loans by the clearing banks might in future be eligible for re-financing at the Bank of England. This is exactly what is required.

There are a number of other assistive measures which the UK government could take to produce a continuing high level of industrial investment. The most obvious is the introduction of higher depreciation allowances for plant and machinery, and those usual in Japan could indicate the scope which is possible. An indicative economic plan for the UK as practised in France and Japan, will also set the scene. Yet past attempts by British governments to plan the economy have usually failed dismally because of a widespread opinion that exhortation to invest would be enough. An indicative economic plan for the UK must not only outline the target growth rates for the various economic sectors, but also must ensure, through voluntary co-operation between government and clearing banks that the required investment resources are made available to British industry. The adoption by the government of a realistic and all-embracing industrial strategy, aimed at helping all of productive industry might help. The current actions of the UK government are less helpful. What is the point of the government reducing its own expenditure so as to leave room for industrial growth if industry does not have the capital finance to take up the capacity thrown free? The policy of cutting the PSBR might help to release savings, but as things are currently arranged it will not help industry much, and UK industry needs more investment funds in the national interest.

7.3 CONCLUSIONS

Many of the propositions in this book can be reduced to potentially testable hypotheses, which could form the basis of an economic model. These propositions are stated, in outline, in appendix C.

The programme suggested for improving the UK's economic prospects is not placed within a phased timetable, but five years might be sufficient to introduce the acceptable face of investment credit. Agreement in principle to such a programme, and the willing consent of the most involved parties, is the first step in that long journey.

We would suggest that there may be one advantage in the programme we propose. It seems to us that there could be a very fair chance that it would work. The French and Japanese industrial miracles have come about through conscious government action to improve industry's ability to invest; we should be prepared to learn from their success. The prospects of the UK economy could be transformed by the creation of a more adequate saving-to-investment transformation process. The British government may sooner or later act on this matter, in the public interest. If it did, then the long decades of UK decline would be over, and, on a higher path of investment, within a few years the UK's growth could converge with that of other nations of Western Europe.

Whether the programme we suggest will gain any kind of practical support appears, for the present, to be doubtful. Yet there seems little doubt about what needs to be done; there is only doubt as to whether as a nation and government, the UK possesses the will to do it. And because the factors leading to low growth in the UK are mirrored in other Anglo-Saxon economies, then they too need to take steps to avoid their relative decline. The implications of such a programme in other Anglo-Saxon economies, however, is too large a subject for this book.

Perhaps the victors of World War II have been resting on their oars since 1945, and should now re-commence rowing. It is not too much to say that the future history of the world may depend upon whether these economies accept their decline or adapt to avoid it.

The stark choice which seems to face Britain is whether the banks and the British government will act to help ensure the provision of more adequate external sources of investment finance for manufacturing industry, or whether, with industrial dependence on inadequate retained earnings to finance investment, the United Kingdom will continue to decline. The difficulties involved in making the necessary changes should not be minimised, but the outcome of a higher future living standard for the British people seems very desirable. The United Kingdom once more could show the way towards balanced growth and future greatness through the creation of a more adequate system of financing industrial investment.

Appendixes

STATISTICAL APPENDIX A

INDEX TO STATISTICAL TABLES

234

TABLE A1   Industrial production indices in five nations (1970 = 100)

Year	France	Japan	W. Germany	UK	USA
1960	56	28.4	57.2	76	62.0
1961	59	33.8	60.7	77	62.5
1962	63	36.5	63.3	77	67.7
1963	70	40.7	68.1	78	71.7
1964	74	47.1	73.4	87	76.6
1965	76	48.9	78.0	89	83.6
1966	80	55.3	78.2	91	91.8
1967	82	65.9	76.2	91	93.7
1968	85	75.9	83.4	97	99.1
1969	95	87.9	94.2	100	103.7
1970	100	100.0	100.0	100	100.0
1971	104	102.7	101.5	101	100.1
1972	112	110.2	105.7	103	108.0
1973	120	127.4	113.2	110	117.7
1974	123	123.5	111.9	106	117.0
1975	112	110.4	105.0	101	106.7

Source: *Main Economic Statistics: Historical Statistics 1960–75*, OECD.

TABLE A2 Industrial production indices in five nations (1960 = 100)

Year	France	Japan	W. Germany	UK	USA
1960	100.0	100.0	100.0	100.0	100.0
1961	105.4	119.0	106.1	101.3	100.8
1962	112.5	128.5	110.7	101.3	109.2
1963	125.0	143.3	119.1	102.6	115.6
1964	132.1	165.8	128.3	114.5	123.5
1965	135.7	172.2	136.4	117.1	134.8
1966	142.9	194.7	136.7	119.7	148.1
1967	146.4	232.0	133.2	119.7	151.1
1968	151.8	267.3	145.8	127.6	159.8
1969	169.6	309.5	164.7	131.6	167.3
1970	178.6	352.1	174.8	131.6	161.3
1971	185.7	361.6	177.4	132.9	161.5
1972	200.0	388.0	184.8	135.5	174.2
1973	214.3	448.6	197.9	144.7	189.8
1974	219.6	434.9	195.6	139.5	188.7
1975	200.0	388.7	183.6	132.9	172.1

Source: OECD data as above, re-scaled to 1960 = 100.

TABLE A3 Production of passenger cars in five nations

in 000s	France	Japan	W. Germany	UK	USA
1964	1351.3	579.7	2650.2	1867.6	7751.8
1973	3202.4	4471.0	3643.0	1747.3	9658.0

Source: *United Nations Statistical Yearbook 1974*, Table 137, pp. 323, 324. Copyright, United Nations 1975. Reproduced by permission.

TABLE A4 Crude steel production in five nations

in 000 metric tons	France	Japan	W. Germany	UK	USA
1964	19780	39799	37340	26651	115281
1973	25264	119322	49521	26649	136803

Source: *United Nations Statistical Yearbook 1974*, Table 126, p. 310. Copyright, United Nations 1975. Reproduced by permission.

TABLE A5   Exports and imports of the UK, 1948–75

Year	Exports as % of GDP at factor cost	Imports as % of GDP	Growth of GDP (%)	Growth of exports (%)*	Growth of imports (%)*
1948	18.22	19.18	–	–	–
1949	19.61	20.06	3.11	10.97	– 7.86
1950	21.69	19.59	3.28	14.24	0.84
1951	20.72	20.23	3.62	– 1.00	6.98
1952	20.29	18.72	0.01	– 2.11	– 7.46
1953	20.19	19.29	4.70	4.19	7.90
1954	20.58	19.30	3.62	5.64	3.67
1955	21.12	20.53	3.48	6.27	10.09
1956	21.62	20.20	1.92	4.36	0.28
1957	21.75	20.31	1.97	2.54	2.51
1958	21.45	20.58	– 0.25	– 1.60	1.09
1959	21.30	21.19	3.50	2.77	6.56
1960	21.50	22.60	4.65	5.64	11.92
1961	21.41	21.72	3.60	3.13	9.93
1962	21.54	21.95	0.99	1.62	2.07
1963	21.57	21.87	4.00	4.15	3.61
1964	21.21	22.53	6.05	4.28	9.24
1965	21.70	22.21	2.40	4.77	0.98
1966	22.10	22.30	2.04	3.93	2.45
1967	21.78	23.18	2.66	1.16	6.72
1968	23.43	23.99	3.68	11.54	7.30
1969	25.21	24.31	1.66	9.38	3.01
1970	25.93	25.03	2.09	4.99	5.12
1971	27.16	25.64	2.30	7.16	4.77
1972	27.30	28.13	1.70	2.22	11.58
1973	28.82	30.09	5.85	11.75	13.23
1974	30.77	30.05	0.41	7.22	0.29
1975	30.11	28.46	– 1.32	– 3.43	– 6.57

* In terms of value, current £.

Source: Calculated from Table 9 of *Economic Trends, Annual Supplement 1976*, HMSO, 1976.

TABLE A6 Growth rate and percentage contributions to GDP in France

Year	Growth of GDP	% of private expenditure	% of govt. expenditure	% Gross domestic capital formation	% Residential building	% Machinery and equipment
1960	–	59.76	14.02	19.93	5.19	6.79
1961	5.37	60.73	13.84	21.26	5.23	7.58
1962	6.68	61.07	13.50	21.76	5.17	7.80
1963	5.74	61.89	12.99	22.27	5.39	8.09
1964	6.59	61.30	12.63	23.78	6.34	8.17
1965	4.65	61.15	12.40	24.36	6.76	8.27
1966	5.60	60.70	12.01	25.02	6.69	8.53
1967	4.94	60.96	11.90	25.30	6.54	8.67
1968	5.00	60.72	11.85	25.42	6.42	8.93
1969	7.75	59.95	11.53	26.16	6.50	9.47
1970	5.81	59.23	11.28	26.57	6.62	9.71
1971	5.06	59.77	11.12	26.57	6.44	9.86

Source: Calculated from Table A7.

TABLE A7 Components of GDP in France, 1960–71

in Frs bn., 1963 prices	GDP	Private expenditure	Govt. expenditure	Gross domestic capital formation	Residential building	Machinery and equipment
1960	346.09	206.84	48.52	69.00	17.97	23.49
1961	364.67	221.49	50.46	77.53	19.06	27.66
1962	389.02	237.59	52.52	84.66	20.11	30.33
1963	411.36	254.59	53.45	91.61	22.17	33.29
1964	438.45	268.77	55.38	104.27	27.79	35.84
1965	458.84	280.60	56.89	111.78	31.01	37.94
1966	484.54	294.11	58.22	121.22	32.43	41.35
1967	508.49	309.97	60.51	128.69	33.26	44.10
1968	533.93	324.20	63.27	135.74	34.28	47.69
1969	575.30	344.89	66.36	150.52	37.37	54.46
1970	608.75	360.54	68.68	161.77	40.32	59.12
1971	639.57	382.28	71.15	169.94	41.18	63.06

Source: Table 2, p. 163 of *National Accounts of OECD Countries 1960–71*, OECD.

TABLE A8   Growth rate and percentage contributions to GNP in Japan

Year	% growth rate of real GNP	Consumer expenditure	Government expenditure	Equipment and non-residential construction	Residential building
1960	–	60.14	19.53	13.27	4.34
1961	14.40	57.01	18.58	15.87	4.20
1962	7.00	58.35	20.05	15.34	4.46
1963	10.44	57.91	20.20	14.63	4.81
1964	13.24	57.08	19.16	15.50	5.38
1965	5.11	57.36	19.92	13.80	6.03
1966	9.79	56.59	19.94	14.03	5.88
1967	12.94	55.22	18.82	15.81	6.08
1968	13.41	53.35	18.06	17.77	6.33
1969	10.76	52.82	17.18	19.44	6.61
1970	10.94	51.33	16.36	20.10	6.73
1971	7.34	51.29	17.27	19.57	6.51
1972	9.07	51.34	18.05	18.95	7.04
1973	9.86	50.60	17.15	20.44	7.42
1974	1.16	51.93	17.15	18.54	6.66
1975	2.02	54.00	18.67	15.55	6.86

Source: Calculated from Table A9.

TABLE A9   Components of GNP in Japan, 1960–75

in ¥ bn. 1970 prices	GNP	Consumers' expenditure	Government expenditure	Equipment and non-residential construction	Residential building
1960	25408	15281	4961	3374	1103
1961	29066	16571	5401	4616	1222
1962	31100	18148	6235	4771	1387
1963	34346	19890	6937	5024	1653
1964	38894	22202	7452	6028	2093
1965	40880	23448	8145	5641	2464
1966	44884	25400	8949	6296	2640
1967	50690	27990	9538	8015	3081
1968	57486	30668	10383	10217	3640
1969	63669	33629	10939	12378	4206
1970	70635	36259	11557	14195	4661
1971	75818	38888	13095	14835	4938
1972	82698	42461	14926	15670	5825
1973	90850	45969	15577	18566	6738
1974	89796	46628	15401	16644	5983
1975	91606	49465	17102	14242	6286

Source: *Main Economic Statistics, 1960–75*, OECD.

TABLE A10   Growth rate and percentage contributions to GDP in West Germany

Year	% growth of GDP	% Consumer expenditure	% Govt. expenditure	Gross domestic capital formation	Residential building	Machinery and equipment
1960	–	55.55	13.97	24.65	6.25	7.90
1961	5.64	55.91	14.06	25.63	6.20	9.18
1962	4.02	56.62	14.99	26.00	6.18	9.18
1963	3.43	56.71	15.48	25.75	6.01	8.88
1964	6.78	55.84	14.42	26.97	6.31	9.05
1965	5.63	56.40	14.30	26.70	6.06	9.32
1966	2.87	56.88	14.22	26.20	6.16	8.85
1967	−0.25	57.64	14.71	24.07	5.87	8.17
1968	7.09	55.76	13.73	24.25	5.51	8.34
1969	8.17	55.53	13.35	25.10	5.04	9.48
1970	5.95	56.06	13.18	26.38	4.83	10.26
1971	2.74	57.56	13.75	26.83	5.13	10.37

Source: Calculated from Table A11.

TABLE A11   Components of GDP in West Germany, 1960–71

DM in bn., 1963 prices	GDP	Private expenditure	Govt. expenditure	Gross domestic capital formation	Residential building	Machinery and equipment
1960	338.56	188.08	47.29	83.46	21.15	26.73
1961	357.64	199.96	50.27	91.67	22.19	32.82
1962	372.01	210.62	55.78	96.71	22.98	34.14
1963	384.77	218.20	59.55	99.06	23.11	34.17
1964	410.82	229.41	59.25	110.80	25.93	37.19
1965	433.96	244.77	62.06	115.89	26.93	40.43
1966	446.42	253.92	63.48	116.98	27.50	39.51
1967	445.31	256.09	65.49	107.17	26.15	36.39
1968	476.89	265.92	65.50	115.65	26.29	39.75
1969	515.83	286.45	68.67	129.45	26.01	48.91
1970	546.52	306.40	72.03	144.16	26.42	56.07
1971	561.52	323.11	77.24	150.64	28.83	58.21

Source: Table 2, p. 179 *National Accounts of OECD Countries, 1960–71*, OECD.

TABLE A12　The declining proportion of British manufacturing investments

Year	Manufacturing investment as a % of total capital formation
1948	24.8
1949	25.6
1950	27.9
1951	29.8
1952	28.3
1953	24.9
1954	24.3
1955*	25.6
1956	28.5
1957	28.7
1958	26.8
1959	23.8
1960	25.3
1961	27.1
1962	25.1
1963	21.8
1964	21.2
1965	22.3
1966	22.4
1967	20.4
1968	20.2
1969	22.5
1970	23.7

Source: Calculated from Table E of *The British Economy: Key Statistics 1900–70, op. cit.*
* Between 1955 and 1956 there was a change in the basis of this series: split between manufacturing and distribution became based on business units, not establishments.

TABLE A13 Growth rate and percentage contributions to GNP in the USA

Year	Growth of GNP	% of Consumer expenditure	% of Govt. expenditure	% Gross domestic capital formation	% Residential building	% Other Construction	% Investments in plant and machinery
1960	–	61.48	23.47	13.71	3.23	5.43	5.05
1961	2.51	61.19	24.20	13.33	3.13	5.39	4.81
1962	5.80	60.43	24.16	13.68	3.49	5.17	5.02
1963	3.95	60.36	23.78	14.05	3.36	5.55	5.14
1964	5.26	60.43	23.18	14.27	3.24	5.57	5.46
1965	5.89	60.28	22.64	14.99	3.11	5.83	6.05
1966	5.95	59.74	23.37	14.74	2.70	5.56	6.48
1967	2.72	59.86	24.64	13.96	2.52	5.25	6.19
1968	4.38	60.22	24.64	14.35	2.75	5.32	6.28
1969	2.57	60.75	23.79	14.60	2.72	5.36	6.52
1970	−0.32	62.21	23.27	13.99	2.57	5.17	6.25
1971	2.99	62.47	22.52	14.47	3.05	5.43	5.99
1972	5.74	62.59	21.61	15.26	3.36	5.56	6.34
1973	5.32	62.13	20.47	15.51	3.16	5.39	6.96
1974	−1.84	62.76	21.00	14.23	2.45	4.77	7.01
1975	−2.03	64.66	21.72	12.55	2.09	4.13	6.33

Source: Calculated from Table A14.

TABLE A14 Components of GNP in the USA

in $bn, 1972 prices	GNP	Consumer expenditure	Govt. expenditure	Gross domestic capital formation	Residential building	Other construction	Plant and machinery
1960	736.8	453.0	172.9	101.0	23.8	40.0	37.2
1961	755.3	462.2	182.8	100.7	23.6	40.8	36.3
1962	799.1	482.9	193.1	109.3	27.9	41.3	40.1
1963	830.7	501.4	197.6	116.7	27.9	46.1	42.7
1964	874.4	528.7	202.7	124.8	28.3	48.8	47.7
1965	925.9	558.1	209.6	138.8	28.8	54.0	56.0
1966	981.0	586.1	229.3	144.6	26.5	54.5	63.6
1967	1007.7	603.2	248.3	140.7	25.4	52.9	62.4
1968	1051.8	633.4	259.2	150.9	28.9	55.9	66.1
1969	1078.8	655.4	256.7	157.5	29.3	57.9	70.3
1970	1075.3	668.9	250.2	150.4	27.6	55.6	67.2
1971	1107.5	691.9	249.4	160.2	33.8	60.1	66.3
1972	1171.1	733.0	253.1	178.6	39.3	65.0	74.3
1973	1233.4	766.3	252.5	191.3	39.0	66.4	85.9
1974	1210.7	759.8	254.3	172.3	29.7	57.7	84.9
1975	1186.1	766.9	257.6	148.9	24.8	49.0	75.1

Source: *Main Economic Indicators, Historical Statistics, 1960–75*, OECD.
Note: Construction (in total) was disaggregated into residential and other construction according to the proportions given on p. 65 of *Main Economic Statistics*, i.e. the assumption was made that inflation rates for residential and other construction are similar.

TABLE A15 Growth rate and percentage contributions to GDP in the UK, 1960−75

at 1970 market prices	% GDP growth	*(as percentages of GDP)* Consumer expenditure	Govt. expenditure	Gross domestic fixed investment	Total construction	Machinery and equipment
1960	−	65.18	19.13	15.02	−	−
1961	3.31	64.57	19.19	15.96	−	−
1962	0.87	65.37	19.62	15.86	8.40	7.46
1963	3.97	65.62	19.17	15.45	7.95	7.80
1964	5.85	64.04	18.17	17.05	8.97	8.07
1965	2.06	63.70	18.51	17.49	9.17	8.32
1966	1.97	63.64	18.67	17.58	9.14	8.44
1967	2.65	63.20	19.20	18.56	9.85	8.71
1968	3.47	62.57	18.62	18.76	9.99	8.78
1969	1.34	61.98	18.08	18.55	9.76	8.79
1970	2.32	62.07	17.94	18.50	9.50	9.00
1971	2.53	62.31	18.02	18.36	9.74	8.62
1972	2.58	64.40	18.22	18.29	9.85	8.44
1973	5.96	63.52	17.91	17.71	8.96	8.75
1974	0.26	62.70	18.38	17.31	8.71	8.59
1975	−1.30	63.33	19.24	17.45	9.30	8.15

Source: Calculated from Table A16.

Financing Industrial Investment

TABLE A16   Components of GDP in the UK

in £m., 1970 prices	GDP	Consumer expenditure	Govt. expenditure	Gross domestic fixed investment	Total construction	Machinery and equipment
1960	38577	25146	7379	5794	–	–
1961	39853	25734	7647	6361	–	–
1962	40199	26279	7889	6374	3377	2997
1963	41796	27427	8014	6458	3324	3134
1964	44239	28330	8138	7541	3970	3571
1965	45151	28760	8357	7899	4141	3758
1966	46039	29301	8595	8092	4206	3886
1967	47259	29869	9075	8771	4657	4114
1968	48899	30598	9103	9175	4884	4291
1969	49556	30715	8960	9191	4835	4356
1970	50707	31472	9095	9380	4817	4563
1971	51990	32396	9369	9544	5064	4480
1972	53329	34344	9716	9754	5253	4501
1973	56506	35894	10118	10008	5064	4944
1974	56653	35521	10413	9805	4937	4868
1975	55917	35413	10760	9760	5203	4557

Source: *Main Economic Indicators Historical Statistics, 1960–75*, OECD, for all data but GDP at market prices, which was taken from *National Accounts of OECD Countries, 1960–75*, OECD.

Table A17 Transformation of saving to lending in France, 1971*

Code	S10	S80	S40	S50	S60	S90	Total
Part I Assets acquired by each sector (sources)							
F20	9976	17088	25967	148	5716	−591	58304
F30	9374	47398	22149	459	1561	26914	107855
F90	384	6678	13	−	21	38	7134
F40	598	−	−11	138	4	−107	622
F50	4685	4012	6374	4732	1028	2064	20177
F60			3832	1026	5084	3406	16066
F10	−	−	980	−	−	891	1871
F70	−5364	−648	39024	1537	2444	−2222	34771
F80	6425	−19	56840	987	3427	3124	70829
Total	26078	74509	155168	9027	19330	33517	317629
Part II Liabilities incurred by each sector (borrowers)							
F20	−	−	33052	−	7687	17565	58304
F30	803	−	86423	736	3427	16466	107855
F90	−	−	−	7159	−	−	7159
F40	−	−	2187	−	−1614	49	622
F50	10611	−	9741	−	−444	269	20177
F60	6699	−	6544	15	3	2805	16066
F10	−	−	891	−	−	980	1871
F70	25896	9938	6615	556	−1663	6571	34771
F80	24468	26722	7563	−33	5754	6268	70742
Total	68477	36660	153016	8433	13150	37831	317567

* Frs m.

Key

F20 Currency and transferable sight deposits
F30 Other deposits
F90 Insurance technical reserves
F40 Bills and short-term bonds
F50 Long-term bonds
F60 Shares and other equity
F10 SDRs
F70 Short-term loans
F80 Medium- and long-term loans

S10 Non-financial corporate and quasi-corporate enterprises
S80 Households
S40 Credit institutions
S50 Insurance companies
S60 General government
S90 Rest of world

Source: Eurostat National Accounts, 1976.

TABLE A18   Transformation of saving to lending in France, 1972*

Code	S10	S80	S40	S50	S60	S90	Total
Part I Assets acquired by each sector (sources)							
F20	18150	22736	36031	708	11862	2812	92299
F30	6928	56342	33754	541	2033	29365	128963
F90	529	7283	14	–	19	41	7886
F40	– 557	–	– 9260	– 111	–	– 15	– 9943
F50 }	2358	4099	10271	6205	1065	1303	22557
F60 }			6103	1456	5414	5957	21674
F10	–	–	1292	–	–	883	2175
F70	6709	2218	83077	1326	4791	2360	100481
F80	5864	– 8	87519	514	1740	2314	97943
Total	39981	92670	248801	10639	26924	45020	464035
Part II Liabilities incurred by each sector (borrowers)							
F20	–	–	71745	–	11066	9488	92299
F30	986	–	101114	560	2504	23799	128963
F90	–	–	–	7909	–	–	7909
F40	–	–	774	–	– 10842	125	– 9943
F50	9662	–	11117	–	961	817	22557
F60	8455	–	7573	67	2	5577	21674
F10	–	–	883	–	–	1292	2175
F70	34244	16925	44479	287	4755	– 208	100482
F80	29965	43854	7631	124	8587	7728	97889
Total	83312	60779	245316	8947	17033	48618	464006

*Frs m.

Key

F20 Currency and transferable sight deposits
F30 Other deposits
F90 Insurance technical reserves
F40 Bill and short-term bonds
F50 Long-term bonds
F60 Shares and other equity
F10 SDRs
F70 Short-term loans
F80 Medium- and long-term loans

S10 Non-financial corporate and quasi-corporate enterprises
S80 Households
S40 Credit institutions
S50 Insurance companies
S60 General government
S90 Rest of world

Source: Eurostat National Accounts, 1976.

Table A19 Transformation of saving to lending in France, 1973*

Code	S10	S80	S40	S50	S60	S90	Total
Part I Assets acquired by each sector (sources)							
F20	13348	16403	10653	442	6122	4351	51404
F30	6282	61497	42595	767	3051	32458	14671
F90	(Not available for 1973)						
F40	−545	−	−15336	−121	−	−	−16002
F50 ⎫	5137	9075	11973	6233	1482	509	28157
F60 ⎭			7785	2924	5468	4754	27178
F10	−	−	−2820	−	−	−	−2820
F70	1372	192	96006	2027	8504	5972	114271
F80	6787	7	90837	538	1924	3351	103444
Total	32381	87174	241692	12810	26551	51395	452437
Part II Liabilities incurred by each sector (borrowers)							
F20	−	−	45973	−	9843	−4412	51404
F30	2023	−	103331	847	2207	38333	146741
F90	(Not available for 1973)					−	
						−	
F40	−	−	83	−	−16061	−24	−16002
F50	7686	−	13832	−	6007	632	28157
F60	12169	−	7955	88	35	6931	27178
F10	−	−	−	−	−	−2820	−2820
F70	43722	9301	50525	808	12684	−2780	114260
F80	35610	45785	10322	14	20	11539	103290
Total	101210	55086	232021	1757	14735	47463	452208

* Frs m.

Key

F20 Currency and transferable sight deposits
F30 Other deposits
F90 Insurance technical reserves
F40 Bills and short-term Bonds
F50 Long-term Bonds
F60 Shares and other equity
F10 SDRs
F70 Short-term loans
F80 Medium- and long-term loans

S10 Non-financial and corporate and quasi-corporate enterprises
S80 Households
S40 Credit institutions
S50 Insurance enterprises
S60 General government
S90 Rest of world

Source: Eurostat National Accounts, 1976.

TABLE A20   Transformation of saving to lending in West Germany, 1971*

Code	S10	S80	S40	S50	S60	S90	Total
Part I Assets acquired by each sector (sources)							
F20	6280	6634	1159	281	4454	2809	21617
F30	9240	37443	692	1931	4516	1466	55288
F90	1058	9906	–	–	18	46	11028
F40	−43	–	14527	–	−548	−539	13397
F50	352	8139	5912	2510	1113	1571	19597
F60	3255	1097	1042	788	703	1127	8012
F10	–	–	721	–	–	627	1348
F70	6549	40	18126	–	570	8079	32224
F80	3069	65	56934	5693	7296	7055	80112
Total	29760	63324	99113	11203	16982	22241	242623
Part II Liabilities incurred by each sector (borrowers)							
F20	–	–	20504	–	–	1113	21617
F30	–	–	54562	–	–	717	55288
F90	–	–	–	11208	–	–	11208
F40	−578	–	−1055	–	–	15030	13397
F50	3773	–	15187	–	1955	−1318	19597
F60	4755	–	950	–	–	2213	8012
F10	–	–	627	–	–	721	1348
F70	24302	3126	3492	737	1353	−786	32224
F80	60426	2718	4	42	11994	4928	80112
Total	92687	5844	94271	11902	15302	22618	242623

* DM m.

Key

F20 Currency and transferable sight deposits
F30 Other deposits
F90 Insurance technical reserves
F40 Bills and short-term bonds
F50 Long-term bonds
F60 Shares and other equity
F10 SDRs
F70 Short-term loans
F80 Medium- and long-term loans

S10 Non-financial corporate and quasi-corporate enterprises
S80 Households
S40 Credit institutions
S50 Insurance companies
S60 General government
S90 Rest of world

Sources: Eurostat National Accounts, 1976.

TABLE A21 Transformation of saving to lending in West Germany, 1972*

Code	S10	S80	S40	S50	S60	S90	Total
Part I Assets acquired by each sector (sources)							
F20	11208	7346	1873	− 70	− 2119	1363	19571
F30	10161	46148	106	2801	8326	636	68178
F90	1607	11544	−	−	37	81	13269
F40	85	−	13373	−	− 501	128	13085
F50	1106	11115	7234	3151	81	7646	30333
F60	364	− 239	1472	928	371	4491	7387
F10	−	−	1304	−	−	620	1924
F70	7038	82	24943	−	1148	1220	34431
F80	2946	95	71065	6688	8223	3994	93011
Total	34515	76061	121476	13498	15566	20179	281295
Part II Liabilities incurred by each sector (borrowers)							
F20	−	−	17718	−	−	1853	19571
F30	25	−	68097	−	−	56	68178
F90	−	−	−	13269	−	−	13269
F40	623	−	2012	−	− 312	14786	13085
F50	3345	−	26602	−	4605	− 4219	30333
F60	3009	−	1350	175	−	2853	7387
F10	−	−	620	−	−	1304	1924
F70	22974	4633	3702	643	− 541	3020	34431
F80	74131	3618	12	6	13254	1990	93011
Total	104107	8251	116089	14093	17006	21749	281295

* DM m.

Key

F20 Currency and transferable sight deposits
F30 Other deposits
F90 Insurance technical reserves
F40 Bills and short-term bonds
F50 Long-term bonds
F60 Shares and other equity
F10 SDRs
F70 Short-term loans
F80 Medium- and long-term loans

S10 Non-financial corporate and quasi-corporate enterprises
S80 Households
S40 Credit institutions
S50 Insurance enterprises
S60 General government
S90 Rest of world

Source: Eurostat National Accounts, 1976.

Financing Industrial Investment

TABLE A22 Transformation of saving to lending in West Germany, 1973*

Code	S10	S80	S40	S50	S60	S90	Total
Part I Assets acquired by each sector (sources)							
F20	−2784	1637	1527	362	6748	753	8243
F30	16497	44590	7574	3432	6707	3443	82243
F90	1743	12726	–	–	36	76	14581
F40	51	444	22339	115	4571	−1030	26490
F50	1100	11972	3547	3068	−252	6128	25563
F60	1766	1673	860	887	170	839	6195
F10	–	–	1803	–	–	–	1803
F70	4677	−13	15565	–	1928	9929	36086
F80	1637	50	64421	6742	13776	7732	94358
Total	24687	73079	117636	14606	33684	27870	291562
Part II Liabilities incurred by each sector (borrowers)							
F20	–	–	6717	–	–	1526	8243
F30	26	–	74648	–	–	7569	82243
F90	–	–	–	14581	–	–	14581
F40	1227	–	5392	–	−374	22699	26490
F50	1205	–	22467	–	2118	−227	25563
F60	2976	–	1078	162	–	1979	6179
F10	–	–	–	–	–	1803	1803
F70	22979	1398	1914	889	3314	1592	32086
F80	76270	2491	115	7	14826	649	94358
Total	102229	3889	112331	15639	19884	37590	291562

* DM m.

Key

F20 Currency and transferable sight deposits
F30 Other deposits
F90 Insurance technical reserves
F40 Bills and short-term bonds
F50 Long-term bonds
F60 Shares and other equity
F10 SDRs
F70 Short-term loans
F80 Medium- and long-term loans

S10 Non-financial corporate and quasi-corporate enterprises
S80 Households
S40 Credit institutions
S50 Insurance enterprises
S60 General government
S90 Rest of world

Source: Eurostat National Accounts, 1976.

TABLE A23 Transformation of saving to lending in West Germany, 1974*

Code	S10	S80	S40	S50	S60	S90	Total
Part I Assets acquired by each sector (sources)							
F20	10780	6500	968	93	−56	1915	20200
F30	−4793	45708	10407	3899	2708	2719	60648
F90	1737	13664	–	–	36	79	5606
F40	696	238	−6325	−11	−1290	−109	−6801
F50	209	10696	18082	4163	−691	−3082	29377
F60	3403	525	197	757	524	1757	7163
F10	–	–	168	–	–	–	168
F70	21900	−26	14111	–	2015	9415	47415
F80	3172	51	60095	7122	10601	4760	85801
Total	37104	77356	97703	16023	13847	17454	259487
Part II Liabilities incurred by each sector (borrowers)							
F20	–	–	18882	–	–	1318	20200
F30	9	–	49899	–	–	10740	60648
F90	–	–	–	15516	–	–	15516
F40	666	–	−990	–	4273	−10750	−6801
F50	1860	–	20328	–	3540	3649	29377
F60	3124	–	1024	312	–	2703	7163
F10	–	–	–	–	–	168	168
F70	25386	−169	1233	1080	−1211	21096	47415
F80	53626	105	45	11	18825	13189	85801
Total	84671	−64	90421	16919	25427	42113	259487

* DM m.

Key
F20 Currency and transferable sight deposits
F30 Other deposits
F90 Insurance technical reserves
F40 Bills and short-term bonds
F50 Long-term bonds
F60 Shares and other equity
F10 SDRs
F70 Short-term loans
F80 Medium- and long-term loans

S10 Non-financial corporate and quasi-corporate enterprises
S80 Households
S40 Credit institutions
S50 Insurance enterprises
S60 General government
S90 Rest of world

Source: Eurostat National Accounts, 1976.

Table A24 Transformation of saving to lending in the UK, 1971*

Code	S10	S80	S40	S50	S60	S90	Total
Part I Assets acquired by each sector (sources)							
F20	713	1156	51	−17	1670	−555	3018
F30	−189	2586	1197	−61	1	3357	6891
F90	−	1930	−	−	−	−	1930
F40	378	−	1159	−	2	451	1990
F50	120	190	2543	889	−2	320	4060
F60	320	1171	352	799	82	216	598
F10	−	−	−	−	135	125	260
F70	121	55	3352	1	1220	−267	4482
F80	416	−93	2426	37	2077	704	5567
Total	1879	4653	11080	1648	4707	4351	28318
Part II Liabilities incurred by each sector (borrowers)							
F20	−	−	1667	−	−306	1460	3018
F30	−	−	6629	−	273	1	6891
F90	−	−	−	1846	84	−	1930
F40	150	−	1502	−	365	−27	1990
F50	291	−	90	17	3599	63	4060
F60	146	−	266	−	−	186	598
F10	−	−	−	−	125	135	260
F70	787	638	514	23	−780	3300	4482
F80	2038	2039	74	−	938	478	5567
Total	3412	2677	10747	1886	4298	5298	28318

* £m.

Key

F20 Currency and transferable sight deposits
F30 Other deposits
F90 Insurance technical reserves
F40 Bills and short-term bonds
F50 Long-term bonds
F60 Shares and other equity
F10 SDRs
F70 Short-term loans
F80 Medium- and long-term loans

S10 Non-financial corporate and quasi-corporate enterprises
S80 Households
S40 Credit institutions
S50 Insurance enterprises
S60 General government
S90 Rest of world

Source: *Eurostat National Accounts, 1976.*

TABLE A25 Transformation of saving to lending in the UK, 1972*

Code	S10	S80	S40	S50	S60	S90	Total
Part I Assets acquired by each sector (sources)							
F20	1167	2023	767	240	−352	−206	3639
F30	487	2946	4920	87	50	6758	15248
F90	−	2601	−	−	−	−	2601
F40	771	−	1953	−	−1	961	3684
F50	224	−324	−592	464	−1	282	153
F60	638	−1060	681	1325	36	112	1732
F10	−	−	−	−	6	124	130
F70	298	45	13738	38	−627	−25	13467
F80	416	15	2856	42	1678	295	5302
Total	4001	6246	24323	2196	757	8401	45924
Part II Liabilities incurred by each sector (borrowers)							
F20	−	−	3661	−	382	−390	3639
F30	−	−	14458	−	733	37	15248
F90	−	−	−	2484	117	−	2601
F40	180	−	3781	−	−437	160	3684
F50	395	−	71	64	−430	53	153
F60	331	−	663	9	−	729	1732
F10	−	−	−	−	124	6	130
F70	2986	2016	1016	17	635	6797	13467
F80	1012	3034	144	15	808	289	5302
Total	4904	5050	23800	2589	1932	7665	45924

* £m.

Key

F20 Currency and transferable sight deposits
F30 Other deposits
F90 Insurance technical reserves
F40 Bills and short-term bonds
F50 Long-term bonds
F60 Shares and other equity
F10 SDRs
F70 Short-term loans
F80 Medium- and long-term loans

S10 Non-financial corporate and quasi-corporate enterprises
S80 Households
S40 Credit institutions
S50 Insurance enterprises
S60 General government
S90 Rest of world

Source: *Eurostat National Accounts, 1976.*

TABLE A26 Transformation of saving to investment in the UK, 1973*

Code	S10	S80	S40	S50	S60	S90	Total
Part I Assets acquired by each sector (sources)							
F20	2091	3520	1153	85	270	1	7118
F30	611	2560	10126	191	90	12906	26484
F90	–	2957	–	–	–	–	2957
F40	31	–	1118	77	301	911	2438
F50	326	390	190	635	3	532	2070
F60	1014	– 1580	38	686	7	335	500
F10	–	–	–	–	– 2	–	– 2
F70	902	65	20444	55	1225	164	22855
F80	976	120	2755	313	1339	935	6438
Total	5951	8032	35824	2042	3225	15782	70856
Part II Liabilities incurred by each sector (borrowers)							
F20	–	–	6352	–	553	213	7118
F30	–	–	25142	–	879	20	26484
F90	–	–	–	2820	137	–	2957
F40	277	–	2286	–	– 295	170	2438
F50	154	–	69	15	1698	134	2070
F60	107	–	258	–	–	135	500
F10	–	–	–	–	–	– 2	– 2
F70	6091	1309	816	51	1641	12947	22855
F80	1188	3054	78	21	1158	939	6438
Total	7817	4363	35444	2907	5771	14554	70856

* £m.

Key

F20 Currency and transferable sight deposits
F30 Other deposits
F90 Insurance technical reserves
F40 Bills and short-term bonds
F50 Long-term bonds
F60 Shares and other equity
F10 SDRs
F70 Short-term loans
F80 Medium- and long-term loans

S10 Non-financial corporate and quasi-corporate enterprises
S80 Households
S40 Credit institutions
S50 Insurance enterprises
S60 General government
S90 Rest of world

Source: Eurostat National Accounts, 1976.

TABLE A27 Transformation of saving to investment in the UK, 1974*

Code	S10	S80	S40	S50	S60	S90	Total
Part I Assets acquired by each sector (sources)							
F20	−226	3363	212	530	22	9	3910
F30	808	1785	2743	719	−82	9146	15119
F90	−	3115	−	−	−	−	3115
F40	−626	−	486	125	−299	1343	1029
F50	143	357	−111	274	−	173	836
F60	484	−1095	−416	229	20	406	−420
F10	−	−	−	−	37	−	37
F70	456	−10	11845	188	947	−186	13240
F80	901	815	2594	211	2978	2117	9616
Total	1940	8330	17353	2276	3623	13008	46530
Part II Liabilities incurred by each sector (borrowers)							
F20	−	−	3189	−	817	42	3910
F30	−	−	14317	−	531	25	15119
F90	−	−	−	2900	215	−	3115
F40	438	−	−1170	−	1576	185	1029
F50	−66	−	97	−	748	57	836
F60	44	−	68	62	−	−546	−372
F10	−	−	−	−	−	37	37
F70	4509	213	−190	−47	331	8424	13240
F80	2781	2291	442	−5	3164	943	9616
Total	7706	2504	18681	2910	7382	9167	46530

* £m.

Key

F20 Currency and transferable sight deposits
F30 Other deposits
F90 Insurance technical reserves
F40 Bills and short-term bonds
F50 Long-term bonds
F60 Shares and other equity
F10 SDRs
F70 Short-term loans
F80 Medium- and long-term loans

S10 Non-financial corporate and quasi-corporate enterprises
S80 Households
S40 Credit institutions
S50 Insurance enterprises
S60 General government
S90 Rest of world

Source: Eurostat National Accounts, 1976.

TABLE A28   GDPs for the five nations, 1960–75

in current prices	France Frs bn.	Japan ¥bn.	West Germany DM bn.	UK £m.	USA $m.
1960	295.53	15503	302.55	25483	506696
1961	324.89	19162	333.45	27202	523624
1962	362.86	21252	366.91	28479	563914
1963	404.40	24542	384.77	30289	594501
1964	445.47	29014	422.14	33064	635030
1965	477.73	32052	462.02	35466	687138
1966	518.87	36921	492.10	37792	752292
1967	558.55	43676	496.86	39921	795354
1968	609.60	51750	540.54	43118	867219
1969	698.52	59838	605.68	46130	934346
1970	782.56	70868	686.96	50707	981199
1971	872.43	79373	762.54	56636	1061113
1972	981.12	90630	834.63	62769	1168326
1973	1113.55	111004	928.18	71759	1302135
1974	1277.56	132486	999.66	81617	1405481
1975	1438.98	145620	1045.52	102969	1513828

Source: National Accounts of OECD Countries, 1975.

APPENDIX B1: DIFFERENCES IN THE SYSTEMS OF NATIONAL ACCOUNTING (SNA) BETWEEN THE FIVE COUNTRIES

1 Within the five nations, there are some differences in the reported systems of national accounting, so far as items included in GDP, gross fixed capital formation and capital consumption are concerned. Japan and West Germany are on the 'former system'; France, the UK and the USA are on the 'present SNA'.

2 The OECD defined these systems, and summarised the differences between them, as set out below.

2.1 GROSS DOMESTIC PRODUCT

In present SNA   The sum of the items in respect of final expenditure on goods and services, in purchasers' values, less the cif value of imports of goods and services: or the sum of the value added of resident producers, in producers' values, plus import duties. The value added of resident producers is equivalent to the difference between the value of their gross output, in producers' values, and the value of their intermediate consumption, in purchasers' values: or to the sum of their compensation of employees, operating surplus, consumption of capital assets and excess of indirect taxes over subsidies.

Differences in the former systems   In the former systems included are (i) operating surplus (net rent) in respect of buildings owned and occupied by government, (ii) motor vehicle duties and similar government levies paid by households and (iii) bank service charges to households: excluded are charges in respect of the consumption of machinery and equipment of government and private non-profit services; private non-profit bodies primarily serving business which are entirely, or mainly, financed and controlled by the public authorities are classified as enterprises (industries) rather than as government services: and additions to, and withdrawals from, stocks of internally processed commodities are, in principle, valued at explicit costs rather than at producers' values.

2.2   GROSS FIXED CAPITAL FORMATION

In present SNA   The outlays (purchases and own-account production) of industries, producers of government services and producers of private non-profit services to households on additions of new and imported durable goods to their stocks of fixed assets, reduced by the proceeds of their net sales (sales less purchases) of similar second-hand and scrapped goods. Excluded is the outlay of government services on durable goods primarily for military purposes. Included are (i) dealers' margins and other transfer costs only in respect of transactions in land, mineral deposits, timber tracts etc., (ii) outlays on the reclaiming and improving of land, (iii) expenditure on developing and extending timber tracts, mines, plantations, orchards, vineyards, etc., and (iv) outlays on alterations in, and additions to, fixed assets which significantly extend their life time of use, or increase their productivity. Outlays on repair and maintenance in order to keep fixed assets in good working condition are classed as current expenditure. Breeding and draught animals, dairy cattle, animals raised for wool clip are, in principle, to be classed as fixed assets, but it may be necessary to include some of these animals in increases in stocks.

The value of the additions to fixed assets should cover all costs directly connected with the acquisition and installation of the fixed assets for use, e.g. purchase price, custom and other indirect taxes, transport, delivery and installation charges, site clearance, planning and designing costs, legal fees. The costs of financing and additions, such as flotation costs, underwriters' commissions, advertising bond issues, are excluded. It may be necessary to value fixed assets produced on own-account at explict cost instead of producers' values.

The acquisition of fixed assets is to be recorded at the moment when the ownership of the goods passes to the buyer. In the case of construction projects this is taken to be at the time that work is put in place.

Differences in the former systems In the former systems included in transactions in second-hand fixed assets are purchases and sales of land, timber tracts, mineral deposits, etc.: excluded are (i) additions to the machinery and equipment of private non-profit bodies mainly serving households or the public authorities. (ii) additions to stocks of breeding and draught animals, dairy cattle, etc. and (iii) the causes of developing and extending plantations, orchards, vineyards and timber tracts excepting land clearance; and outlays of an extra-territorial body of a foreign government on construction are allocated to the country where the investment is located instead of the country of the foreign government.

2.3 CAPITAL CONSUMPTION

In present SNA The normal wear and tear, forseen obsolescence, and probable (normally expected) rate of accidental damage not made good by repair in all fixed assets valued at current replacement cost. Charges are not included in respect of unforeseen obsolescence or the depletion of natural resources. No attempt should be made to allow for arrears in the consumption of fixed capital because earlier estimates have been at a lower price level. The charge for the probable rate of accidental damage might be based on past experience or on the net premiums paid for such insurance of the fixed assets.

Differences in the former systems In the former systems excluded are charges for the consumption of the machinery and equipment of government services and private non-profit services to households.
Sources: From *National Accounts of OECD Countries, 1975*, Volume 1, pp. 6, 8 and 13.

APPENDIX B2: EQUIPMENT INVESTMENT IN THE UK AND ELSEWHERE

1 Japan's Economic Planning Agency derived estimates of the UK investment in plant and equipment by deducting investment in dwellings and public investments from total gross domestic capital formation. A replication of that process is in Table B2.1, and shows that, as Table 3.15 indicates, UK 'equipment investment' is about 6.9 % of GDP during the period 1956–63. However, as this estimate was derived as a residual by deducting public sector investments plus dwellings from total investments, it may be doubted whether it does reflect plant and machinery investments.

TABLE B2.1   A replication of the procedure used by Japan's Economic Planning Agency to estimate UK equipment investment*

Year	(1) UK GDP	(2) Total GDCF	(3) Public sector investment	(4) Dwellings	(5) Equipment investment	(6) (5) as % of (1)
1957	22769	3712	1653	682	1377	6.05
1958	22701	3737	1626	644	1467	6.46
1959	23489	4025	1749	742	1534	6.53
1960	24641	4418	1806	834	1778	7.22
1961	25514	4847	1957	895	1995	7.82
1962	25765	4829	2028	924	1877	7.29
1963	26758	4907	2132	944	1831	6.84

* in £m., 1963 prices
Note: (5) is derived from column (2) minus (column (3) plus column (4))
Source: Tables A and J of *The British Economy: Key Statistics 1900–1970*, published for London & Cambridge Economic Service by Times Newspapers Ltd., 1971.

2 Table B2.2 gives the figures for plant and machinery investment and GDP for the period 1957–63. The average value of plant and machinery investment is 6.94 %, hence the estimate derived by Japan's Economic Planning Agency is reasonably accurate while wrongly derived.

3 This raises the question of the extent to which other estimates of equipment investment in Table 3.12 may be accurate. It is interesting to derive recent estimates of equipment-output ratios for France, West Germany, the UK and the USA, so that a comparative analysis may be

TABLE B2.2 UK equipment investment as a %
of GDP, 1957–63, Current Prices, £m

Year	GDP	Plant and machinery investment	Plant and machinery as % of GDP
1957	19377	1296	6.69
1958	20206	1338	6.62
1959	21261	1420	6.68
1960	22647	1532	6.76
1961	24237	1808	7.46
1962	25298	1820	7.19
1963	26931	1926	7.15

Source: Tables 8 and 40 of *Economic Trend,
Annual Supplement, 1976*, HMSO.

done with the benefit of sound data. Unfortunately, Japanese equipment-output ratios cannot be realistically calculated, for where data refers to total investment in Japan, this includes business structures, while where Japanese equipment investment is available in aggregate, this includes shipbuilding (which is a sizeable Japanese export, not an addition to Japan's capital stock).

4 Incremental equipment-output ratios for four countries are calculated in Table B2.3. France, the USA and West Germany seem to acquire more output for a given level of investment in equipment than the UK. The principal reason for this may be that investment in the UK is low where investment productivity is high (in private sector manufacturing industry) and much of UK investment is in social overhead capital. See Section 3.4 for a fuller explanation of this argument.

APPENDIX B3: THE EFFECT OF ECONOMIC GROWTH AND INFLATION ON POTENTIAL PURCHASING POWER

1 The purpose of this appendix is to calculate the rate of inflation which must not be exceeded if the total potential purchasing power of households (defined as the purchasing power of earnings plus savings) is not to fall. This is done by:

(i) Giving a practical example, based on Japanese data, of how increase in the real earnings of households may be partially offset by the fall in the purchasing power of savings;

TABLE B2.3   Equipment-output ratios for four countries

Country	Period	Equipment investment as % of GDP	Average GDP growth	IEOR*
France	1961–65	7.98	5.57	1.43
	1966–70	9.06	5.81	1.56
	1961–70	8.52	5.69	1.50
West Germany	1961–65	9.12	5.09	1.79
	1966–70	9.02	4.72	1.91
	1961–70	9.07	4.91	1.85
UK	1961–65	7.46	3.20	2.33
	1966–70	8.21	2.35	3.49
	1961–70	7.84	2.77	2.83
USA	1961–65	5.82	4.62	1.26
	1966–70	6.97	3.10	2.25
	1961–70	6.40	3.86	1.66

Source: Tables A6, A10, A13 and A15 of the statistical appendix.
* Incremental Equipment-Output Ratio

(ii) Deriving a formula relating the inflation rate to the real growth of earnings and the ratio of household saving to earnings;

(iii) commenting on this formula.

2 Consider Japan: in its growing economy, the major source of growth is that given by an increase in purchasing power of wages and salaries — or to put it slightly differently, the real gain to households is the average earnings multiplied by the difference between earnings increases and the inflation rate. Earnings in Japan between 1960 and 1970 increased on an average financial rate of about 17% a year; inflation accounted for a 6% rise in prices; living standards therefore rose at about 10% a year. As earnings in Japan constitute some 65% of GNP, the real rise in earnings is about 6.5% of GNP annually.

3 The losses made by the average individual are largely the reduced purchasing power of past savings, which increase at various interest rates while their purchasing power has been eroded at the inflation rate. We will assume for the purposes of the discussion which follows that the average interest rate paid on savings in Japan is about 4%. In 1968, 46% of Japanese savings were in time deposits, 17% in currency and demand deposits, and the rest in securities or pension funds. It is difficult to calculate what the actual interest rate might be without knowing the proportions in each kind of financial asset. However, assuming 4% may

be a reasonable estimate, then 2 % of the purchasing power of savings was lost due to 6 % inflation. Savings would therefore have to equal over 3.25 times earnings (or 6.5 divided by 2) before the loss in the purchasing power of saving would cancel out the increase in earnings. Now the ratio of the total funds of all Japanese financial institutions to GNP was about 1.5 in 1975. If the average Japanese individual possessed savings in proportion to his share of GNP, then the purchasing power of his earnings plus his savings increased. In fact the average Japanese family possessed savings in excess of 1.5 times its income, as Japanese households are a major source of uncommitted saving, but taking that into account, it was not the case that the purchasing power of the combined savings plus earnings of households fell. (In 1968, outstanding personal financial assets in Japan were 1.623 times disposable income. See Table 80, Economic Survey of Japan 1969/70, *op. cit.*).

4 This argument can be generalised to calculate an 'allowable rate of inflation', below which total potential purchasing power will rise, and above which it will fall. If household earnings are e, and the rate of real growth in earnings is g, then the increased purchasing power of households is $(e \times g)$. If households savings are S, and they are increased by the interest rate i and diminished in purchasing power by the inflation rate of f, then the exact change in purchasing power of savings is given by $(S \dfrac{(1.0 - i)}{(1.0 - f)} - S)$ but to a first approximation, if i and f are both reasonably low, this is equal to $S(i - f)$.

5 If the total potential purchasing power of earnings plus savings is to rise, then the sum of the increased real earnings plus the change in the real value of savings must exceed zero, i.e.

$$(e \times g) + S(i - f) > 0.0$$

If the ratio of household savings to earnings is m, then we can write:

$$g + m(i - f) > 0.0$$

6 There are two uses to which we can put this equation. First, if we know the relevant figures, we can use it to calculate the change in real purchasing power for savings plus earnings in an economy; and second, we can alter the equation slightly to show the inequality which must hold for a real rise in purchasing power. This inequality is simply:

$$m(f - i) < g$$

or the loss in real purchasing power of savings (scaled to a proportion of earnings) must be less than the percentage increase in real income.

Another slight re-arrangement allows us to see that, for an increase in potential purchasing power, the inflation rate must not exceed the interest rate by more than the growth rate divided by the ratio of saving to earnings, (or $(f-i)$ must be less than g/m).

7 For example, if the growth rate is 5% and households possess savings equal to half their earnings, the inflation rate would need to exceed the interest rate by 10% before there would be a reduction to real potential purchasing power. In theory it is possible, using this equation, to calculate increases in real potential purchasing for the five nations. Unfortunately, the ratio of household savings to earnings is not available for all these five economies. It is difficult to establish the level of household savings in an economy because the distinction between savings and circulating credit is not very clear. The nature of bank deposits offers no solution, for some demand deposits (especially in France, and the USA) are actually household savings, left in demand deposits to ensure rapid withdrawal if needed or resulting from banking practice on loans.*

8 Interest and inflation rates have also varied so widely recently that the calculations made relate only to more stable past periods or to individual years.

9 Any general large-scale withdrawal of savings would probably cause additional inflation if these savings resulted in increased economic demand which could not be met. To an extent, therefore the trade-off between the purchasing power of savings and earnings is theoretical, due to the potential rise in inflation if large proportions of total savings were encashed. However, in normal economic experience only a small proportion of savers choose to encash their savings in any one year, so the effect of increased inflation due to withdrawal of savings is literally incalculable.

10 Nonetheless, this equation allows us to understand the apparent paradox that some nations can prosper on higher rates of inflation, because the potential purchasing power of households has increased although both inflation and growth may be high. Before potential purchasing power falls, inflation can exceed the interest rate by upto g/m, i.e. the growth rate divided by the ratio of savings to earnings. This condition obviously becomes harder to meet as (and if) the ratio of savings to earnings rises, and for household savings less than earnings, inflation can exceed the interest rate by more than the growth rate before potential purchasing power falls.

* In the USA, 20% of the capital value of a loan may be required, by USA banking practice, to be kept in an interest-free demand deposit.

11 The ratio of household savings to earnings — ,can be thought of as a kind of capital-output ratio for households, for it represents the savings resources households are able to loan (via credit institutions) to the rest of the economy divided by household earnings from the economy. In most cases where data is available, this ratio seems less than 2. This is not the case for the USA, where the ratio of personal financial assets to disposable income exceeds 3. A tentative conclusion might therefore be that in most nations the inflation rate may exceed the interest rate by up to half the growth rate before total potential purchasing power falls. But there is a need for considerable caution in suggesting any such solution. Inflation generally increases prices and current incomes at the expense of savings and fixed incomes. Any calculation based upon the statistically average individual may be misleading for large groups of people. Those people who are retired and on fixed incomes may suffer particularly, as their savings will be eroded by inflation without the benefit of any compensating advantage of increased real income. It is not enough to say that they will receive social security benefits; these do not cover everyone. Also, savings are by no means equally distributed among households. For any particular level of inflation which exceeds the interest rate, those who have saved large sums of money, without investing them in real assets, are disproportionately penalised.

12 Finally, to ensure potential purchasing power does not fall is only one way of looking at the trade-off of economic growth with inflation. Other criteria are obviously possible, and these would provide different results; there is perhaps no particular reason why potential purchasing power should be selected as a criterion for calculating a trade-off rather than others. Ideally, the impact of inflation and economic growth upon all the assets and liabilities of households need to be taken into account to asset the nature of the trade-off, but there seem to be no studies which do this in the detail it may deserve.

APPENDIX C: SOME COMPONENTS OF A PROPOSED ECONOMIC MODEL

1 The primary purpose of this book is to provide information about the financing of, and thereby partially to explain differences in the level of industrial investment. However, an economic model has suggested itself to the authors, arising naturally out of the research for the book. In this short appendix we cannot hope to do more than outline the model,

which may be capable of partially explaining some of the differences in the levels of saving, investment and economic growth between nations.

2 In proposing an economic model, it is usual for the assumptions underlying the model to be explicitly stated. It is difficult to do this when our touchstone is not an abstract ideal economic world, but is based upon the data collected and published by various sources. It would be presumptious, and inevitably incomplete, to attempt to outline the assumptions which may exist, underlying the real economic world. The propositions suggested below are not intended to provide a closed system of exhaustive abstractions, but a tentatively proposed series of working hypotheses, which further research could confirm or refute.

3 The following propositions, which the mathematically minded could re-write as equations, seem to have some evidence in their favour; the figures in brackets after the propositions relate to the sections in this book in which the subjects are discussed.

(i) The primary source of uncommited saving in a country is the saving of individuals (Chapter 4).

(ii) The level of individual saving may be increased by increasing wage awards in the form of periodic bonus payments, lower social security, and higher inflation, and decreased by the increased provision of consumer credit, and, for each of these factors, vice versa (section 6.1).

(iii) The transformation of short-term saving to longer-term lending by the banks may be assisted by more term saving by depositors, long-term bonds being raised through inter-bank lending, the discounting of industrial bonds by the central bank, deliberate risk-taking by banks transforming funds from short- to longer-term, and central bank guarantees that these banks (advancing industrial credit) will not be permitted to fail because funds will always be available, at a price, from the central bank. The proportion of funds transferred by the financial system to final users as medium- and long-term funds sets a boundary upon the maximum rate of fixed investment in the economy (Chapter 5).

(iv) Business fixed investment depends upon the availability of medium- and long-term finance for that investment, which equals gross business savings plus capital consumption allowances plus borrowed external capital, which is borrowed up to the point at which the rate of return from marginal projects is equal to the repayment rate of that borrowed capital. The cheapness of external finance to cash flow depends upon the length of term of the loan more than on the interest rate. External capital, once provided, creates depreciation provisions and hence higher future gross business savings. Depreciation allowances in excess of capital consumption produce an investment multiplier (Chapter 5).

(v) The increase in output and employment, due to investment in various economic sectors, can usefully be analysed in each of the economic sectors of the personal sector, the non-corporate private sector, the corporate companies sector, public corporations, and government (sections 3.4 and 6.4).

(vi) Investment may have three effects:

(a) An immediate employment effect, resulting in the employment of manpower while the investment is being put into place (i.e. additional employment in capital goods industries, or additional employment in the building industry while the factory is being built); this additional employment produces additional demand.

(b) Economic capacity may increase (if the investment produces marketable goods and services) after the investment is in place.

(c) Possibly a continuing employment effect due to the need for some manpower input to produce the additional goods and services. Investments in social overhead capital (e.g. road-building) are high in the effects listed in (a) and largely absent in those in (b) and (c). Investments in public corporations in the UK are high in (a) and low in (b) and (c). Investment in private companies are high in each of (a), (b) and (c) in the UK. The difference between the immediate employment and demand effect of investment and its long-run effect on employment and output may be largely responsible for the increasing unemployment and low output growth of the UK economy (section 6.4).

4 There are obviously other propositions, derived from accepted economic theory, which we either accept or take a view upon, and for which there may be some evidence. For example, we accept the Harrod-Domar model of economic growth, and wholly reject the marginal theory on which much of Denison's work is based. The propositions in paragraph 3, however, seem enough for this book.

Notes

PREFACE

1 See the *Guardian*, 21 September 1977, p. 16.

CHAPTER ONE

1 *National Accounts Statistics, Sources and Methods*, CSO.

CHAPTER TWO

1 OECD, *Economic Survey of the United Kingdom*, 1962.
2 Richard E. Caves *et al., Britain's Economic Prospects*, Allen & Unwin, 1968.
3 The Hudson Institute, Europe, *The United Kingdom in 1980*, Associated Business Programmes Ltd., 1974.
4 See, for example, R. C. O. Matthews, *Some Aspects of Post-War Growth in the British Economy in Relation to Historical Experience*, in Derek H. Aldcroft and Peter Fearon (eds.), *Economic Growth in Twentieth Century Britain*, Macmillan, 1969.
5 Edward F. Denison, 'Economic Growth', Chapter 6 of Richard E. Caves *et al., Britain's Economic Prospects*.
6 See Tables A1 and A2 in the statistical appendix.
7 See Table A3 in the statistical appendix.
8 See Table A4 in the statistical appendix.
9 See, for example, Nicholas Kaldor, 'The New Monetarism', p. 261 *et seq.* of *Money and Banking*, ed. A. A. Walters, Penguin Modern Economics Readings, 1973. Friedman's comments on Kaldor's article follows immediately on p. 279 in that book.
10 W. A. Eltis, 'Economic Growth and the British Balance of Payments' in D. H. Aldcroft and P. Fearon (eds.), *op. cit.* (This article was first published in December 1967 in the *District Bank Review.*)
11 See appendix A5 for data.
12 Data from *Economic Progress Report*, No. 83 (Feb. 1977) HMSO.
13 See Tables 3.21 and 3.22, and Section 3.4, where this is more fully discussed.
14 This suggestion has apparently found official favour — See 'Top Whitehall Training To Copy France', p. 5 of *The Times*, 3 May 1977.
15 Prentice-Hall International, London, 1971. The comment is in the appendices, p. 215.
16 *Finance for Investment*, NEDO, May 1975.
17 *Ibid*, Chapter 7.

18 Industrial areas, throughout much of the developed world, tend to be areas of low unemployment. Unemployment is partially structural (i.e. related to a geographical imbalance between job-offers and job-seekers) and inevitably cyclical, with the booms and depressions of each economy. USA, UK, and West German unemployment figures should not be compared directly, because USA statistics collect data about all persons seeking work; UK figures largely register those unemployed who are eligible for benefits; and West German figures may (or may not) include guest workers from outside the EEC.

19 R. Bacon and W. A. Eltis, *Britain's Economic Problem: Too Few Producers*, Macmillan, 1976.

20 R. Bacon and W. A. Eltis, *op. cit.*, p. 22.

21 From 'A Macro-Model of Inflation', *Economic Journal*, Vol. 85 (June 1975). Quoted in Bacon and Eltis, p. 26.

22 R. Bacon and W. A. Eltis, *op. cit.*, p. 64.

23 *Ibid.*, p. 90.

24 David Smith, 'Public Consumption and Economic Performance', *National Westminster Bank Review*, Nov. 1975.

25 R. Bacon and W. A. Eltis, *op. cit.*, p. 116.

CHAPTER THREE

1 G. W. Southgate, *English Economic History*, Dent, 1958, p. 115.

2 See, for example, Southgate on the textile industries; *ibid.*, pp. 126–35.

3 John Hicks, *A Theory of Economic History*, Oxford University Press, 1969, p. 145.

4 Paul A. Samuelson, *Economics*, McGraw-Hill, 1967, p. 48.

5 Adam Smith, *An Inquiry into the Nature and Causes of the Wealth of Nations*, Dent, 1910.

6 *Ibid.*, Vol. 1, pp. 9–10.

7 T. R. Malthus, *An Essay on the Principle of Population as it Affects the Future Improvement of Society*, London, 1798; reprinted in a Pelican Books edition, edited by Antony Flew, 1970.

8 See, for example, Donella H. and Dennis L. Meadows and others, *The Limits to Growth*, Earth Island Ltd., London, 1972; and for the other side of the argument, W. Beckerman, *In Defence of Economic Growth*, Jonathan Cape, London, 1974, especially Chapter 6 ('Resources for Growth', pp. 215–40).

9 Karl Marx, *Estranged Labour and Capital*, 1844, reprinted in *A Critique of Economic Theory*, ed. E. K. Hunt and J. G. Schwartz, Penguin Books, 1972.

10 John Hicks, *op. cit.*, p. 149.

11 *Ibid.*, p. 149.

12 Say does not seem to have said that 'supply would create its own demand' as is widely assumed. See J. B. Say, 'Treatise on Political Economy or the Production, Distribution and Consumption of Wealth', translated by C. R. Prinsep from the 4th French Edition (Longman, 1821).

13 Michael Stewart, *Keynes and After*, Penguin Books, 1969.

14 See, for example, Part II ('Inflation and Deflation') of J. M. Keynes, *Essays in Persuasion*, first published 1931, re-issued by Hart-Davis, 1951.

15 J. M. Keynes's *General Theory of Employment, Interest and Money* was first published in 1936.

16 R. F. Harrod, *Towards a Dynamic Economics*, Macmillan, London, 1948.

17 E. D. Domar, *Essays in the Theory of Economic Growth*, Oxford University Press, 1947.

18 J. A. Schumpeter, *Business Cycles: A Theoretical, Historical and Statistical Analysis of the Capitalist Process*, McGraw-Hill, New York and London, 1939.

19 B. Higgins, *Economic Development*, Constable, 1959, p. 212.

20 Edward F. Denison, *Why Growth Rates Differ: Post-War Experience in Nine Western Countries*, Brookings Institution, 1967.

21 J. W. Kendrick, *Productivity Trends in the United States*, National Bureau of Economic Research, Princeton, USA, 1961.

22 E. F. Denison, *op. cit.*, p. 34–6.

23 Maurice Dobb, 'The Trend of Modern Economics', in *A Critique of Economic Theory*, ed. E. K. Hunt and J. G. Swartz, Penguin Books, 1972, p. 48.

24 E. F. Denison, *op. cit.*, pp. 352–4.

25 D. H. Aldcroft and P. Fearon (eds), *op. cit.*, p. xiii.

26 That is, by Denison's method.

27 Joan Robinson, 'Capital Theory Up To Date', pp. 233–44, in E. K. Hunt and J. G. Swartz, *op. cit.*

28 *Ibid.*, p. 235.

29 J. Meade, *A Neo-Classical Theory of Economic Growth*, Allen & Unwin, 1961.

30 Joan Robinson, *op. cit.*, p. 237.

31 *Ibid.*, p. 238.

32 J. B. Clark, 'Distribution as determined by a law of rent', *Quarterly Journal of Economics*, Vol. 5, no. 3 (1891) (Quoted by Joan Robinson, *op. cit.*).

33 Joan Robinson, *op. cit.*, p. 241.

34 E. F. Denison, *op. cit.*, p. 34.

35 Joan Robinson, *op. cit.*, p. 233.

36 Quoted in Joan Robinson, *op. cit.*, p. 233. Source, C. E. Ferguson, *The Neo-classical Theory of Production and Distribution*, Cambridge University Press, 1969.

37 *National Accounts Statistics: Sources and Methods*, Chapter XII, part 5. p. 387.

38 D. H. Aldcroft and P. Feason (eds.), *op. cit.*, p. xiii.

39 E. F. Denison, *op. cit.*, p. 141.

40 See *National Accounts Statistics: Sources and Methods*, p. 384.

41 and 42 *National Income and Expenditure, 1973*, HMSO. Table 57 (p. 71) and the depreciation table in the notes, p. 113.

43 In the UK, the reliability of gross investment statistics is assessed as $\pm\ 10\%$ See *National Accounts Statistics: Sources and Methods*, p. 382.

44 Sir Sidney Green told the TUC (see the report in the *Guardian*, 8 Sep. 1972) that almost two-thirds of British plant and machinery was over 10 years old, and a substantial proportion of it was over 20 years old.

45 See, for example, Erik Lundberg's *Instability and Economic Growth*, Yale University Press, 1968, where this problem is outlined for the UK, Sweden,

Holland, Japan, the USA and Canada.

46 See Tables A6 and A7 in the statistical appendix for the percentage allocation of France's GDP from 1960–71.

47 In 1970, for example, FRS 97.6bn. (78.8 %) out of productive investments of FRS 123.9bn. was in private industry. See *XXI Rapport du Conseil de Direction de Funds de Développement Economique et Social*, June 1976, p. 14.

48 Only Japan invests 15–20 % of its national income in plant and machinery. See Tables A8 and A9 in the statistical appendix.

49 Erik Lundberg, *op. cit.*, p. 322.

50 Reproduced by permission, from *The Structure and Operation of the Japanese Economy*, by K. Bieda, John Wiley and Sons, Australasia Pty. Ltd., Sydney, 1970, p. 56.

51 Economic Planning Agency, *Economic Survey of Japan 1965–66*, p. 61; OECD, *Economic Survey of Japan 1970*, p. 39. Quoted in Andrea Boltho's *Japan—An Economic Survey 1953–73*, Oxford, 1973.

52 Tables A8 and A9 in the statistical appendix refer.

53 See Tables A10 and A11 in the statistical appendix.

54 Growth estimates include the Saar and West Berlin on both dates; these areas were incorporated in West Germany in 1960.

55 See Table A12 in the statistical appendix.

56 At the time of writing there are reports of unflattering comments by German managers working in Britain about their British counter-parts, as reported in *Der Spiegel*. Mr Deitrich Loesewitz, representing machinery construction firms, is reported as having said: 'It is unbelievable what old junk they are still using for production here' (Britain). See the *Guardian*, 1 Aug. 1977, p. 13.

57 See Tables A13 and A14 in the statistical appendix.

58 It should be remembered, in the comparison, that there are slight differences between the definitions of GDP, fixed capital investment, and capital consumption; Japan and West Germany are on the former system of national accounting while France, the UK and the USA are on the present SNA. See Appendix B1 for details.

59 Notes to Table 5, *Economic Survey of Japan 1965–66*, Economic Planning Agency, Tokyo, 1968.

60 See Appendix B2 for fuller information on this topic.

61 See, for example, Appendix B2, where equipment-output ratios for the 1960s are calculated on the same basis for France, West Germany, the UK and the USA.

62 See, for example K. C. O. Matthews, 'Some aspects of post-war growth in the British economy in relation to historical experience', in D. H. Aldcroft and P. Fearon (eds.), *op. cit.*, Chart 2, p. 87, shows a constant-prices capital-output ratio which has varied between 4.0 and 4.3 for the post-war period (1946–65).

63 Although a continued decline in Britain's economic performance can produce, and some would argue has produced, a lower quality of life in the UK. See *The United Kingdom in 1980*, *op. cit.*

64 Angus Maddison, *Economic Growth in the West*, Allen & Unwin, 1964, p. 75.

65 Letters to the Editor, *The Times,* 22 Apr. 1977. The ultimate source of this quotation is *British Trade with Japan* (Japan Information Centre, Embassy of Japan, London, January 1977).

CHAPTER FOUR

1 The amounts shown as 'total assets acquired' do not equal the 'total liabilities incurred' because one tiny economic sector — private non-profit making institutions — has been deleted from the original data to form Table 4.1.

2 There are four years of such data for France — 1970 in Table 4.1, and 1971– 73 in Appendices A 17–19.

3 From the chapter on the French financial system, Peter Readman with J. Davies, M. Hoare and D. Poole, *The European Money Puzzle*, Michael Joseph, London, 1973, p. 40.

4 1973 has been chosen for the purposes of illustrating the operation of the French medium- and long-term financing system. There is no particular merit in that year. Similar tables for 1974 and 1975 are available in the quoted source, and tables for previous years can also be found in earlier *Statistiques et Études Financières* of the Ministère de l'Économie et des Finances.

5 Except for the financial market, where the 'closing position' is shown, it would be equally logical to exclude the financial market from the total of line 11, and only add them in to calculate total resources. As the table is made up, the sum of new funds at lines 12(a) and 12(b) are bracketed and ignored in the totals column for they have been already added to derive a grand total.

6 The total of columns 7(a) and 7(b) rows 1–5 inclusive, equals the borrowings on the capital market entered as debentures or shares in lines 12(a) and 12(b) of column 8, in Table 4.5.

7 Readman *et al.*, *op. cit.*, p. 48.

8 G. C. Allen, *A Short History of Modern Japan*, Allen & Unwin, 1972, p. 170. The estimate of the amount of housing and other capital stock destroyed is from J. B. Cohen, *Japan's Economy in War and Reconstruction*, (University of Minneapolis Press, 1949).

9 For some details of the 'special procurement procedure', which, in Allen's words, enabled Japan to some extent to 'solve her balance of payments problems without damping down economic growth,' see G. C. Allen, *Japan as a Market and Source of Supply*, Pergamon Press, 1967, p. 38–9.

10 Reproduced by permission, from *The Structure and Operation of the Japanese Economy*, by K. Bieda. John Wiley and Sons, Australasia Pty, Ltd., Sydney, 1970, p. 141.

11 G. C. Allen, *A Short History of Modern Japan*, p. 190.

12 For a list of the numbers of those operating in 1968, see K. Bieda, *op. cit.*, pp. 133, 134.

13 *Ibid.*, p. 161. More was borrowed than loaned, therefore some sources of interbank call money finance are not covered in the above data.

14 G. C. Allen, *A Short History of Modern Japan*, p. 191.

15 Reproduced by permission from K. Bieda, *op. cit.*, p. 145. The 'as well' refers to the banks' provision of long-term loans, mentioned in a previous sentence.

16 Consumer and mortgage credit are relatively under-developed in Japan. This topic will be covered in section 6.2.

17 K. Bieda, *op. cit.*, p. 145.

18 See James Abegglan, *Business Strategies for Japan*, Sophia University, Tokyo, 1970, p. 61; Kunio Miki in R. Ballon, *Doing Business in Japan*, Sophia University, Tokyo, 1967, p. 79; and K. K. Kurihara, *The Growth Potential of the Japanese Economy*. The Johns Hopkins Press, Baltimore, 1971, p. 74.

19 P. Readman *et al.*, *op. cit.*, p. 62.

20 *Ibid.*, p. 63.

21 A. Tillett, T. Kempner and G. Wills, (eds.) *Management Thinkers*, Penguin Books, 1970, p. 20.

22 P. Readman *et al.*, *op. cit.*, p. 61.

23 See Table 4.19 and Tables A20 to A22 in the statistical appendix.

24 P. Readman, *et. al.*, *op. cit.*, p. 78.

25 See *Companies in 1970*, Dept. of Trade and Industry, HMSO, 1971.

26 See the subsidiary and associated banks listed in J. E. Wordsworth (ed.), *The Banks and the Monetary System in the UK, 1959–71*, Methuen, 1973, pp. 506–7.

27 The figures in this paragraph are from *The British Economy, Key Statistics 1900–1970* (published for the London and Cambridge Economic Service by Times Newspapers Ltd., 1971), p. 16.

28 *Economic Trends*, HMSO, July 1973, p. 40.

29 There are some errors, presumably due to rounding, in Table 4.25: the lines do not always add to the totals shown. This inaccuracy is unusual for Eurostat tables; however the authors have no special knowledge which would enable these tables to be corrected.

30 Hakan Hedberg, *Japan's Revenge*, Pitman, London, 1972.

31 That is, by inflation and by population growth to calculate GDP growth per head.

32 Gunnar Myrdal, *Challenge to Affluence*, Gollancz, 1963, p. 15.

33 Peter Readman *et al.*, *op. cit.*, p. 54.

34 For a list of the 33 members of the Mitsubishi kinyu keiretsu, see Bieda, *op. cit.*, p. 213.

35 *Ibid.*, p. 214.

36 *Finance for Investment*, NEDO, May 1975, p. 203.

37 As R. Grierson has remarked in the NEDO study of *Finance for Industry*, it has been suggested that 'imagination is the only limit to the types of security which can be used to raise funds in the US' (p. 194).

CHAPTER FIVE

1 See Table 'Interest rates, security prices and yields', in *Economic Trends, Annual Supplement 1976*, HMSO.

2 For a fuller exposition of the arguments, see A. J. Merrett and Allen Sykes, *The Finance and Analysis of Capital Projects*, Longman, 1963, Chapter 15, *Optimal Financing*, pp. 393–422.

3 H. Kahn, *The Emerging Japanese Superstate*, Prentice-Hall International, London, 1971, p. 106.

4 F. Modigliani and M. H. Miller, 'The cost of capital, corporation finance, and the theory of investment', *American Economic Review*, June 1958.

5 See, for example, A. J. Merrett and Allen Sykes, *op. cit.*, pp. 407–22.
6 Robin B. Fox, 'Leverage in U.K. companies 1967–73—An empirical investigation', *Management Decision*, 1977, Vol. 1.
7 K. Bieda, *op. cit.*, pp. 117, 118.
8 Indeed, if only the historic cost of capital is recovered, the net capital stock (if there are no external sources of capital) could decrease.
9 A. Glyn and B. Sutcliffe, *British Capitalism, Workers and the Profits Squeeze*, Penguin Books, 1972.
10 James C. Abegglan, *Business Strategies for Japan*, Sophia University, Tokyo, 1970, pp. 58–68.
11 Kenneth K. Kurihara, *The Growth Potential of the Japanese Economy*, The Johns Hopkins Press, Baltimore, 1971, p. 77.
12 *Ibid.*, p. 136. Dr. O. Shimomura has been described as the father of Japan's 'Income-Doubling Plan' and the initiator of the growth controversy (K. K. Kurihara, *op. cit.*, p. 2). See also O. Shimomura, 'Basic Problems of Growth Policy', *Economic Studies Quarterly*, Mar. 1961.
13 Assuming, of course, these are non-Japanese bankers. Japanese banks loan out up to 100 % of deposits plus borrowings.

CHAPTER SIX

1 See Notes to Table 188, p. 649 of *United Nations Statistical Yearbook 1974*, United Nations, New York, 1975. The exchange rate used was the par value of the currency, where fixed official exchange rates were the norm, and the quarterly average of the official rates, where there was a single fluctuating rate.
2 Milton Gilbert *et al., Comparative National Products and Price Levels*, OEEC, Paris 1958.
3 Wilfred Beckerman, *International Comparison of Real Incomes*, OECD, Paris 1966.
4 *Economic Progress Report No. 88*, July 1977, HMSO; from the first article, entitled 'What the pound buys abroad'.
5 Data taken from the *Economic Statistics Annual 1970*, Statistics Dept. of the Bank of Japan, Mar. 1971, Table 166. See Table 4.16, where this data is reproduced.
6 *Economic Survey of Japan, 1969/70*, Economic Planning Agency, Japanese Government, p. 72.
7 R. Stone *Private Saving in Britain, Past, Present and Future*, MS, May 1964. Professor Stone found that a factor for hire purchase regulations was a significant variable in explaining the personal saving level between 1949 and 1962 in the UK economy. Quoted in *The U.K. Economy*, ed. A. R. Prest, Weidenfeld & Nicolson, 1966.
8 See K. Bieda, *op. cit.*, p. 155.
9 *Economic Survey of Japan*, OECD, June 1972.
10 Michael Stewart, *Keynes and After*, Penguin Books, 1967, p. 189.
11 This calculation is done in appendix B3.
12 M. C. Kennedy, in A. R. Prest (ed.), *op. cit.*, assesses the multiplier as 1.3 over about two years, but points out the tendency of the multiplier to rise above

this level. An estimate of about 2, on the basis that increases in output in manufacturing results in similarly sized increases in services, seems to be of the right approximate size, although it could be on the high side. However, a high estimate, when assessing possible inflation rates following the printing of money to finance investment, seems prudent.

13 This certainly happened prior to the oil crisis of 1973; the picture since then has been less clear.

CHAPTER SEVEN

1 See, for example, 'Where finance fails investment,' *Management Today*, Feb. 1976.
2 The authors produced an article published on p. 19 of *The Times*, 17 July 1976, entitled 'Britain and Japan — Is the difference the cost of capital?'
3 Those of Australia,Canada, New Zealand, the UK and USA.
4 See the 'Banks Debate Broadsheet No. 1', for example, published in most UK morning national newspapers on 19 May, 1977.
5 *Banking and Finance*, a Labour Party pamphlet produced in Aug. 1976.
6 Andrew Glyn and Bob Sutcliffe, *British Capitalism: Workers and the Profits Squeeze*, Penguin Books, 1972.
7 *Ibid.*, p. 208.
8 *Ibid.*, p. 76.

Index